MW01123967

The iPath

How I Became Conscious of an Invisible World

By: Michael Stepakoff

Except where otherwise indicated,
all Bible scripture quotes are taken from the Tree of Life Version.
Copyright © 2014 by the Messianic Jewish Family Bible Society.
Used by permission of the Messianic Jewish Family Bible Society.

"TLV" and "Tree of Life Version" are trademarks registered
in the United States Patent and Trademark office by the
Messianic Jewish Family Bible Society.

Copyright © 2017 by Michael Stepakoff
All rights reserved. No part of this book may be reproduced,
scanned, or distributed in any printed or electronic form without
permission.
First Edition: 2017
Printed in the United States of America

ISBN-1544695721
ISBN-9781544695723

CONTENTS

PREFACE

"My kingdom is not of this world." Those are the words of the greatest Teacher who ever walked the earth.

The statement itself implies that there is a world, other than the one in which we currently seem to be living. An imperishable world which is not governed by the laws of this temporal, perishable world, but by the law of eternal life. Not a world of flesh and blood, where death and change are ever-present, and in which might and power have dominion. But a world consisting of grace, love, peace, infinite joy and eternal Life. A world wherein God is the only authority.

That Kingdom which is not of this world is no romantic dream, but the very substance and Reality of the universe. The Teacher came to reveal it to humankind, that we might not perish, but have everlasting life.

We are living between two worlds. Between an exterior world which we see with our eyes, and an interior world which is invisible. Although we cannot behold it with our senses, the paradise in which Mankind once dwelt remains fixed and permanent, always right there in the midst of us.

If only we could see it. If only we could establish contact with the invisible world. Then, the healing Life of God would shine through mortal flesh into this perishing world of strife and turmoil. And thereby, glorify God, and bear witness that there is salvation through the Teacher. Who came for this very cause. To bear witness to the Truth. That we might have Life. And have it abundantly. Both now and forever. Shalom.

Michael Stepakoff

1

Who Am I?

A Story to Tell:

Who am I? If someone were to ask you that question, would you be able to answer? Oh, you might think you can answer. Most people do think they can. And so did I.

But when I realized that I did not really have the answer, it changed everything. It opened up a whole new world to me. Because on its face it's an absurd question. Yet, once I thought about it, I realized I didn't know. Do you? Well, in my case, I had to have the answer to that question. And that's how I got onto the iPath.

Let me just say, I am no different than anyone else. The only reason I have a story to tell, is because, quite simply, something happened to me when I started asking the question—*Who am I?*

My name is Gary Goldman. But that's not who I am. For the most part, I am an ordinary human being. But something extraordinary happened to me. And as a direct consequence, I experienced something, the nature of which I can only describe as "transformative."

This transformative experience is how I got onto the iPath. And I am quick to recognize, and will never forget, that it was not my own doing. I didn't choose to be on the iPath. It just happened.

If I must pinpoint a moment when it began, then okay. It began when I started asking the question—*Who am I?*

The thing is, I don't know why I ever asked that question to begin with. How or why was it ever on my heart to ask such a ridiculous question? I don't know. I cannot say that it was my idea. It was just something that happened.

The Wilderness Experience:

Now, let me be more specific:

I had just begun my sabbatical year. It was October now, and we were a couple of weeks into the new year. The Jewish new year.

It had been fourteen years and this was my first time taking a sabbatical from my duties as the Rabbi. So I had no idea what Sabbatical can do to you. It messes with you.

You see, so long as we stay busy doing what we normally do, then we don't think about what we're doing, or why we are doing it, or if we are doing it well. We just do it. Well, something weird happens when all of a sudden you aren't doing it anymore. What happens is you start thinking about things.

It's like being beamed up to a spaceship where you spend a year, isolated from planet earth, while the whole world goes on without you. And meanwhile, up on the ship, you are shown pictures of yourself, doing whatever it is you do. And then you are asked questions by those who beamed you up. Like what do you intend to accomplish if we let you go back?

That's what it's like. I don't care who you are, a year off from your normal occupation causes you to contemplate and reflect on things you ordinarily will not think about. Like what the heck am I doing with my life? What is my life all about? Will it have made any difference in the world, or even any difference in me, when I am gone from this life? Am I wasting my time here? And, quite possibly, the question which was the hydrogen bomb of my life—*Who am I*?

Sabbatical is a wilderness experience. And you know what happens in the bible every time someone goes into the wilderness—self-discovery and personal transformation. Whether it's forty days, or forty years, or in my case one year, people don't often come back the same. Some might even come back with a face that shines so bright that you have to wear a veil over it so you don't freak people out. That's what happened to me. Minus the shining face and the veil. Isolated and living in my sabbatical shell, I was transformed. I may look the same. But I assure you I am not.

Sabbatical is a different angle. If only we could maintain that kind of angle on life, without being on Sabbatical. Well, that's sort of what happened to me. I learned how to do that. I brought it back with me.

When it was all over, it wasn't over. It never ended. I was still seeing the world, and my life in it, in the way I was seeing it when I was living in that vacuum, because of being airlifted out of the world. Because of sabbatical.

Which, I note, the root of "sabbatical" is "Shabbat." The Shabbat, or Sabbath day, in Jewish tradition, is the day of rest. A day of refreshing and renewal. A "sabbatical" year is like a whole year of Shabbat.

But what if you could approach Shabbat, not as a day of the week, but instead, as a state of being? A state of rest.

If you could do that, then you've perfected the art of living. For being at rest, even when you are working, even working hard, well, that is the art of living.

And I'm telling you, indeed, there is a Shabbat that never ends. Because it has no beginning nor end. It is simply a time which IS. Although, it really is not a "time" at all. Because it's beyond time. That, my friend, is the iPath.

Why Me?:

Okay, but I'm getting ahead of myself here. I have a story to tell. And when I share this story with you, I know that you might ask, why me? And all I can say is, I don't know. But to that I would also add, why not you? If it could happen to me, I guarantee you, it could happen to you. Because I'm no different than anyone else.

I had mixed feelings about taking a year off from my rabbinical duties. On the one hand, it seemed like a good idea. I mean, who would turn down a year off with full pay? On the other hand, the problem was, I didn't know what to do with myself. So, I spent the first two weeks pretty much dazed and confused about it.

When I started my sabbatical, I had all this alone time. And nobody was around to tell me how wonderful my Shabbat sermon was; or what a beautiful wedding ceremony I performed; or how thankful someone is that I prayed by their husband's bedside when he had his surgery; or how the advice I gave them in my office may have saved their marriage; etc. etc.

I had my family, of course, but they were busy going about their lives. My two middle school age kids—one boy, one girl—were busy with school, and activities. And my awesome, devoted wife, Laura was immersed in her career as a full time social worker.

Sabbatical meant that I was now dwelling in a vacuum. Time and space went on without me. I was alone. While the world continued to turn, and go about its business, I had to try and find my place in a world in which I now seemed not to exist. I thus saw my life from a different angle. The angle that makes you ask the question—*Who am I?*

It all started at the Starbucks. The one in my neighborhood. I had started hanging around Starbucks in the mornings, because what else does one do with oneself on Sabbatical? I surely didn't know. I couldn't go into the office. I was on Sabbatical. I don't like to work at home. Do you see the problem? That's why I was at Starbucks. I had nowhere else to go.

What was I doing? Other than drinking coffee, reading, and jotting down a few notes, I wasn't really doing anything. I know it seems kind of pointless. It was. I was on sabbatical. I was hoping to find a point, to an otherwise pointless way of life. Because I did not know what the point was. Nor what to do about it. Except that I maintained, quite steadfastly, the belief that there was a point. And I just needed to find it.

But I can tell you this—not having a point can actually be quite liberating. Because it opens the door to possibilities that wouldn't have otherwise been possible.

Most of the time, most of us are too occupied with our occupations to be worrying about whatever the point is. I know I am. And in that scenario, the point always seems to be whatever you do to occupy yourself. Nothing more.

But in the day that you cease to occupy yourself in the usual way, you suddenly realize that your occupation is not the point. You suddenly see that there is some point to the occupation. But you don't know what it is. Do you?

So, then, you might try to find a new point by occupying yourself in some new way. But that doesn't work. Otherwise, take it from me, what does work is when you get right down to the heart of the whole matter. And the only way to do that is to ask yourself the bottom line question—*Who am I?* Because that is the point. Not what you do, but who you are. And when you find that, well, then you're on the iPath.

I also found, if you get the answer to that question, then you can bring it with you, back into whatever it is you do to occupy yourself during whatever number of days you might have under the sun. But the difference is that the point is no longer how you occupy yourself, the point is knowing who you are in the midst of that scene. That is the nature of the iPath.

Yesterday's Manna:

The idea that I had going into sabbatical, was that I would use the time to write a book. That was the official plan. I was certain that God wanted me to say something of great value to the world. It would be sort of a gift from God, who would use me as his instrument, to present a manuscript for the good of mankind.

There was only one problem—I quickly realized I had nothing of great value to say to the world. Nor anything that would be of any particular benefit to mankind.

Now maybe you think, well, hey, if you're a Rabbi, then surely you must have had something to say? You're darn right I did. And when I set out at first with the idea to speak my peace to the world, by putting my message into book form, I definitely had plenty that I could have said. Tons.

Having something to say was not the issue. The issue was in the *value* of it. The world is already full of voices. The world does not need another banging gong or clanging cymbal, giving the world more of what it already has.

Of course, there certainly would be no point in spending my sabbatical drafting a book that makes people go, "Ho hum." Or at best, they might go, "Hmm." Perhaps, even with an eyebrow raise.

Either way there's no point. Because there's no value. Because the world does not need to go "Ho hum," nor "Hmm." The world needs to go, "Ahhh!"

But I'll tell you something I learned about that. You can't make anybody go, "Ahhhh!" until you've had something happen to you that makes you go, "Ahhhh!"

Because it's hard enough to bring someone to where you are at. But it's flat-out impossible to take anyone further than you've gone yourself.

But I've said too much. I'm getting ahead of my story. So just suffice it to say for now that, indeed, there are better ways for a man to spend sabbatical then writing a book which would have to be entitled *Zero Impact*. Because that's exactly what my book would have been, if I'd gone forward with it at that time.

Undoubtedly, it would have been up to par, from an academic standpoint; and I feel confident that it would've made people go, "Hmm," but nobody would've gone "Ahhhh!" It was zero impact stuff. Low-impact at best. It would've been nothing more than an addition to the great stockpile of what the world already has.

What I needed was fresh manna. But I had no idea where or how to acquire fresh manna. For the meantime, all I had to give out was yesterday's manna. That is, the manna that the world already has plenty of. The manna which is not life-giving, but is already rotting and decaying. Which is what manna does if it sits too long.[1]

And even though the world doesn't realize they are eating yesterday's manna, and even though those who give it to them don't necessarily realize that is what they are doing, nevertheless, I suddenly realized it. And that was the problem.

Because I couldn't ignore it. I couldn't lie to myself. Nor could I waste my sabbatical year working on a project that would result in me giving more of yesterday's manna to the world. I needed today's manna. And so does the world.

But, as I said, I was no different than anyone else. Yesterday's manna was all I had to consume. And, therefore, it was all I had to give out.

Who Do People Say That I Am?:

So it was, that in the first few days of my sabbatical, though dead set on writing a book for the benefit of the world, I quickly realized that I had nothing worth saying to the world.

But I didn't give up. I continued daily to try and overcome. To somehow rise above this situation. I did not concede defeat. I strove with it. Like Jacob wrestling with the angel of the Lord.

I suppose what I actually was doing, was wrestling with myself. I was engaging in an inner confrontation. Who was I confronting? Me, I guess.

Although, I want to be clear that I did not set out with the intent to do that. It just sort of developed that way. I struggled within myself, with myself. But at all times,

---

[1] Ex. 16:20.

7

without me thinking about what I was doing. In fact, I didn't even know what I was doing. I wasn't aware of it, really. It just sort of unfolded.

I think it was maybe that first or second morning at Starbucks. I had not quite yet started asking myself—*Who am I?*—as I was too busy trying to figure out what I could say to the world in book form, and why it was that I had nothing worth saying.

So, during the first two days, right before I started asking myself—*Who am I?*—I was actually pondering something else. And it was this other thing, that led me to start asking *Who am I?* Which, as I said, was really the starting point of the whole thing.

I guess you could say that this first thing that I was asking, and contemplating, sort of primed the pump. So that when I started asking—*Who am I?*—the well opened right up.

So, at first, when I clicked open my bible program on my laptop computer, somehow my attention was drawn to a certain incident. The incident is described in Mark 8:27-30 and in Mat. 16:13-17. I read over it several times. Contemplated it. Digested it. Drank coffee. Contemplated some more.

It says that Yeshua[2] separated from the masses, and gathered together with his inner circle, his closest followers. And to them, he posed two questions: The first was this— *"Who do people say that I am?"*

And his inner circle of talmidim[3] informed Yeshua what the people were saying about him. They reported that many people thought he was one of the prophets risen from the dead. Maybe Elijah, or Jeremiah. Or John the Immerser. They were mistaken. He was none of these.

Now, in spite of what the talmidim said in response to Yeshua at that moment, I think it's clear that many thousands of the Jewish people in the land at that time also

---

[2] Yeshua is Hebrew for "Jesus."
[3] Talmidim are "disciples."

believed that Yeshua was the Messiah. Or at least they hoped that he was. And they were surely talking all around the land about whether or not he might be the Messiah. Undoubtedly, there were those hailing him as Messiah all over the land.

As I read through it, and poured over it in my mind, I wondered what our generation would say if asked that same question—*"Who do people say that I am?"* I mean, would the answer be any more "accurate" today than it was then?

And it came to mind, that today, there are supposedly 2.2 billion people in the world who believe Yeshua is the Messiah. That's about one-third of the world's population. Do that many people really know the answer to—*"Who do people say that I am?"*

No way. If one-third of the world actually knew God, the world would be quite a different place. Moreover, the other two-thirds would see, and would probably quickly give in.

For me, when that question is posed—*"Who do people say that I am?"*—the fact is plain and obvious, from my point of view, that the masses of the world don't really know who he is. They never have known. Not in Yeshua's time. Not historically. And not today either. Even if they give the "correct" answer, doctrinally, that doesn't mean they know who he is.

As sort of a side-bar, a phrase came to mind, and I typed it into the search window—"narrow gate." I clicked onto the verse, where Yeshua said:

> *"Enter through the **narrow gate**; for the gate is wide and the way is broad that leads to destruction, and there are many who enter through it. For the gate is small and the way is narrow that leads to life, and there are few who find it.*[4]

---

[4] *NASB*, Mat. 7:13,14.

Whatever this might mean, needless to say, one-third of the world's population is not a "narrow" portion of humanity.

Look, I have a story to tell. But, I just want to be clear about something up front, that I hold dear to my heart. You see, I believe that God loves everyone. Yes, everyone. The whole world. God's love for mankind is universal and unchanging.

And God sent his son, Messiah Yeshua for the sake of the *whole world*. He's the atonement for the sins of the *whole world*. He's the lamb who takes away the sin of *the world*. Because God so loved *the world*. Etc., etc.[5]

But here's the thing. Even though God's love is universal, not everyone is aware of that love. And, moreover, I think people are easily deceived to believe that they are walking in that love, just because their religious beliefs tell them so, even when they are not.

In reality, while Messiah has come for the world, the world has not received him. Including that massive part of the world which claims to have received him. It hasn't. And history testifies to it.

But as long as people *believe* they have received him, well, it's a barrier. For no one will receive what they believe they have already received. And people can be made to believe that. Easily.

In which case, they won't go any further, because they think they are already there. This is the key problem with getting onto the iPath. You have to first overcome your own religious beliefs. You have to lose your religion. But, that's sacred ground, isn't it? So therein lies the problem. Religion has posited itself as the way to God. But it's really the barrier.

Because God so loved the world he gave his only Son. Yeah. But the world has not accepted the love of God. Nor the Son. Because it either doesn't believe in the Son outright; or it does believe, but can't take the Son as he is. So it reinvents him.

---

[5] *See*, 1 John 2:2, John 1:29, John 3:16.

Yeshua had masses of people following him around, but not everyone could grasp what was going on, because they didn't know who he was. As I mulled this over, there in the Starbucks, another verse came to mind, in which Yeshua separated himself from the masses, and said to his inner circle of followers:

"To you has been given to know the secrets of the kingdom of heaven, but to them it has not been given."[6]

Why are some able to discern the secrets of the kingdom and others are not? I do not know. I just know that the trap of ignorance comes about when we have convinced ourselves that we already know the truth—even though we don't.

I cannot explain it. This is just how it is. But I do know that the first step on the spiritual path is to recognize one's own ignorance. Indeed, easier said than done. But without that recognition, growth is impossible.

It's like a seed refusing to be planted in good soil because it imagines itself already to be a full grown, fruit-bearing tree. It will never transform into what it thinks itself already to be, because it refuses to be planted in soil. Even though it is no more than a seed, full of potentiality, yet still, it is convinced that transformation has occurred—even though it has not.

Yeshua described this scenario in which there are those close disciples who know the secrets of the kingdom of heaven, are enriched by God's grace more and more, while the masses go on in their ignorance:

"For whoever has, to him more will be given and he will have plenty. But whoever does not have, even what he has will be taken away from him."[7]

[6] Mat. 13:11.
[7] Mat. 13:12.

11

The reason the masses go on in their ignorance is because they have been convinced that they know the truth. But, in fact, it is this very belief they have of already knowing the truth that keeps them from knowing the truth which they think they already know. As it says in regard to the masses:

"Because seeing they do not see, and hearing they do not hear nor do they understand."[8]

In that regard, when you look at history, there is one principle that proves true time and time again. It is easier to fool people than it is to convince them that they have been fooled.

Truth be told, the world at large has either rejected God, or reinvented him. It's a rejection either way. But for those who have reinvented him, it's easier to jump over the moon, than to convince them of their error. Only a work of God's grace can bring it about, so that "the secrets of the kingdom of heaven" might be revealed.

The story of reinventing God is an old one, and goes back to the beginning. It is the reason why there were countless wars in Europe that turned "Christian" nations against one another, including two World Wars. It also is the reason why the worst war in American experience—the Civil War—was fought between a Union and a Confederacy which both considered themselves to be "Christian" and bible-based nations. Moreover, it's the reason why there was a holocaust against the Jews in "Christian" Europe. We Jews can see this plainly. Because we have been the victims of it time and time again.

The iPath begins at that narrow gate. That gate where God cannot be reinvented, because God is not defined by ideals of man, but God simply IS. Anyone can go through that narrow gate, and all people are invited. From every nation, family, tribe, or language. All races, Jew and Gentile,

---

[8] Mat. 13:13

all colors, every person on the face of the earth can walk on that true path of the Messiah. But it isn't up to me. All I can do is share my story of how it happened to me.

And it can happen to anyone, but you have to be willing to press on, not as if we have already attained, but onward, to the higher calling in Messiah.[9] Are you willing to do that?

But now I am beginning to sound like a preacher. I do that sometimes. Forgive me.

Who Do *You* Say That I Am? :

All of these thoughts were circulating in my mind. All this stuff about the ignorance of the masses, etc., most of it was not new to me. I had considered much of that before.

But then I came to the second question which Yeshua posed during that incident. The second question he posed was—"*Who do you say that I am?*"

So, you see, there is what "people" say—referring to the general population of followers. And then there is what "you" say—referring to the inner circle, the talmidim. And I pondered this. What was their answer? What would be my answer?

I find it quite easy to see the ignorance of the masses, and if necessary, to cite examples from history as proof. But when confronted with the question—"*Who do you say that I am?*"—I paused.

Now, of course, I could rattle off the standard, cookie-cutter, doctrinally-correct answer. But I wasn't so sure that really was the answer. Because, that answer was not significantly different than the answer the masses would give. They obviously don't have the answer. Did I? Why would I think so, if my answer was the same as theirs?

I mean, of course, I could just give the theologically-correct answer, "You are the Messiah, son of the living God."[10]

---

[9] *See,* Phil 3:12-14.
[10] Mat. 16:16.

But so would 2.2 billion today. So would 99% of Germany during World War II. What was so different about my answer. Do you see? I had never thought of it this way.

So, maybe there is more to being a follower of the Messiah than just holding to the right doctrine? Obviously the ability of one third of the world today to give the answer—*"You are the Messiah, son of the living God"*[11]—has not brought peace on earth, or a higher civilization. Something is missing. Even though the answer is correct on its face, it's still not the answer. And so, I saw that in asking this provocative question, Yeshua must have been probing at something more. Something hidden.

As was, even Yeshua's closest followers didn't know how to answer the question. Even though they were in the inner circle. Only one, only Shimon, also known as "Kefa" (Peter), seemed to have the actual answer. Shimon responded, *"You are the Messiah, son of the Living God."*[12]

But as I considered this, I thought, there has to be more to the answer than just what Shimon stated. Because he was not the only person during that generation to believe, or hope, or say that Yeshua is the Messiah. Lots of people believed and hoped and said that he was the Messiah. Crowds hailed him as the Messiah when he entered Jerusalem.[13] It was not some novel idea, as if Shimon was the first to think of it, or the first who was bold enough to say so.

A mere statement by Shimon of the fact that Yeshua is Messiah was only adding to the stockpile of what plenty of others were already saying about him all over the land of Israel.

Shimon must've seen something about Yeshua at that moment, which wasn't readily apparent to everyone. As Yeshua told him, *"Flesh and blood has not revealed this to you,"* (Mat. 16:17).

---

[11] Ibid.
[12] Ibid.
[13] Mat. 21:9.

I wasn't sure what it was. But I knew that the answer was not the answer as put to words and stated. The answer was something which came into his heart, which came to him by spiritual revelation.

And, yet, even for Shimon, that moment of revelation was a flash-in-the-pan. Shimon quickly lost sight of whatever it was he had seen there. As we know, because not long after that, Shimon denied ever having known Yeshua.[14] Furthermore, the same crowds who hailed him as Messiah, only days later shouted "Crucify him!" and "We have no King but Caesar!"[15]

Shimon had to be brought back into knowing the Reality. And he was brought back to it, afterwards, along with all of the close followers of Yeshua, who thereafter, went forth and imparted to the world what they had come to know from the Rabbi, after he rose, and by spiritual revelation, after he ascended to heaven.

And I found later on, that Truth works in this way. It calls out to you, and draws you in. But it has to take root, and be nurtured, and grow up in a person. Otherwise, as it happened with Shimon, you may see it one day, and it's gone the next. Like a seed planted in the wrong kind of soil.

Even on good soil, it has to sink roots, and settle down deep, and be given time to engage you in its processes, before emerging as fruit. Otherwise, its revelation can be fleeting...but, now I've said too much. I'm getting ahead of my story again.

What's the Big Deal?:

Now, maybe you're reading this and thinking, what's the big deal about the question—*Who do you say that I am?* Maybe you think you already know the answer to that.

---

[14] Mark 14:66-72.
[15] John 19:15.

Well, believe me when I tell you, it won't do you any harm to reconsider. I thought I knew it too. And I am no different than you. And you are no different than me. So, hear me out on this.

The Truth is out there, calling out to you, and to me, and to everyone else. But you have to be drawn to it. And when you are drawn, hopefully you respond to the call. Because that's how you get onto the iPath.

But you won't be drawn if you think you're already there. I know that sounds simplistic, but most of the world is stuck in this way of thinking.

As for me, the question—"*Who do you say that I am?*"—was indeed a big deal. Because I realized that my answer to it was a "ho hum" answer, to be thrown into the stockpile of the masses, along with the billions of others, who answered in the same way. I had nothing to say about it that was worth saying. Certainly not anything worth spending a year drafting a book so that it could be said to the world.

Of course, I could answer with an Hebraic twist. There are plenty of people out there who like that sort of thing. It's unique. It makes them go, "Hmm." That is better than "Ho hum." But not much. And it just wasn't worth it to me.

Decorative, cultural flair, even Jewish cultural flair, might be interesting to many people. But it isn't transformative. It is little more than window dressing. Even at best, it certainly isn't life-changing, not in the sense of being revelatory or liberating. Do you see where I am coming from?

So as to the question—"*Who do you say that I am?*"—I had nothing of great value to say to the world about it. Nor about any other issue that I could think of. Nothing that would make anyone go, "Ahhhh!" Because they've heard it all before. And I knew it. And did not deny it. I embraced it. But I did not give up.

Mi Anokhi:

And, so it was, on the third day at Starbucks, as I continued to agonize over the idea of writing a book which I could not write, because I knew the world did not need a book like that from me, and because I didn't feel I had anything to add to the world's great stockpile of answers to Yeshua's question—"*Who do you say that I am?*'—that I stumbled across something else in the scriptures.

It was something that Moses said to God at the burning bush, when the Lord told Moses that he had been chosen to lead Israel up out of slavery. Moses responded:

"*Mi Anokhi?*" That is the Hebrew for, "*Who am I?*"[16]

And I thought, well, I may not have a good answer to Yeshua's question—"*Who do you say that I am?*"—but at least I ought to be able to answer the question—"*Who am I?*"

After all, the whole world seems to have missed the point of who Yeshua is. And perhaps I was no different in that respect. But every one ought to have an answer for—"*Who am I?*" Including me.

Moses was 80 years-old. He was herding sheep in the desert. He didn't speak well. "*Who am I*," he said to God, "*that I should go to Pharoah, and bring the children of Israel out of Egypt?*"[17]

And I thought, Moses must've got the answer to that question. Because he did exactly what he was told by God to do. He went to Pharoah, spoke his peace, and brought forth the children of Israel. Moses must've found out exactly who he is. Perhaps, this was Moses' secret? Sort of the key which unlocked his life that he could be the Deliverer of Israel?

I am not comparing myself to Moses. He was in a league of his own. I just knew that I was supposed to write a book. Which I fully knew was a book that the world does not need. So, there was no doubt in my mind. I needed to find out who

---

[16] Ex. 3:11.
[17] Ibid.

I am, as Moses did, so that I might impart my message to the world. Otherwise, I had no idea what to say to the world.

And so as I sat in this neighborhood Starbucks, morning after morning, this went on for about two weeks. And each morning, I thought about this question. I contemplated it. The same question that Moses asked—"*Who am I*"? The more I realized that I didn't really know, the more I knew that I had to know.

Do you know who you are? Before you answer, let me just say, there is great power in questions. More so, I think, than in answers. We have to ask questions in order to move forward in life. Otherwise, we just keep doing what we are doing because it's what we do.

Questions are the key to advancing, spiritually. And the most powerful question I ever asked, was the one I started to ask right there in the Starbucks, as I was in the third day of my sabbatical, in which I was at a loss to figure out what to do with my time—*Mi Anokhi? Who am I?*

I asked myself that question—*Who am I?* And, I realized that I did not have an answer. No more than I could answer Yeshua's question—"*Who do you say that I am?*" I couldn't answer either one of those questions. At least not in any significant way.

Of course, you see, I could say, "I am Gary Goldman," or "I am a messianic Rabbi," or "I am the husband of Laura Goldman and father of two kids." But you know what? I might as well have said, "Blah, blah, blah." Because it didn't mean a thing. Because, in reality, I am none of those things.

What would you say? C'mon. You'd say the same kinda stuff, I guarantee you. And it wouldn't mean a thing for you either. Because it's not the answer. I knew that. I didn't know the answer, but at least I knew that I didn't know the answer! And that was encouraging. That was progress.

So I pressed on. I continued my—whatever it was. I really don't know what it was that I was doing. But as the days went by, during that first two weeks of sabbatical, I kept asking myself that question—"*Who am I?*" That is really how it all started.

18

And I didn't just ask it. I dwelt upon it. And then, the floodgates opened up. Right there in Starbucks.

But again, maybe I've said too much. I'm getting ahead of my story again. And trust me, there is a story here. An extraordinary story.

Something Lacking:

As I continued daily in the Starbucks, asking myself— *Who am I?*—I simultaneously was going through my computer files to see what, if anything, I might have of value to impart as a message to the world.

I thought, perhaps, I could take some older materials and get some ideas for writing a new book? Or maybe even take what I have and, with some editing, simply assemble it into book format?

I had plenty of solid material. Of course, I had fourteen years of bible teachings. Thousands of them, filed away on computer, which could be assembled, edited, and published into book format, without me ever having to come up with anything new.

But as I went through years of my teaching materials, I felt more and more convinced that something had been lacking in my teachings. Though I wasn't sure what it was at that point.

I just knew that the world-at-large does not need to have me tell them that Abraham had faith in God, and therefore, so should you.

Or that Jacob's faith carried him through tough times in the house of Laban, and the same will work for you.

Or how the woman with an issue of blood had lost all hope until she came to Yeshua, and was healed, and so you too will be healed if you just reach out and take hold of God.

Or look how Joseph never lost faith, so God raised him out of the pit to become the right hand of Pharoah, and so too, God will raise you up out of your situation.

Or look how Moses was the Prince of Egypt, and could have ruled the world, but instead chose to follow the Lord, and so he became even mightier than Pharoah, and so you too will overcome opposition if only you humble yourself and obey God as Moses did; etc., etc.

The religious world is built upon such teachings. Life-application teachings.

Taking a bible story, usually one that has to do with overcoming hardship, and applying it to your life situation, is the fabric upon which the religious world is built. The religious world thrives upon these kinds of messages.

Yes, I am a worker in that world. And, yes, I have given thousands of those kinds of teachings. Good ones, if I may say so. Lots of them. And I could have assembled a nice book chock-full of those kinds of teachings.

But when I started going through my old sermon notes, thinking I might adapt some of them into book form, I quickly saw the futility of such an endeavor.

Because life-application teachings are not life-changing. It is the Life itself that changes lives. Not the application of scripture to a person's life, but, rather, the impartation of the Life itself.

Yeshua used to say, "I am the Life." You see? Life isn't something to be applied to life. Life IS Life.

Please don't get me wrong. I'm not saying it's wrong to give life-application teachings. I'm saying that it doesn't give people what they need. Take it from me, as one who has given literally thousands of them in the past.

Yeshua didn't go around giving life-application teachings. Nor did the Apostles. They imparted Life. And people were inspired. Set free. Healed. Encouraged. Joyful. Because of the Life. Because in him was the Life and the Life was the light in the midst of them.

But I did not know how to do that. All I had was life-application teachings. The Messianic Jewish version of them. Perhaps different and unique, in that respect. But still, life-application teachings.

And, therefore, whatever I had to say, had already been said and was continuing to be said every day. Because there are life-application teachers on every street corner. But the Reality is that life-application teachings are not life-changing. They are *info*rmative. Not *trans*formative.

So, at that time, as I sat there in Starbucks, a man on a mission, to write a book, a book which the world did not need, I was not yet on the iPath. I was just a man who knew that something was lacking. Even though I could tell you the Lord is my Shepherd, I lack nothing,[18] something was indeed lacking. And that's why I was sitting in Starbucks every morning, asking myself the ridiculous question—*Who am I?*

Because one thing was for sure, another book full of life-application bible teachings was the last thing the world needed from me. It would just be another piece of hay added into a giant haystack that's already out there.

I deeply wanted to say something of value to the world. In point of fact, I had nothing of the kind. But I was not giving up.

Who Are These People?:

So it was, that during the first two weeks of my sabbatical, I would come into Starbucks, have my coffee, do some reading, ask—*Who am I?*—and then try to begin writing my book. The one that the world did not need.

Day after day, there I was. Waiting for that epiphany moment. A breakthrough, I guess. I had no idea if or how I might ever have one. Or what might be needed to help it along. However, for this great task which I had taken upon my shoulders for the good of mankind, I knew one thing that I needed—to be left alone.

Hardly anybody knew me at Starbucks. Even if they knew me a little bit, they didn't know much about me. And I wanted to keep it that way.

---

[18] *NIV*, Ps. 23:1.

Now maybe you're one of these people who drives thru Starbucks and gets your coffee, but if you've never hung around Starbucks in the mornings, then you couldn't know what it's like. So I'll just tell you. There are a lot of weird people hanging around at Starbucks in the morning. And I clearly was one of them.

As I passed my mornings there, I began to wonder. Who are these people? What are they doing here? Why are they spending their mornings at Starbucks? Shouldn't they be at work? Don't they have anything better to do to occupy themselves than to hang around here? Surely, they don't have a great contribution to make to humanity such as I. Do they?

But then after spending a few mornings there, it occurred to me that many of these people likely were wondering the same things about me. Who is this guy? What is he doing here? Doesn't he have a life? He sure is weird.

Nevertheless, I had work to do. I didn't want to network and develop relationships with anyone. I would never get my contribution to humanity finished if I started schmoozing with the morning crowd at Starbucks.

I was a man on a mission. And I needed to keep my identity a secret. I didn't want anyone to know who I was or why I was spending my mornings at Starbucks. Even though I am certain they were wondering. Even as I was about them.

So I found a spot in the corner, by the storefront window, where no one would bother me. I was there to write a book. It would take effort. And time. Probably a few months. But I would write my book. Because mankind needed this book.

Except as the days passed, I knew that Mankind did not need this book. Not unless I might actually have something of value to say to mankind. Which I didn't.

But, during those first two weeks, I was trying. And as the days went by, I sat in my private corner of Starbucks, in a sea of weird people, saying to myself—*Mi Anokhi? Who am I?* I often said it out loud. But when I did, I said it only in

Hebrew, since I doubted very much anyone would understand, even if they did happen to overhear me.

Day by day, I did this, drinking coffee, producing nothing, looking at the diverse people, wondering what they were doing there, and them wondering what I was doing there. I was beginning to wonder what I was doing there too.

Because I had nothing of value to say. Not to the world anyway. But, even though I didn't know it at the time, there was great value in what I was saying to myself, and contemplating—*Mi Anokhi? Who am I?*

There can be moments in a person's life where something happens, and you don't know what it is. Or how it could have happened to begin with. But when it happens, it catapults you onto a new trajectory, and gives you a totally fresh vision of life.

That's what happened to me one day at Starbucks. The Starbucks in my neighborhood. So, let me tell you about my neighborhood.

The Renter:

My neighborhood is in a totally suburban, residential area, on the Gulf Coast of central Florida. We live in the Tampa Bay area, specifically, in the city of Clearwater, Florida. Ours is a very quiet neighborhood, in a beach community.

By most standards, our neighborhood would be considered rather upscale. Even posh. It is a neighborhood which, quite honestly, would normally be out of my league, economically speaking.

But I'm not ashamed to admit it. You see, I am a renter. And by being a renter, I've been able to live with my family in an upscale neighborhood, that would otherwise be out of our league.

It had been ten years at this point, that I began to rent the house. The owner was Tiffany Feingold-Spiegelman. The hyphenated Jewish surname was the result of marrying Jews, although, Tiffany herself is not Jewish. Tiffany is a Christian, and active in a neighborhood megachurch.

Tiffany had gotten the house in a divorce settlement. The reason for the hyphenated name? After Tiffany divorced her ex-husband, Jay Feingold, she married her ex-husband's law partner. Or I should say, her ex-husband's ex-law partner, Murray Spiegelman.

So, upon divorcing Feingold, she married Spiegelman. Then, she moved, along with her hyphenated Jewish surname, into a nicer house, owned by Spiegelman.

All of this worked to my benefit, because Tiffany Feingold-Spiegelman decided to rent out her former house, which she acquired by divorcing Feingold. So that's where I came in. Ten years earlier. When I rented the house.

I note here that Jay Feingold and Tiffany had a son, Andy Feingold. Andy played on my youth football team. I was the head coach. I'll get into that later in my story.

For the most part, I dwelt happily and peaceably with my family in the house owned by Tiffany Feingold-Spiegelman. We paid our rent every month, and all was well.

Tiffany Feingold-Spiegelman rented the house to me pretty cheap. Perhaps she might have intended to sell it after a couple of years, but when the bottom fell out of the market, nobody was selling their houses unless they had to. So it's a good deal for her and for me.

On her end, she has a steady stream of rent coming in every month, from a decent, trustworthy tenant. And on my end, I've been able to provide my family with a home in a beautiful, quiet neighborhood, with excellent schools, which would otherwise be out of my league.

Being able to live in that house has been a blessing for my family. It's a quiet, peaceful neighborhood with lots of lakes, streams, and ponds. Streets are lined with beautiful, old, moss-decorated southern live oaks. Acres of conservation inviting lots of deer to roam around. My wife, Laura, takes the dog on long walks. Our kids, have been able to attend some of the best public schools in Florida.

The only problem has been that certain people in neighborhoods like ours don't like renters. Take, for example, Theresa, my backyard neighbor. Or as Laura and I call her, "Mother Theresa."

Mother Theresa is mid-40's, divorced, and lives all alone in her big, four-bedroom house with her dog, Pierre, a nasty little yapper, of a breed I do not recognize.

We call her Mother Theresa because she serves on the board of the homeowners association, which in her mind, seems to indicate that she rules over the rest of the neighborhood as a parent to us all.

If your trees need to be trimmed, if your driveway is moldy, if your lawn is not in top condition, etc., you can expect Mother Theresa to correct you on such shortcomings. She will usually give people the benefit of a word of correction. But if you don't respond to her admonishment by making the correction, you can expect to get a threatening letter from the homeowner's association.

Mother Theresa made it plain to me from day one, as we unloaded the moving van, that renters ought not consider themselves actual citizens in our neighborhood. Apparently, our presence drives down the fair market value of everyone else's house. Or so she told me. So she'd be watching me. Always watching.

She wasn't kidding. Mother Theresa routinely uses her pull on the board of the homeowner's association to oppress me. I never get the benefit of an admonishment. If I leave a trash can out overnight, or if one of the palm trees has a branch that is brown and hanging low, or if my lawn has a dead spot, or if one of my backyard shrubs that block the view between my house and hers is looking slightly ill, you can bet I'll get a threatening notice from the association, generated by Mother Theresa's complaint.

Pierre, her faithful canine companion, who typically barks at me upon sight, also apparently does not approve of renters.

"Pierre doesn't like you," she sniveled at me as we crossed paths one day, while walking our dogs.

I am thankful for our home and I do love living where I do. But Mother Theresa's overzealous commitment to keep the neighborhood free of renters, is a burden that is hard to bear.

God's Awesome Ladies (GAL's):

When I was hanging around at Starbucks, trying to write a book for the benefit of mankind, a book in which mankind would have had no interest if ever it had actually been published, I was doing my best to keep to myself and keep my identity hidden.

But there were two people at the Starbucks who knew me. I wasn't sure if they knew what I did professionally, but both Tiffany Feingold-Spiegelman and Mother Theresa were there. And they knew me from the neighborhood.

The reasons that both Tiffany and Mother Theresa could be seen at Starbucks regularly is because they were active in a Christian women's group at the neighborhood megachurch called "GAL's."

GAL's, which stands for "God's Awesome Ladies," was for Christian women who were zealously committed to physical fitness. Mother Theresa is the leader of the group.

GAL's is affiliated with Sunny Lake Community Church, a non-denominational megachurch, located in our neighborhood. Sunny Lake is one of the top 50 largest churches in America.

There was a YMCA across the street from Starbucks, and Sunny Lake megachurch was just a couple of blocks from there. God's Awesome Ladies worked out together at the YMCA. They presumably played tennis, did aerobics, yoga, or whatever might suit their fancy for exercise, and after the workout, they would congregate at Starbucks.

Along with their tennis outfits and athletic gear, they often wore T-shirts bearing the name of their church, "Sunny Lake" along with a motto like: "Firm Believer" or "Bod4God."

That's Me in the Corner:

One of the things I like about this particular Starbucks is the music piping through the speakers at all times. Typically it's the classics of the 60's and 70's. They play many of my favorite bands. Grateful Dead. Allman Brothers. Skynard. Beatles. And, of course, as would be expected for that genre of music, they play a lot of Dylan.

It isn't just that I love Bob Dylan music, which anybody who knows me, knows that I do. But there is nothing quite so inspiring as to hear "Like a Rolling Stone" piping into a place filled with God's Awesome Ladies, dressed in tennis outfits and spandex yoga pants, who spend their mornings sipping non-fat lattes, discussing the bible, praying and engaging in idle gossip.

I typically would try to get my stool along the window, in the corner, facing the parking lot, away from everyone else, where I could keep to myself. But, when you show up every morning at a certain place, certain people are bound to wonder what you're up to. And who you are. And what the heck you're doing in the corner all the time, with your back to the rest of the establishment.

The staff at Starbucks mainly knew me as "Gary," because that's how I introduced myself when asked. None of the staff knew that I was a Rabbi. And I felt no inclination to make that known. In fact, I preferred not to. I had work to do. I was busy writing a book for the good of mankind. Even though I had nothing to say to mankind.

Latasha was the one who started the rumor that I was a writer by trade. And I was fine with that rumor. A rather hefty, African American girl with strands of pink mixed into her hair, Latasha had a voice like Aretha Franklin. And Latasha liked to sing. She was always singing a tune. Never the tune that was being piped through the speakers in the ceiling. But always her own tune. And in a voice that sounded too perfect to be real.

The iPath

Latasha was my favorite Starbucks staff worker. Latasha always had my order working the moment she saw me walk in the door—a grande Pike Place coffee, in a "for here" mug. I greatly prefer the taste of coffee in a ceramic mug, instead of those paper cups. And Latasha always accommodated me.

Latasha had the rare distinction, as sad as it may sound, of being about the only African American at this particular Starbucks. Including patrons. She didn't seem to care.

Latasha was probably the first to ever ask me my name, and when she asked, I was honest with her.

"Gary Goldman," I told her.

"Go-man," she said. Not that she didn't understand me, but Latasha had creative license. She interpreted things her way. I liked that about her.

It was on the second day of my sabbatical, she said to me, "You a writer or something?"

"Something like that," I said, hoping that her words were prophetic.

"You alright, Go-man." Latasha made you feel like if you had her approval, it was as good as God's.

"Thanks," I said sheepishly.

"Hey, I'm a writer too. I write songs."

"Oh?"

"Mostly jazz. I sing at night. You know? Downtown Clearwater." She handed me a card. "You should come see me sometime."

And so it was born, thanks to Latasha, that I became known to the Starbucks staff as "Go-man, the Writer." Anyone not privy to that, probably just knew me as the man in the corner.

I guess Latasha thought I was a writer because she saw me typing and/or writing notes all the time. Of course, nothing I was writing was of any value. But I was writing. I was trying to write a book for the good of the world. The trouble was, I had nothing worth saying to the world.

But I stayed in my corner, and confronted myself. Dwelling on the question—*Who am I?*

28

The King:

Another person who was at Starbucks every morning was Pastor Buddy MacSwain. Pastor Buddy was the Sr. Pastor of the Sunny Lake Community megachurch. He was an incredibly popular and successful megachurch Pastor. And for good reason. Buddy had the dynamic personality, the people-skills, the drive, the looks and the determination to lead a massive body of people in the way that such a group expected of their leadership.

Back in the 80's, Buddy played quarterback at a Christian college in Texas, and then went on to play a few years as a backup quarterback in the NFL.

Buddy's wife, Melanie, was one of the original Hooters girls back in the 80's. One of our claims to fame in the Tampa Bay area, is the very first Hooters located in Clearwater, Florida. Melanie "Melons" MacSwain helped put Hooters on the map.

Of course, all of that was back in the '80's. Buddy and Melons had been founding members of Sunny Lake Community megachurch in 1994, along with Mother Theresa and her former husband, who was the founding Sr. Pastor. Buddy was part of the church leadership and board, and eventually was one of the assistant Pastors on staff.

A couple of years before I moved into the neighborhood, apparently Mother Theresa's ex-husband fell into a scandal with a church secretary. The board dismissed him, and named Buddy MacSwain the new Senior Pastor. Under Buddy and Melons, that church grew exponentially. Sunny Lake has become the 27th largest megachurch in America.

Tampa Bay, like practically every major city in America, is home to several massive, protestant megachurches located in suburban areas. But among megachurches in Tampa Bay, Pastor Buddy is King. Nothing compares in size or stature to Sunny Lake megachurch. And no one compares to Buddy. Buddy is Elvis.

Buddy's big-man-on campus status was plain to see every morning at the Starbucks, where he never lacked a crowd. Especially if the GAL's, a/k/a God's Awesome Ladies happened to be there. They adored their Pastor. Their unwavering devotion to their Pastor and to their church was plain to see every morning at Starbucks.

Pastor Buddy was extremely affable and personable. He liked to go around the room to shake hands and introduce himself, as if he were the owner of the establishment. Which, for all practical purposes, he was. At that particular Starbucks, there was no doubt about it — Buddy ruled.

That's just how it was. If Buddy had his own TV show, it would have to have been called *Everybody Loves Buddy*. Because they do.

Buddy was a great people-person, a charmer and an effective networker. And then there was me. Over in the corner. By the window. Keeping to myself. With my laptop and reading materials, asking myself—*who am I?*—and trying to write a book for the good of the world, unto which I had absolutely nothing of value to say.

And, well, neither did Buddy. He had nothing of value to say either. But no one cared. He had lots to say, and lots of people to listen. So, why couldn't I just be like Buddy?

Well, naturally, I can't be like Buddy, because Buddy is outgoing and affable, likeable, and extroverted. He doesn't sit around in the corner asking himself—*Who am I?* Buddy is a people person. Well-liked. Nobody cares whether he has anything of value to say. He's Buddy McSwain. He's the King. Everyone loves the King. It is enough to just shake his hand. Or to have him come over and say, "What's cooking?"

As for me, I am an introvert. Hopelessly. I know this about myself. I accept it. I can't change.

Yes, I tried group therapy for this. I was invited once to an I.A. meeting. You know, Introverts Anonymous. Total waste of time. Nobody had anything to say.

Okay, not really. LOL. I made that up. But I am an introvert. That part is for real. And I just embrace it. I am as

God made me. No excuses. You have to be honest about these things.

But nobody cares about an introvert. Because the introvert reaches out to no one. The introvert reaches only unto himself. So why should anyone be interested in hearing from someone who is not reaching out, but is instead looking within? They aren't interested. But sometimes they are drawn.

Take Moses for example. Moses was not a man of words. The Torah says so.[19] He was slow of speech. He was not a people person. He spent 40 years in a desert wilderness. But he did pretty well in spite of it. So, maybe I could too?

I just wanted to be left alone, in the corner, by the window, to read, think, and maybe write a few notes in my laptop. I didn't want anyone to know that I was a Rabbi, or let alone, that I am a messianic Rabbi—a fact which always seems to give rise to questions. I didn't want to answer any questions. I just wanted to be left alone.

Buddy's List:

The problem was, if anyone happened to be sitting at the Starbucks enjoying their coffee, Buddy would not leave you alone. Buddy was King. It was his Starbucks. And you couldn't walk into Buddy's Starbucks and expect to be left alone. Not by him anyway. No sir, you could always expect Pastor Buddy to at least say hello to you.

Now, if Buddy happened to think you might be an "unbeliever," then your name would be placed onto Buddy's "unsaved" list. It didn't take long before my name was placed on that list.

I'm not sure how it happened. Probably because one of the GAL's tipped Buddy off. Probably Tiffany Feingold-Spiegelman. Or maybe Mother Theresa. Both of those ladies knew that I am Jewish. And that I am a Rabbi, of sorts.

---

[19] *See*, Ex. 4:10.

In any case, I don't know exactly how he found out, but sure enough, Buddy found out that I am Jewish. And that made me a target. And he also knew that I was some kind of a Rabbi. That made me a double target. He probably had lots of stars next to my name. Stars of David.

In any case, I was definitely on Buddy's unsaved list. And once you're on that list, there's no getting off. No sir. Not until you "make a decision."

To "make a decision" means that you had to pray with Buddy to receive Jesus into your heart. Until you did that, your name's not coming off that unsaved list. Not unless you qualified for an exemption. And I'll explain how exemptions work later on. They're hard to come by.

But so long as you are placed on the unsaved list, and do not qualify for an exemption, then you'd better not expect to be left alone to mind your own business at Starbucks. No matter how hard you try. And that included me. Because sure enough, I was on that list.

Therefore, every morning at Starbucks, in spite of my best efforts to hide in the corner by the window, Buddy would approach me in his affable demeanor, and then try to engage me in conversation, which usually began with some word about mankind's hopeless state of depravity.

Not that I necessarily disagree. I took no issue with the idea that mankind is hopelessly depraved. But I steadfastly refused Buddy's repeated invitation to "make a decision for Christ."

I wasn't there to make a decision. I was there to write a book. Granted, a book which would contribute nothing to the world. But that didn't matter. I was entitled to my freedom as an inalienable right. But Buddy apparently didn't see it that way.

And so, the terms of my freedom were made clear to me—unless and until I made a decision, I wasn't getting off of that list.

The problem was that it was Pastor Buddy's Starbucks. Not mine. Therefore, like it or not, Buddy would be approaching me again day after day, to check if I'm ready to make a decision.

I had to endure this treatment daily for two weeks. I would show up, committed to write a book. I would find my spot, isolated in the corner, by the window, and would try and keep to myself. Reading, making notes. Getting nowhere. Asking myself—*Who am I?*

Then Buddy would approach me by the window. He'd greet me in his affable, friendly manner. Then he'd go right on to tell me about the total depravity of mankind, and ask if I'm ready to make a decision.

And all the while, God's Awesome Ladies would be huddled together on the other side of the coffee shop, in their workout gear and Bod4God T-shirts. Oh, they'd try to be nonchalant about it, but I knew what they were doing. They were interceding! Praying for me!

I was out of my league. Pastor Buddy and the GAL's were not backing down. No sir. This megachurch Pastor, with the loyal, support, of an elite, physically fit detachment of die-hard, suburban, Protestant, white women, were wearing me down. I am not easily broken. But I was beginning to wonder how much longer could I resist?

As much as I valued my incognito status, after a couple of weeks of this, I needed resolution. I had to have closure. There was no avoiding it. One way or another this thing was going to come to a head.

Pastor Buddy and the GAL's had fervently prayed the prayer of faith, and they were not backing own. They were on a mission to reach the lost and spiritually dead at this Starbucks. And, there was no doubt about it. As far as they were concerned, that definitely included me.

The Jig is Up:

I was simply trying to remain anonymous and keep to myself, in order to write a book which the world did not need. And would never need. Or read, for that matter. But, God was taking me in another direction.

Something new was being birthed. Something was happening. I didn't know what it was. Nor how nor why it was happening. But, now, looking back, I know that something indeed was happening. Something life-changing. Transformative.

But for the meantime, I was stuck on Pastor Buddy's unsaved list. And I wasn't getting off that list. Not without making a decision. Which I flat-out was not going to do.

Buddy clearly knew I was a Jewish Rabbi. And I didn't want to get into the fact that I am a messianic Rabbi. I simply wished to remain anonymous and to avoid drawing attention to myself. But I realized that unless I had a heart to heart with Buddy, he'd never leave me alone. I assumed a simple explanation would clue him in, and get him off my case.

"Listen," I said to Buddy, in a hushed tone. "I'm trying to keep this on the down low. Okay? I am a *Messianic* Rabbi."

And Buddy just stood there with his grin and nodded, as the GAL's were huddled up across the room. I could plainly hear one of them rebuking the spirit of unbelief. Buddy's expression didn't change one bit. Obviously, he was not tracking with me. So I tried again.

"Messianic Jews are Jews who believe in Yeshua," I said. "You know, Jesus?"

But Buddy just grinned, and nodded in his polite and affable way. And then he put a gentle hand on my shoulder.

"Rabbi," said Buddy in his southern drawl, "we're all flawed. Hopeless sinners. There's no hope for mankind except through the blood of Christ."

"I know," I said. "I get all that."

"Are you ready, then?" said Buddy.

"Ready for what?" I said.

"Do you think that you might like to make a decision today?"

In spite of my attempts to try and explain to Buddy that I was a messianic Jew, and a *messianic* Rabbi, and had been for quite some time now, this fact made no difference to him.

It wasn't getting me off of Buddy's "unsaved" list. I gave him my card, to verify my credentials. No dice.

"I'm already saved," I protested to Buddy.

"It just doesn't work that way, Rabbi," he responded.

And then he'd go right on with telling me about the state of mankind's depravity, and how the only hope for mankind was to make a decision right now to accept God's plan for salvation.

"It's so simple," he said. "All you have to do is say this little prayer. It's called the sinners' prayer. Won't you pray this prayer with me right now, Rabbi?"

I just wanted to be left alone. I was tired of this daily charade. It was really stressing me out. But I was not going to pray the doggone sinner's prayer with Pastor Buddy.

And no matter how much I tried to explain to Buddy that I am a Messianic Jew, and what that meant, and that I was surely already saved, ol' Buddy just wouldn't accept it.

In fact, now that the jig was up, things only got worse. Because the revelation of my identity as a messianic Jewish Rabbi only gave rise to more questions on Buddy's part.

Like whether I believed in the same "Jesus" as him; and whether I believed the "right" things about that "Jesus;" and whether I accepted the new Testament or just the Old; and whether I belonged to a religion of works as opposed to faith; and did I accept that righteousness is only through the blood of the Lamb; and why did I still keep the Sabbath, and feasts, and all those dietary laws; and don't I know that circumcision availeth nothing, etc. etc.

So now that I came forward with the fact that I am a Jewish believer, hoping that it would get Buddy off of my case, instead, Buddy became Torquemada the Grand Inquisidor.

All I wanted was to dwell in peace and harmony with all members of the human race at Starbucks. I took issue with no one. I had no problem with anyone else's religious beliefs. Why couldn't I be left alone regarding mine?

All I needed was a private space to focus on writing my book that the world did not need. But Pastor Buddy wouldn't have it. Not in his Starbucks. No sir.

The man just wouldn't leave me in peace. Messianic or not, and no matter what I might say in response to Buddy's theological inquiry, unless and until the day that I might agree to make a decision, there would remain an air of suspicion toward me.

Because after all, the bottom line for Buddy is, how can anybody believe in Jesus and still be Jewish? Right? Something must be wrong with me.

So, no matter what I might say to try and explain that I did not need to be "saved," that I already am saved, the Pastor and his gang of bible-toting work-out queens would be continually praying for the Lord to fully open my mind to the truth.

And the fact that I, too, am a zealous believer in physical fitness, and, in fact, a committed jogger, and have been for many years, well, that did not change anything either.

Because so long as I was Jewish, it didn't matter if I was physically fit or not. Or if I believed in Yeshua or not. I was going to hell, unless I made a decision and said the sinner's prayer. Right? And, furthermore, until I said the prayer, I wasn't getting off of Buddy's list.

Lightning Strikes:

Oftentimes, when the Lord is about to do something magnificent in your life, the pressure builds, like a woman about to have a baby. It build and builds, and then suddenly, the release comes—the thing is birthed.

And so it happened that on one particular day in October, after about two weeks into my sabbatical, that lightning struck. On that day, Pastor Buddy greeted me loudly, from across the room, for all to hear, just before he sat down for coffee with God's Awesome Ladies. That was the day that Buddy said, loudly, in his deep Southern accent:

"Shalom, Rabbi!"

I nodded and silently saluted back to him, hoping to go unnoticed. However, to my chagrin, the Pastor's greeting caught the attention of Evan. Evan was Jewish.

Now, Evan worked at Starbucks. He was an early 20's kid with a bone through his nose, golden lip ring, and large stainless steel gauges, which were disfiguring each of his ears.

Basically, every visible part of Evan's body was covered with body art. Face, neck, fingers, elbows. Every visible body part. And I suspect it can be safely assumed that many of Evan's non-visible body parts may have been tattooed as well.

Let me just say that I am completely hip about body art. Okay, I admit, I counsel my own children against it, but I have nothing against it generally. I sincerely admire some works of body art, and oftentimes, I think it can be quite beautiful.

In any case, body art is traditionally frowned upon in Judaism. This is due to certain Torah commands concerning markings on the flesh. Moreover, due to the history of Jews being tattooed with numbers in the Nazi death camps, it is not well-thought of in traditional Judaism. Many Jewish mothers warn their children that some strict Jewish cemeteries actually will not bury people who have intentionally undergone tattooing.

But this generation of young Jewish millennials have a different view, and, personally, I am fine with that. As I said, I think body art is beautiful. I just feel, it would be wise to leave at least some part of the human body in its original condition. So, maybe in that respect, I'm old school. Otherwise, I would have no objection to Evan's violation of the long-standing Jewish legal injunction against body art.

Now another thing that is traditionally frowned upon in Judaism, is when Jewish people believe in Yeshua. Believing that Jesus is the Messiah, could also keep you out of a lot of Jewish cemeteries, not to mention quite a few other mainline

Jewish institutions. In this respect, therefore, I sympathize with Evan's situation. On the other hand, there's no guarantee that he would sympathize with mine.

Evan clearly took notice of Buddy's acknowledgement of me as "Rabbi." And since Evan was Jewish, I knew right away that this greeting of me as "Rabbi," was likely to give rise to certain questions. Because Evan already knew that I was Jewish too.

He knew I was Gary Goldman. He'd seen the star of David I wore on my necklace. Though I was not decorated as he was, still we were members of the tribe, and therefore, brothers.

But he did not know that I was Rabbi Goldman. He thought I was Go-man, the writer. Thanks to Latasha. But now, thanks to Pastor Buddy, my cover was blown.

So, Evan came over to where I was sitting. Evan began changing out the trash near my stool by the window. But I knew that trash can didn't need to be changed. He was going to ask me questions. And I was bracing for it.

I note, I never before had tried to talk to Evan about Yeshua. For one thing, I didn't feel he was open to it. What could I do to reach Evan? Tell him about mankind's state of moral depravity and ask him to make a decision? Not gonna work.

I treated Evan just the same as anyone else in the world. I treated him kindly. Respected him. And remained ready and willing to share with him about Yeshua, should there at any time be an opening to do so. What more could I do?

Otherwise, I tried to stay busy with my work. Whatever that was. I still did not know.

Exemption:

Now maybe you are thinking that since Evan is Jewish, he, too, was a target on Buddy's unsaved list. But not so!

At first, this seemed unfathomable to me. But, I assure you, Evan clearly was not targeted for "salvation" by Pastor Buddy and his gang of GAL's. Why not?

At first I asked that same question. Then I figured it out. It was abundantly clear to me what was going on. Call me a conspiracy theorist, I don't care. There was a secret policy, which granted exemption only to certain people.

You see, there were certain people who were not placed on Pastor Buddy's list, even though they fit the profile in every way. Even though they should have been categorized as "unsaved," just as I was. Quite clearly, some people had been given an "exemption."

Take Evan, for example. He was Jewish. Just like me. And clearly Jews were placed on the unsaved list. But not Evan. Evan was left alone. He was able to move about freely in Starbucks. He could go about his business, unmolested by the God-squad.

Evan and Buddy, were openly co-existing, notwithstanding Buddy's mission for reaching the lost. Even though, I personally believe that Evan really was quite lost. And he was Jewish. Which meant that Evan should have been on that list. But he wasn't. No attempts whatsoever to save Evan.

Clearly, Evan was exempt. How did he do it? Well, I figured it out. The exemption policy, was a secret policy, never vocalized, but completely understood, quite intuitively, by all parties involved in efforts to reach the lost. And the way it worked, if you could be considered "undesirable" by the good folks at Sunny Lake Community megachurch, you were exempt. You were not on the list.

Take Evan. Evan was a Jew, like me. But Evan was no ordinary Jew. Evan was a totally-tattooed Jew. With bone in nose. Too scary for Sunny Lake. And that's why he was exempt. And I wasn't. A few tattoos, that would've been different. Then Evan would have been on Buddy's list for sure. But totally tattooed, with nose bone, well that clearly qualified for an exemption.

Okay, admittedly, this exemption theory involves some speculation on my part. But I'm quite sure of it.

As further proof I offer this: Only one other person at Starbucks had an exemption—Latasha. Even though a Jazz singer and at times openly stated that she was not a Christian, she was never targeted for salvation by Buddy and the GAL's. Why not? But, of course. Latasha was black.

So, I figured out the secret. Heavily tattooed and/or African American people were automatically exempt from this white, affluent, suburban megachurch in our neighborhood. Oh sure, the doors of that church were open to all. But no special effort was being made to reach out to certain folks. But as for me, there was no free ride.

Perhaps I should have been flattered. It is good to be wanted. But I was not flattered. To me, this whole scenario seemed unfair. It was discriminatory. And I, too, wanted to be discriminated against.

But rules are rules. So I began to wonder—was there something I could do to qualify for an exemption? I began to seriously ponder this.

Maybe I could make myself "undesirable" in some way? Maybe if I shoved a bone through my nose, and covered myself from head to toe in body art, then Buddy and the GAL's would leave me in peace too? Unfortunately, that was not an option for me. Nor was becoming an African American.

Thanks to discriminatory practices, Evan and Latasha had a free ride. But as for me, there was nothing I could do to get one. How unfair life can be at times.

Co-existing:

I note that not only did Evan's exemption enable him to move freely about the room, unmolested, also Evan had great rapport with Pastor Buddy. Evan always greeted Buddy with a friendly smile. He'd say, "What up, Pastor?" and Buddy was like, "My man, Evan!" and that sort of thing.

Latasha didn't go for it. One time while waiting in line for a refill, Buddy said to Latasha, "Sistah!" and she looked at him like he was the devil.

That was the end of that. Buddy and Latasha still co-existed, but in a different way than Buddy and Evan.

As for Evan, Buddy and him had an implicit understanding. It was never stated, but at all times implied. Evan would be nice to Buddy, so long as Buddy wouldn't try to "save" Evan.

In the beginning, I co-existed with Evan as well. However, that all changed on this one particular day. The day that Buddy said from across the room, in a loud voice that all could hear, "Shalom, Rabbi." That set in motion a chain of events that changed everything. And it would catapult me in a new direction in life.

My Confession:

So it was, on that day, Evan heard Buddy call me "Rabbi." And that was the shot heard round the world. It was the tiny spark that changed everything. I couldn't conceal it anymore. I had no choice. I had to confess to Evan.

I told him the truth and the whole truth about who I am, professionally-speaking, and what I do. To which Evan squinted like he'd just bit into a lemon, and made the inevitable, obligatory response, with a lisp, due to the stud in his tongue: "You mean Jews for Jesus?!"

Which I, of course, emphatically denied. And then I proceeded with the usual litany of how I am not a Jews for Jesus, though I have nothing against Jews for Jesus, they are wonderful people, I have many friends who are Jews for Jesus, but I am not one of them, since they are really Jewish Christians, but I am not a Christian, although I have nothing against Christians either, they are wonderful people too, I have many friends who are Christians, but I am not one of them—

And, as Evan crossed his arms across his chest and shook his head in the negative, I then continued with the whole schmear about how I am simply a Jewish person who

41

practices all the Jewish customs and keeps Jewish holidays; and my son was circumcised on the eighth day; and I personally trained both of my kids for bar and bat mitzvah; and I fast every year on Yom Kippur; and keep a kosher home; and eliminate all leavened bread products from my home the day before Passover; and often eat bagels and lox on Sundays; and I am the hugest fan of Bob Dylan and Jerry Seinfeld—

And then, judging by the look of disgust upon Evan's face, I quickly added the whole bit about how even though I am Jewish, and even though I do in fact believe Jesus *is* the Messiah, we call him "Yeshua," not "Jesus," because, after all, he was Jewish, and nobody ever called him "Jesus" in his time, because they didn't actually speak English in those days, and his mother and all of his original followers were all Jews, and blah, blah, blah, blah blah—

And of course, Evan was thoroughly confused. And thoroughly not buying it. Not one bit. Then, as it often happens, Evan proceeded to pitch a fit and went on to berate me.

"You're no different than that Pastor over there!" He angrily exclaimed.

"But I thought you were okay with him?" I said.

"How would you know?"

"I've seen you co-existing with him."

"Well," Evan paused, then continued, "that's because I am okay with him."

"Then how come you're not okay with me?" I said. "After all, you said I'm no different than him."

"But he's not Jewish!"

"So?" I said.

"He's got a right to believe what he believes. You on the other hand—"

"But I don't necessarily believe what he believes," I said.

"Oh yes, you do!" argued Evan.

"Well, Buddy sure doesn't think so," I said.

"I don't care what he thinks," said Evan. "You can't be Jewish and believe in Jesus."

"Well, I am Jewish."

"No you're not."

"Yes, I am. But if you say I'm not, then what's the problem? You should be okay with me. Just like you're okay with Buddy."

Evan took a deep breath. He gathered his thoughts, then looked at me angrily.

"I am not okay with you. Because you say that you are Jewish. But you're not. You're a Christian."

"Well, Buddy doesn't think I am," I protested.

"I don't care what Buddy thinks! I say you're a Christian. And I don't know if Jews believe in hell. But if we do, then you're definitely going there."

What does one say to that? I was condemned to Jewish hell by Evan, the totally tattooed Jew. And while I stood condemned by Evan for the alleged offense of becoming a Christian; I stood condemned to Christian hell by God's Awesome Ladies and their beloved Pastor-King for the offense of *not* becoming a Christian. Was there no hope for me?

In the background, Latasha was singing one of her songs. I don't know what it was. But it was melancholy. Sort of Billie Holiday-ish. It was soothing. Healing. Because there was something sincere about it. A song of truth, in the midst of darkness and ignorance.

It helped me regain a semblance of normalcy in the midst of this coffee-shop-from hell. You see, to me, believing in Yeshua is the most Jewish thing a Jew can do. But some Jews and some Christians insist otherwise. It's one thing Jews and Christians seem to agree on: That if you believe in Jesus, you aren't Jewish anymore. It's absurd. But for a messianic Jew, rejection can come from every angle.

Now that Evan had finished lambasting me, he drifted back to his position by the Espresso machine. And I tried to go back to writing my book. The book that was of no value to the world.

So I pulled up that scripture verse. From Exodus 3:11. I pulled it up on my laptop. The one that says, *"Mi Anokhi? Who am I?"* And I dwelt on it. Contemplated it. As I'd been doing for days now. And I said it out loud. Softly. *Mi Anokhi. Who am I?*

I was okay with Evan, even though he was totally tattooed, which violates Jewish law. So Evan should've been okay with me. But he wasn't.

And I was okay with Buddy, even though he was a Christian, and believed that everyone not of the same mind as him needed to get saved. So Buddy should've been okay with me, but he wasn't.

Meanwhile, Evan was okay with Buddy, and Buddy was okay with Evan. They had an understanding. But Buddy was not okay with me. And neither was Evan. And I couldn't qualify for an exemption from either one of them.

And, from my point of view, all of this was not okay. My only intention was to write a book. A book that the world did not need. But, I swear, I never intended any harm to anyone in the process. So why was the world closing in on me? How come everyone was out to get me? And who am I to think that I might have anything of value to give to the world?

Stop Praying, Let God Pray in You:

Yeshua taught that we should pray for those who persecute us and bless those who treat us wrongfully. That in doing so, even if they don't change, we are able to overcome evil with good, and rise above the chaos of a perishing world.

So, I started praying. And then it happened. I had closed my eyes and I was praying for Evan. And for Buddy. Softly, but audibly. I was asking God to open their eyes. "Father open their eyes to understand, to see the Truth. Open their eyes to see and know who the Messiah really is—"

Right then, I was interrupted by a man's voice. Just as I was praying, in this way, suddenly I heard a voice to my right. A voice which said: "Stop praying."

I opened my eyes. A bearded, early 30's young man wearing an "I love Israel" hoody sweatshirt was sitting in the stool next to me. He had been sitting there all along during the confrontation with Evan. I had seen him peripherally, but had not taken notice of him, as he seemed to be just minding his own business. I realized now, he probably had witnessed this whole scene with Evan.

The young man was drinking a cappuccino, and the foam was upon his mustache, which actually looked quite ridiculous.

He had a large "Chai" hanging from a thick gold necklace. He was kind of olive-skinned. He had distinct, pointed, facial features, light brown hair, and although his hair was rather straight and flat, he had managed to form it into long dreadlocks. I assume that takes a lot of work for people with straight hair. I also noticed that he wore a lot of patchouli.

"Excuse me?" I said.

"Stop praying," he said. He took a sip of cappuccino. "You don't know what you're doing."

The young man spoke with sort of an African accent.

"I'm praying to God," I replied.

"Really?" he snickered.

"Is there a problem?" I said.

"Listen to me," he said. "Stop Praying. Let God pray in you." He took another hearty sip of cappuccino.

"Who are you?" I demanded.

"Don't worry about that," he said. "You need to know who you are."

"Oh yeah?"

"That's right. If you knew that, then you'd know who I am."

I chuckled, as if I was unmoved by this remark. But I was hiding my true feelings. And he seemed to know it.

"Hey, I got work to do here," I insisted.

It was then I noticed that "Ballad of a Thin Man" was playing in the background.

"Oh yeah. You're supposed to be a Rabbi, right?" he said.

"That's right." I said. "Are you Jewish?"

"Beta Israel. Thru my mother. My father was white. European. I never knew him."

I knew, of course, that the Beta Israel are the Jews from Ethiopia, who lived there for at least 1500 years, practicing all common Jewish rites and customs. Many of them have made Aliya, which is to say, they've immigrated to Israel.

But many Beta Israel are still in Ethiopia. And they are under persecution by the Ethiopian government. But most cannot make Aliya, even though there is no doubt of their Jewish ancestry. The problem is many of the Jews in Ethiopia over the years came to believe that Yeshua is the promised Messiah.

Hence, even though they continued to practice Judaism, and even though their Jewish ancestry is not in dispute, but is an established fact of history, because of their belief in Yeshua, the State of Israel will not grant them the citizenship offered to all Jews under the "law of return." Not without denying their faith in Yeshua anyway.

So, the Beta Israel are rejected by their own people on account of being believers in Yeshua, and are persecuted by the government in Ethiopia on account of being Jewish.

"If you're a Rabbi," said this young man, "then you should know that God doesn't need to hear from you. It's you who needs to hear from him."

"I'm a *messianic* Rabbi, ok?"

He snickered and took another dose of cappuccino, freshly foaming up his mustache.

"Oh, is that what you are?" he said, sarcastically.

At that point, I didn't know where this guy was coming from. I felt that I had already reached my quota for the day as far as arguing with people who objected to me based on some religious ground.

Hence, rather than engage in another argument, I tried to ignore the young man. To no avail.

"You don't know who you are," the young man said. "That's your problem."

"I know exactly who I am," I responded.

"Nah, ya don't. You were saying, '*Mi anokhi*'? out loud. I heard you."

Obviously, he understood some Hebrew, which was cool. But I felt pretty embarrassed.

"You shouldn't eavesdrop on people, it isn't nice." I said.

"Well, you should know who you are. You are a teacher of Israel and you don't know these things?"[20]

"Yeah, so what's your point?"

"If you knew who you are," he said, leaning forward, eyes squinted, and left index finger pointing directly at me, "if you had even a mustard seed of knowledge of who you really are, you wouldn't be praying for anyone to see the Truth. You would hold the Truth in your heart, in your eyes, in your lips, and even in the palm of your hand. Like bread. And people would be coming to you, to eat the bread that you have to give them. Including that boy with all the tattoos. And a whole lot of other people. They'd be sitting at your feet and learning from you. But you got nothing to give. Because you don't know who you are."

"Whatever," I said.

I went into defense mode. I waved him off with my right hand, trying to extricate myself from this situation. But Mr. Jewish Bob Marley, with the cool dreads, would not back off.

"You don't have a clue who the Messiah is either," he insisted.

Again, I tried to ignore him, pretending to be reading on my laptop. But my non-response to his provocative statement only left him staring at me.

"You're no different than that Pastor over there, the guy with all the work-out queens."

At this point, I had heard that comparison made one too many times.

---

[20] John 3:10.

"Look, bud, I am busy here. Now, I respect your opinions, but I really don't want to have an argument with you. Okay?"

He stared at me intensely. There was something about his stare, something that seemed to say he knew something that I did not know. Was that even possible? Could I possibly be enlightened by a guy who reeked of patchouli?

"Alright, Mr. Messianic Rabbi," he said. "Have it your way, if you like, I'll leave ya alone."

"Who do you think *you* are?" I proudly retorted, folding my arms across my chest.

He leaned toward me. His stare deeply penetrated my eyes at this point, as he continued.

"I know who I am and where I am going. But you know neither who I am, nor where I am going."[21]

I smirked. But I was thrown by that statement. I was indeed surprised that he seemed to be quoting from the New Testament. Then he went on:

"My sheep hear my voice,"[22] he said. "You don't know who I am, because you haven't been listening."

I took a deep breath. I do that when I'm frustrated with a person. It seems to help me not to be rude.

"Okay," I said. "So you obviously know some New Testament. Who are you?"

He finished his cappuccino, crumpled up the cup. He wiped his mustache with his sleeve, and I was glad. That foam on his face was really bothering me.

"I am who I am," he said.

"Can you be a little more specific?" I responded.

Flipping his dreadlocks behind his shoulders with a flick of his head, he said: "He who has seen me, has seen the Father.[23] But you have not seen me. Therefore, you don't know who I am."

---

[21] *See*, John 8:14.
[22] *See*, John 10:27.
[23] *See*, John 14:9.

With that, Marley (as I call him), tossed his cup into the new trash liner, which had been placed there courtesy of Evan, and he went on his merry way. My eyes followed him out the door. Then he stopped, turned back, re-entered the building, and came back toward where I was sitting.

Marley had this very slight, confident, Mona Lisa type of smile, the kind that seems to say that he knows some secret that hardly anyone else knows. And that he couldn't explain to you if even if he wanted to, because you wouldn't understand.

"Just remember one thing," he said pointing at me. "You did not choose me. I chose you.[24]"

I didn't know who he was, didn't have his name, didn't have any idea why he confronted me. Nor did I have any idea if I would ever see him again.

I could have easily brushed off this incident and ignored it. I could have filed it away as nothing more than a confrontation with an oddball. But I didn't. I don't know why, I didn't. But I didn't.

An impression was made. He spoke not as Rabbis speak. Not as I was accustomed to speaking. He spoke as one who had authority.[25]

I was amazed. I didn't understand it. I just knew that I wanted to speak the way he spoke. Not in terms of what he said. But with authority.

From then on, I remembered this incident with Marley, and the things Marley had said. It just kinda stuck with me in my mind. I could've easily dismissed it. But I didn't. Instead, I listened. I retained it. So, it impacted me. In a deep and mysterious way.

Something was happening, but I didn't know what it was. Nor how, nor why it was happening. I was on a new trajectory. I did not yet know this. But I was. I did not know because I did not choose to be on a new path. I thought I was

[24] *See*, John 15:16.
[25] *See*, Mark 1:22.

fine where I was. But I was propelled onto it. Although, I didn't yet know it, because it wasn't my own doing, nevertheless, I was just beginning to walk along the iPath.

So, why me? I do not know. I am no different than anyone else. Nor did I do anything to deserve or even to incite it. All I did was ask myself a simple question, sincerely, and from the depths of my heart. The same question which Moses had asked. And I'm not even sure why I asked it.

I just asked—*Mi Anokhi? Who am I?* And then, it was as if a door had opened up in heaven, and the universe was collaborating to show me the answer.

So, yes, I have wondered—*Why me?* Maybe that's what you are wondering too. And the answer I have to that is— *Why not you?* I guarantee that I am no different than you.

What happened to me, can and will happen to you. But only if you ask the question. And I know you won't ask the question, unless you are prompted. As I was.

But, that's not up to me. All I can do is teach what I have learned. I've got a story to share, and I will share it. And I just know that if it incites you to ask, in sincerity, as I did, then it will happen. You, too, will be drawn onto the iPath.

Ask and it shall be answered. So, if you want to know who I am, then I say unto you—*Who are you?*

I was just beginning to discover it. And I sat there, bewildered, looking through the plate glass storefront, as Marley exited the Starbucks, with "Ballad of a Thin Man," by Bob Dylan, piping thru the speakers in the background, and rich, white, suburban women, all zealous Protestants, dressed in tennis outfits and spandex athletic gear, were laughing it up and drinking lattes with their beloved all-star Pastor.

2

The Captain

A Change of Scenery:

It was mid-November. Just over six weeks into my Sabbatical. After the incident with Marley, I did not return to Starbucks often. I just couldn't take too much more of that scene. I decided to limit that to small doses. And the few mornings I was there, I did not see Marley. Which was disappointing.

But instead of that scene, I started taking long walks in the morning, and then, after Laura and the kids were gone, I brewed up my own coffee at home, and nestled into a comfortable patio chair on my screened-in back porch.

The daytime weather in Florida is perfect between about November and April. During those mornings, as I sat on my back porch, new ideas starting pouring into me like fresh manna. And then I'd spend the day taking notes.

All I was doing was having my morning devotional time, reading scriptures, over coffee, as I had done for many years. But I was seeing it all differently now. And after reading, contemplating, then a stream of thoughts would come to me, from I don't know where. It poured into me, like a stream of consciousness.

As the thoughts poured in, then I'd sit there, furiously trying to scribble it all down. If I didn't get it down into notes, I'd forget it. So I scribbled down whatever I could. In a month's time I must've gone through about six or seven yellow legal pads, which I kept locked away in a safe.

But then, after a few weeks of this, the stream slowed down. The incident with Marley was etched upon my memory, but it was fading. Inspiration ebbs and flows, like the tide goes in and out. And it was definitely going out. I didn't understand any of this, but I just felt I needed another change of scenery.

So, I was on an airplane, headed for the mountains of Utah. The news was that Utah had been blessed with some major snow storms. These major dumps already had amounted to several feet through the late October and early November. That meant early season skiing was now open.

Back in Florida, by November, we are still looking at the tail end of summer. Temperatures still run close to 90 degrees by day. That's when the snowbirds start pouring in. The retirees from the Northeast and Midwest, who spend their winters in Florida, then return to NY or Chicago for the summer.

As for me, I was looking forward to some snow, and some nice, refreshing, cold weather. A change of scenery, and a few days of alone time in the mountains might be just what I needed.

It was the culmination of football season. As a youth football coach, my team was heavily engaged in a playoff run. But I needed a few days off from that as well. The stress of the season was starting to wear on me.

It was not unusual for me to take a trip to Utah for some skiing. Usually, Laura goes with me. But she couldn't take off from her social work, and in any case, she seemed to understand that I needed to do this alone.

"I'm fine with it," she said. "Go and do whatever."

The word "whatever" was Laura's way of saying "you need to go and get your head straight."

So with her full approval and consent, I was off to the mountains of Snowbird, Utah for four days of, well, "whatever."

I didn't know what I was going to do either. I just knew I needed to do something, so that whatever was happening to me, even though I didn't know what it was, would continue. The idea of retreating to the rocky mountains was with the hope that it would help me to somehow continue to be revived and refreshed. After all, that is the point of sabbatical, I guess.

So maybe by going away to some isolated place of great natural beauty, where I could be alone with my thoughts, and be in touch with God's natural creation, fresh manna would continue to fall on me, and I would come back with a newer, even brighter vision for life.

Universal Law:

As my plane to Utah took off, I was reminded how much I love to fly. Something about being up in the air causes me to have amazing thoughts.

I tend to become extremely creative up in the air. I always try to get a window seat. I really enjoy the views from the air. I have a little MP3 player, with sport headphones that I use for jogging. I like to listen to inspirational music, as I peer out the window, and marvel at how different the earth looks from the air.

I also like to read on airplanes. Something about that aerial perspective fills my head with ideas. Some of my best ideas come out of flying. My MP3 player doubles as a recording device, so I often dictate my thoughts into it so that I make a record.

I also sometimes enjoy watching a film while up in the air. I actually don't know how to download a movie to my iPhone, but with the help of my preteen kids, I am usually able to arrange it. My daughter agreed to help me out this time, and when she asked what movie I wanted, I just told her to pick one.

So, between my music, reading materials, and a downloaded in-flight movie, I was all set, and was really looking forward to the 4.5 hour flight as a time of relaxation and inspiration, as much as the Rockies themselves.

However, upon take-off, as we ascended, and as I was enjoying the view out of the window over the Gulf of Mexico, I suddenly became extremely upset. For as we reached about ten thousand feet and began our Westerly course, the captain introduced himself over the loudspeaker.

Some captains do that. Others do not. I greatly prefer the ones who do not.

You see, when I get on an airplane, I don't want to know anything about the guy in the cockpit. He is the captain. Period. I don't want to know his name. I don't want to know where he's from. I don't want to know what he looks like, nor what his voice sounds like. In fact, I don't even want to know that he's human. I prefer to believe that he is not human.

I say, leave that particular mystery behind the veil. Lock the cockpit door and let El Capitán do his job. Which is to fly the plane. That's it. Don't talk to us. Fly the plane.

One of the reasons I don't want to know the captain's name, is because then it is possible that the worst could happen. In fact, I might find out that the captain has a last name like Silverman or Horowitz.

You see, in my understanding of how the universe works, Jews don't fly airplanes. Jews are good with a stethoscope. Jews do your taxes. If you need investment advice, you can always count on a Jew for that. But when it comes to operating heavy machinery—forklifts, backhoes, and of course, airplanes—you do not want a Jewish person.

It is a universal law, or at least should be, that Jews don't fly airplanes. Gentiles fly airplanes. We Jews are too neurotic for that kind of thing.

Probably because we've been through too much, historically. We are a persecuted people. Whatever the reason, it doesn't matter.

All I want to know when I get on board an airplane is that Captain Johnson is in the cockpit. Or Captain Thompson.

I want that guy who was raised on sausage and biscuits; who went off to school each day to the sound of his mother's voice saying, "I love you, son." Not the guy whose mother said, "Put a coat on, for God's sake, you'll catch cold and die."

I want the guy who flew F-15 fighter jets for the U.S. Air Force. Or F-16's, or F-4's. Actually, I don't care which F he flew. What I care about is that his nickname was "Iceman;" he retired at the rank of Colonel, and he is now flying commercial jets for absolutely no reason other than the fact that his one true passion and purpose in life is to fly jets.

So long as the man in the cockpit is *that* man, then I know I'm okay. And if that's not the case, then I'm not okay. In which case I don't want to know about it. Especially not if he has a Jewish surname.

Nevertheless, as our jet ascended a voice came over the loudspeaker. And the voice which came over that loudspeaker was the worst of all possible scenarios. To my horror, it was a voice which introduced itself as "Captain Morris Rosenblatt."

Captain Rosenblatt, in a New York City accent, not only introduced himself, but went on to state that through some wicked combination of El Niño and the jet stream, we were *possibly* in for some turbulence along the way. He wasn't kidding.

My usual plan for quiet enjoyment of the flight was blown apart. For the next five hours, I was a nervous wreck. I couldn't possibly read, sleep, listen to music on my Mp3 player, or relax as if everything was okay. Our plane was being flown by a man named Rosenblatt. And that was not okay!

Let God Pray in You:

Not only was the very idea of a Jewish commercial airline pilot, in and of itself, a clear violation of universal law, but moreover, Captain Rosenblatt's jet was bouncing all over the sky—upward, downward, and sideways.

A steady stream of apologies and explanations flowed forth from the cockpit, from a voice which, in a more perfect world, might have served humanity as a Nobel peace prize winning physicist, the inventor of the microchip, a real estate lawyer in Manhattan, or hotel owner in Miami Beach—but who certainly in God's plan for creation could have no business being in the cockpit of a 737!

55

All I could do was hold on to the seat and pray. And as the plane hit turbulence, causing it to jolt up and down several times in a row, I was praying for my dear life. It was then, that suddenly a voice popped into my head:
"Don't pray to God. Let God pray in you."
From where did this voice come? I don't know. I should say, it was not exactly a "voice," but more like a thought. Yet, it clearly wasn't my thought. It was someone else's thought. Coming from beyond myself. I knew this. Though I didn't know what it was. Except that it was like a voice, but one that was inaudible. Or audible only to me.

Then I remembered. The word was basically what the Jewish Rasta-man had said to me at Starbucks. And then, within myself, I heard it again:
"Don't pray to God. Let God pray in you."
I shifted in my seat. I repositioned my body. I was too anxious, I thought. For now, I needed to do something to set myself at ease. I took my headphones out of my MP3 player, and plugged them into the socket my iPhone.

In doing this, I was now plugged into the movie that my daughter, Ariella, had downloaded for me, before leaving town.

"You will *love* the movie I downloaded, Dad," she said with a grin, as I hugged her goodbye earlier that morning.

I figured, at least, perhaps, it might take my mind off of this roller coaster ride in the air, orchestrated by the Jewish "Iceman." Or more accurately, the Jewish "Goose."

Now I could just sit back and watch the film. Not a bad idea, I thought. Except for one problem. Of all the thousands of films out there, the movie that my daughter downloaded into my iPhone was *Alive*, the story of the Uruguay National rugby team, whose plane crashed high in the Andes mountains when the pilot made a wrong turn and flew accidentally into the peaks. The team survived only by eating the frozen body parts of their dead friends. Terrific. Oh well, at least it wasn't *Snakes on a Plane*. So, I watched it anyway.

Landing in Salt Lake was horrifying. Snow was pouring out of the sky, blowing everywhere. The plane jerking up and down. I couldn't see hardly anything out the window where I was sitting. Except tall, rugged, ice-covered peaks. Just like the ones in the movie.

Okay if I Sit Here?:

When we finally landed, in what looked to me like a blizzard, I felt relieved. I thought, yes, this was exactly how the Uruguayan rugby team must've felt when they were at last climbing into the rescue helicopter.

My plan was to rent a car and drive to the hotel at the ski resort. However, hey, I'm from Florida. When I saw the snow coming down, no way was I driving into that.

So I cancelled the car rental, and booked a ride on the next shuttle. Consequently, I had an hour to kill at the airport. Tired, hungry and still feeling a bit uneasy, I located a Starbucks and nestled in for one of those delicious marshmallow Rice-Krispy treats and a hot cup of Pike Place coffee.

I was a bit disappointed that they didn't have the ceramic mug option, but I was so thoroughly relieved to have my feet on the ground, that I was content to just drink out of the Starbucks standard-issue, grande-size paper cup.

I love to people-watch in airports. And as I sat there, on a stool by the window, I enjoyed watching all the diverse people walk by. I amused myself, wondering to what destination each person might be headed, and where they might be from, and what their lives might be like, and what things they might be trying to accomplish. Slowly but surely, I began to feel relaxed.

But then I heard a voice to my right, which said, "Okay if I sit here, pal?"

The voice sounded vaguely familiar, but I did not at first recognize it. Then I turned and saw a portly, long-bearded man, who looked like Blackbeard the Pirate. He was wearing a Southern Airlines pilot outfit with a nametag. And the name which the man bore upon that nametag was none other than the dread "Captain Morris Rosenblatt."

I quickly noticed the flight attendants, all ladies, were sitting together at their own table. But Blackbeard the Pirate, for whatever reason, wanted to sit by me. Which caused me to observe some curious things about him.

Not only was he the absolute worst pilot ever, but, I couldn't help noticing that he was grossly over the normal body weight for an airplane pilot. In fact, Rosenblatt may have been well-suited to put on an eye patch and sail an 18th century Spanish galleon in the Bahamas, but, it seemed clear to me that he had no business being in the cockpit of a 737.

This made me wonder, aren't there FAA regulations on these things? Aren't commercial pilots required to be slim, trim, athletic, neatly-kept retirees from 20-plus years in the military, who look like they still are in the military?

And all FAA regs aside, how does Capt. Rosenblatt physically manage to get his big ol', bloated, jelly-belly into the cockpit of an airplane?

There were plenty of open seats elsewhere. But before I could say anything, Rosengrubbs planted his big tuchous down on the stool next to me, grunting as if he had some kind of digestive pain.

How's the caw-fee?" He said in that annoying Brooklyn accent which, frankly, makes my skin crawl.

I gave him the thumbs up, to which he picked up his cup, and said, "L'khayim."

Out of common courtesy, I lifted my cup. Rosenblatt clinked his into mine. He clinked it so hard, it spilled some on my hand. He chuckled about it, and did not apologize. He did offer to wipe it off, reaching into his front right pocket and offering up what clearly was a dirty hankie. With a wave of the hand, I declined. I proceeded to get up and retrieve a few napkins.

When I returned, my book was in his hand. Typical New Yorker, I thought to myself. No manners. No boundaries.

As I approached, he put it down on the breakfast bar where we were sitting. I got resettled and Capt. Rosenblatt began to unwrap a turkey sandwich.

"Whatcha reading?" he asked.

"Not reading anything," I said.

He pointed to the book on the breakfast nook, as he stuffed the sandwich through the pie hole, hidden somewhere in that dense forest of thick, black, facial hair. The book was my favorite print bible—the green, leather-bound Tree of Life version, messianic Jewish bible.

One thing I like about it is the language. It says 'Yeshua" and "the Messiah," instead of Jesus Christ. I know it's all the same, but let's face it, Yeshua was Yeshua, and nobody ever called him Jesus. Language has a way of communicating meaning. So, yeah, I know, a bible is just a bible. A name is just a name. And God is God. And there is one God who hears all languages.

No, I do not believe you get special favor with God because you use a certain language. LOL. But I just like to read "Miriam" instead of "Mary" because it has a different feel to it. And "Mashiakh ben Elohim" feels different than Christ, son of God—even though the same concept is intended. Concepts are only concepts, and language is based on concepts. So, one way or another, we'd all be lost without the Spirit to reveal God in the hearts of men and women!

"Reading the bible, are ya?" He said, as he choked down the food which he stuffed into his mouth.

"Yeah," I said, with a quick flip of the bible into his view.

"Is that your path to God?" He said, chuckling. He then proceeded to shove another mass of food into his black hole.

"You could say that." I shrugged.

"I just did!" He laughed, making no effort to hide the mass of food in his mouth. "You said, I could say that, and I said it. Ya get it?"

Capt. Rosenblatt obviously found himself amusing. I did not. And I made little attempt to conceal it. But he didn't seem to care.

I, Too, Read the Bible:

"Hey look, I don't mean any offense, pal. Lemme tell ya something. I been all over this world. I seen a lot of people, been a lot of places. I, too, read the bible. As much as you. Probably more. Not a day goes by where I don't read that book. "

Considering the way Rosenblatt flew an airplane, it shouldn't have surprised me at all that he reads the bible every day. In fact, he ought to be providing a complimentary copy to each of his passengers.

But it did surprise me. Because not many American Jews actually read the bible. I realize that bible reading is quite common and normal for tens of millions of gentile Christians in the U.S., who personal read the bible, outside of church, and on their own time, for inspirational and/or religious reasons. But Jewish people generally do not.

For Jewish people, unless they happen to be a Rabbi, a professor or scholar of some sort, and are studying scripture in relation to their particular work, it is quite uncommon to see one of us reading a bible. Messianic Jews do regularly read the bible for personal inspiration, but we are the exception in this regard.

Now, I am a regular bible reader. And I have been for quite a long time. I read it both in public and in private. But when in public, I try to keep it on the down-low. I don't like for people to see me reading the bible.

The reason I don't like to be seen reading it in public is because I hate the way that certain people out there jump to inappropriate conclusions about me just because they see me reading the bible. There are two conclusions of this type:

Either, number one, they think that I am a religious fanatic, and therefore, they despise me for it. Or number two, they are a religious fanatic, and therefore, they think that I want to engage in a conversation about God and/or religion with them.

Let me just be clear about this: A) I am not a religious fanatic; and B) I don't like to engage in dialogue with people who are.

It is not on account of religiosity that I read the bible. I read it for inspiration. Personal inspiration.

Nor do I believe that every person who reads the bible is necessarily of like mind as me. Or someone with whom I am joined like family into an international band of brothers and sisters. That may be the case. But not necessarily.

Avid bible readers can indeed be wonderful people. Or they can be proud, rude, and even complete butt-heads. I find, the fact that a person reads the bible, or not, doesn't necessarily indicate what kind of person they are.

I think it's good practice to read the bible. That's why I do it. Not because I'm a Rabbi and I have to prepare teachings. But because it's inspirational. But I won't deny that some of the warmest, kindest, most loving people that I know, are not bible-readers. People who read the bible ought to take notice of that.

And, moreover, some of the biggest butt-heads I've ever met could quote scriptures to you all day long standing on their head. That, too, should be taken notice of by bible readers.

I hope I've been clear on this point. I am an avid, devoted, reader of the bible. I would encourage others to be as well. I believe in the great value of it. But I make no judgments on that account. If someone reads the bible, it proves nothing about them. And the fact that I read it proves nothing about me either. Nor would I expect anyone to think that it does.

Which is why I don't wear it on my sleeve. I never have. I have always preferred to do it privately. Oftentimes, when reading the bible in public places, I would use my computer or cell phone bible app. They are great tools, with amazing search functions. And that way, unless someone is super nosy, I avoid calling attention to what I am doing. But sometimes I prefer the print bible.

Rosenblatt had seen me reading the print bible. And he seemed to want to engage me in a dialogue about it. Typically, I'd be inclined to think, more likely than not, he was just another religious fanatic. But a Jewish religious fanatic? Not likely. Not unless he was wearing a black robe and black hat, instead of the garb of a commercial airplane pilot.

God is the Path:

As disinterested as I was at that moment to engage in a conversation with this portly Jewish airplane pilot, who had just taken me on the aerial version of Mr. Toad's wild ride, nevertheless, I could not deny that the dread Captain had my attention.

I suspected he was going to try to challenge me in some way. Which I wasn't really in the mood for. But for whatever reason, I decided to go along with it. So, as I regathered my thoughts, I responded to him.

"I'm sorry, what was that you said?"

"I said I read the bible every day. Probably more than you do," said Rosenblatt.

"I see," I said.

"Why do you read it?" he asked.

"Well, I think it's pretty important to know what's written in this book."

"You're missing the point, pal," he said.

I don't like being called "pal." It's just so New York. It annoys me. But I tried to be polite, and not show it.

"What point?" I said.

"There are no paths to God. God IS the path," said Rosenblatt.

I had to stop and think about that. He was definitely on to something there. I liked that saying. I connected with it. Maybe Rosenblatt had some wisdom to impart, after all, in spite of his great lack of ability to fly an airplane.

"Could you say that again?" I asked.

"Sure. There are no paths to God. God IS the path."

That saying struck a deep chord in me. It resonated. It ignited something within me. He went on:

"As long as you're on a path to God, you're never arriving at the destination. Because you're on the path. Not the destination. What I'm saying is, get to your destination. Then you eliminate the path to the destination. Because the destination IS the path."

He had a point. So, with this point, Rosenblatt had my attention. And what transpired from that moment on, is difficult to explain. But essentially, the Starbucks at the Salt Lake City airport was transformed into a center of supernatural, cosmic revelation. Something like the cold, snowy place where Superman used to go to discover the mystery of who he was and why he was put on earth.

Something was happening. Was I about to learn some great secret of the universe? Granted, I was not placing crystals into a rock to access pre-recorded video messages from planet Krypton, taken before it blew up and all life was destroyed therein. But I was receiving wisdom from the Tree of Life, imparted to me secretly, via America's one and only Jewish commercial airplane pilot.

Hence, as Rosenblob continued, I tuned in. I heard him out. And although his tendency to speak with large chunks of food in his mouth did repulse and annoy me greatly, I nevertheless found the strength to dismiss this as a petty distraction, a necessary evil, which I must endure for wisdom's sake. For my sole interest was in receiving wisdom, and I suppose that wisdom has its price. Thus, I sat and listened. Even when flecks of food spewed forth from his mouth, I quietly endured it. He talked. And I listened.

The Wheel:

He did not seem to mind that I pushed the record button on my MP3 player and placed it on the table so that I might not miss whatever it was that I was about to hear. He said:

"There are no paths to God. God IS the path. When you realize this for the first time, it changes everything. The reason it changes everything, is because it eliminates your concept of God. Look, you can spend your entire life thinking about how it should be lived. But when you are walking with God you are living it without thinking about it. It's just happening.

"The problem is, you don't know how it is supposed to be lived, or why, or for what purpose. Now, most people never think about this stuff to begin with, and they live empty, materialistic lives. That is the life of the masses, the bulk of humankind. They live lives without point or purpose. For many, despair sets in. But the meaninglessness of it all is too horrible to think about, so they rationalize, forget it, shelve it away somewhere. And they trudge on. You see?"

"I follow you," I said.

"Others, realizing their state of despair, become cynical, and turn to a life of immorality. These live for no reward other than to get paid, get laid, get drunk, get stoned, or all of the above. The life of sex, drugs, and rock n' roll is a dead-end. Right, my friend?"

I consented with a nod. But I was deeply puzzled. Though I fully understood the concept Rosenblatt expressed, I struggled to understand how he could know much about it.

In any case, as he chuckled over his own comment, he nearly choked. He then recovered, and went on to another point. And I was glad about that. Although, I wish he had done so without shoving in more food.

"But, then, when you start wanting to live right," continued Rosenblatt, "you start thinking about how to do it. You start asking yourself, 'what is right living as opposed to wrong living?'"

He slapped his hand on the table.

"And, you see, that's where religion comes in. Life becomes moralistic. A path to God. You get out of the darkness of your former life of being a party animal..."

Again, I wondered how he could possibly speak to that issue, as he popped himself in the chest, and chased down the food with some coffee. Then, he went on:

"...but only to take on another kind of darkness. Take yourself for example. Probably married, with children and a steady job, right?"

"Yeah, that's right," I said. "They're the most precious thing in the world to me."

"Of course. Sure. You love them. And why shouldn't you?

"That's right," I said.

"And you love your career. You are glad to be doing what you do. It's a wonderful life, you're so thankful, it's all a blessing, etc., etc. right?"

"All of the above," I said confidently.

"But not necessarily out of the darkness. Still not fulfilled. Are you?"

"Well—"

"Be honest now."

"But nobody is completely fulfilled. We're only human," I protested.

"But you're rationalizing. Don't you see?" he responded. "Also because you're only human."

"Maybe to rationalize is the best we have. I mean no one's perfect. So we make the best of it," I said.

"Oh? You mean put on a happy face and go forth with a can do attitude?"

"Maybe. So what if we do? What are you saying?"

"The problem is you can have a great life, and feel blessed, and thankful, but still have no idea what the point of it is," he said.

"It happens," I said.

"So, you go to work, do your thing, try to make a living, go to sleep, start over again. But you don't dare think about why you're doing it. Or what's it all about? Right?"

"I see your point," I said, "but that's not me."

"Sure it isn't," he said, as he shoved in more food. "But if it was you, then you wouldn't face up to it. No, you'd rationalize. You keep a positive outlook. And in those darkest moments, when you would be wondering what is the meaning of life, you'd pacify yourself to believe that nobody really knows what life is about, and anyway, all that really matters is how you are going to spend eternity? Which in your case, is nothing to worry about, because your particular religion tells you that you are good for the long haul. Right?"

"I don't know. That's a pretty dark view of humanity." I said.

"Look, pal, I didn't make it up. Either it's true or it isn't. And it if it is, then something ought to be done about it. Don't you agree?"

"If it is, then yeah, I guess."

"Otherwise, a man is just a hamster on a wheel," he said. "Day in and day out, the same routine. If you are that man, then you're just like the hamster who thinks he's on his way somewhere but he's not. He's tricked himself by getting on the wheel. The wheel is going round and round and round, creating the illusion that he is going somewhere. But he's going nowhere. And if you're that man, something inside of you is screaming 'what am I doing? Why am I doing this?' But you can't deal with it. You can't answer it. So you try not to think about it.

"Just like the hamster, who doesn't dare think that he's on a wheel. Headed nowhere. You're on a path that leads to nowhere. But you comfort yourself with the notion that you are on a path to God.

"And what I'm saying is that there is no such path. God is God. You're either with God or not. If you're on a path to God, then you're not with God, you're trying to get to him. But it's too horrible to admit. So you convince yourself being on a path to God is good. As if you'll be there one day. Even though today, you aren't there. Am I making sense?"

Wisdom is Supreme:

I did not answer. As Rosenblatt stuffed his pie hole with more food, I sat there stone-faced. He was an offensive man. Not only in word, but in his manners and appearance as well.

And yet, I knew that he was saying something of value. So as I watched him chew, wishing that he would close his mouth when he chewed, I couldn't stop myself from thinking that this encounter with Rosenblatt was some kind of divine appointment.

I am a rather private person, and not often inclined to converse with strangers in public. Yet, there was something about Rosenblatt that grabbed my attention there in the Salt

Lake City airport. Although he was, in various ways, obnoxious, the guy had a certain charisma about him. It was something that I can only describe as "dynamism."

It wasn't the kind of dynamic personality of a guy, say, like Pastor Buddy. No, he was not that kind of guy that has the looks, the charm, the people skills, the popularity to rely upon.

Rosenblatt's dynamism was different. Because you couldn't see it. Outwardly, he was ill-mannered, and, to be perfectly frank, kinda stinky. He was not pleasant to be around. Nor to look at. Yet, there was something mysterious about Rosenblatt, hidden away secretly and sacredly, somewhere beneath all that fat he was toting around. It was an inward dynamic that sort of grabbed you and said, "this guy has something worth listening to."

So, since I had a bible out, as Rosenblatt chewed, the word "wisdom" came to mind. And I took a quick moment to flip over to Proverbs 4:7, and I read to myself.

> *"Wisdom is supreme—acquire wisdom! With all your acquisitions, get understanding."*

Some time ago, I had scribbled in the margin next to Proverbs 4;7, the Hebrew word "reishit" which is translated "supreme." Other bible versions translate it as "the main thing" or "the principal thing." But "reishit" really means "the beginning." In other words, what King Shlomo was saying there, is that wisdom is the beginning. It's the first thing. It's where it all starts.

Rosenblatt saw what I was reading. He burped a couple of times. Then grabbed the bible, flipping a few pages.

"My favorite from Proverbs, right there," he said, as he slid it back my way, with his finger pressed onto Proverbs 8:35, which also speaks of wisdom.

I read it aloud:

> *"He who finds me finds life."*

As I sat there in Starbucks at the Salt Lake City Airport, being instructed by the world's worst commercial airplane pilot, I began to feel that Capt. Morris Rosenblatt had some wisdom to impart. And wisdom is good medicine.

As wisdom says of itself, "he who finds me, finds Life." So I took all of that medicine that I could get.

You Wanna Know What Life Is?:

"I'm gonna tell you something," said Rosenshlubbs, as he choked down what appeared to be an egg salad sandwich. He offered me a bite of that sandwich.

"No thanks," I said.

"You wanna know what life is?"

"Okay," I said.

"Are you listening?"

"Yeah."

"You sure?"

"Pretty sure. Yeah."

He put the sandwich down and took a big gulp of his coffee. He almost wiped his face with his sleeve, but I quickly intervened by offering a paper napkin. He wiped with the napkin, but it didn't do much good. His beard was still full of crumbs.

"Alright. I'll tell you what life is. *I* am the life," said Rosenblatt. He emphasized the word *I*, in saying this. It was as if he was not talking about himself when he said it.

"You are?" I responded.

"Not you are. *I* am."

"You are what?"

"I didn't say you are. I said *I* am," repeated Rosenblatt.

"I heard you," I said, shaking my head. "I'm confused."

"Yeah. Because you didn't hear me."

"I didn't?"

"No. Because you are not listening."

"But I heard you," I insisted. "You said you are the life."

"No, I did not say you are the life. Listen to me. *I* am the life."

"Not sure I see the difference."

"Exactly. That's your problem."

"What's my problem?"

"You don't know who *I* am."

"You're right about that."

"I know," laughed Rosenblatt. He seemed to be enjoying this.

"I don't know what we're talking about," I said.

"Open that bible of yours."

"This bible?"

"Yeah. Open it to John 8:31."

"Okay." I did as he suggested.

"What's it say?"

I read out loud: "*If you abide in my word, then you are truly my disciples...*"

"You see that!" said Rosenblatt.

"See what?"

"Read the next verse."

I read on: "... then you will know the Truth and the Truth will make you free."

"Now that's what I'm saying," he said.

"I still don't get it," I responded.

"If you hear me, and continue to live in my word, then you will know the truth, and the truth will make you free."

"Free from what?" I said.

"Free from not knowing the Truth."

I pondered that for a moment. "What Truth?" I said.

"*I* am the Truth."

Somehow I thought he might say that. But I still didn't understand. And he knew I didn't. So he continued.

"Look. God is the Truth. But you don't know God."

"I don't?"

"No. Not really."

"But—"

"Just hear me out," he continued. "I know you think you know God, and I realize how devoted you probably are to that thought. But just listen."

"Fine," I said. "Go ahead."

"What is keeping you from God is your idea that you are on a path to God. This is a mistake. There is no path to God. God IS the path."

"I know, I know. You said that already."

"Yeah, but you weren't listening. That's why you aren't getting it."

"Alright," I consented, but reluctantly.

"You see, the path to God is your delusion. It's like the hamster on the wheel," said Rosenblatt.

"Enough with the hamster," I said.

"But, don't you see? You're the hamster."

"Why am I the hamster?"

"What? You don't want to be the hamster?"

"I would very much like not to be the hamster."

"Okay, then. You must get off the hamster wheel. Then you won't be the hamster anymore." Rosenblatt laughed. He was quite amused.

"Okay, fine. That sounds simple enough, I am now officially off the hamster wheel." I said.

"Well, no. Not really. You can't just get off like that. If it was like that, everybody would do it."

"Then how do I get off the hamster wheel?"

"One day, hopefully sooner than later, you are going to realize something. Here it is. Are you ready?"

"I'm ready."

"I don't think you're ready."

"Yes. I am definitely ready."

"Ok. Here goes: *I* am the resurrection, and *I am* the life."[26]

I sighed, "I already know that."

"No you don't. And that's the problem."

"What problem?"

"You think you already know it. So you don't."

"I don't?"

"No. You don't. But anyone who knows it, even if he were dead, he will live. And if he is alive, he will never die."

---

[26] John 11:25.

70

"I don't see how you can be resurrected when you are alive?"

"Because resurrection is an ever-present reality. It's the *I am* of this present life. *I am* the resurrection. Not you will be resurrected. *I am.* Do you see that?"

"Ok. Sort of."

"Life, my friend, doesn't start tomorrow. It's a present tense issue. I am the same yesterday, today, and tomorrow.[27] Right?"

I nodded in the affirmative, but my confused look betrayed the fact that I did not really follow.

"To get yourself off the hamster wheel, you've got to get rid of the idea that you are headed somewhere. Be where you are. When you start *being* right where you are, poof, no more wheel."

"I don't know what that's supposed to mean," I said.

"Of course. Because *being* is something you likely never learned how to do. It's not natural. It's the law of the kingdom of heaven. Not a law that says, 'Thou *must.*' It's a law that says '*This IS.*' You see what I'm saying?"

"Hmm," I said. I pondered this for a moment, then he went on.

"You've got the teachings of the Rabbi right there in your hand. Right there in that book. He says, 'if you abide in my word, then you will be my disciples, then you will know the Truth, and the Truth will set you free,' "[28]

"I see," I said.

"Because you say 'I see,' you are blind. When you see your own blindness, then your eyes will start to be opened."

"Opened to what?"

"Opened to what the Rabbi said, '*In that day you will know. I am in the Father, you are in me, and I am in you.*"

"John 14:20," I said.

"Okay, you know the verse. Good. But do you know this 'I' of which the Rabbi spoke, that 'I' which is not only in the

---

[27] Heb. 13:8.
[28] John 8:31.

Father, but in him, and in you as well? When you know that, so thoroughly and completely, then you'll be permanently and forever off the hamster wheel."

Digesting It:

I took a sip of coffee and digested what Rosenblatt just said. I didn't really understand at that point. But I did understand in part. And sometimes a tiny little mustard seed is just enough to bring forth a magnificent and majestic tree, into which many birds will make their nest.

True, I could've easily blown off this whole wacky incident as ridiculous. Why did I ever agree to sit and listen to this man? I could've shelved it away, and forgotten about it. Just like I could've done with Marley in the coffee shop back home. But I didn't. I'm not sure why I didn't.

At this point, I understood only in part. Shall I say I had one foot down, but not both feet? Whatever, it was just enough to keep me on the hook. Probably because I recognized that I was blind. But in this respect, I'm no different than anyone else. So, how did I ever come to know it? Or to recognize it?

It was the grace of God, operating on me through the mystery of the invisible Ruakh, the Spirit, that was drawing me onward, to some higher calling in Yeshua, to be more effective, all for the glorification, the magnification, and the exaltation of the one I serve. Yeshua HaMashiakh. The Son of God.

So, although I did not totally understand the message delivered to me by the dread Captain, I was on my way to this higher calling in the Lord.

I was being liberated. Yes, set free. And having gone through this experience, I want to testify to something here. In the early phase, the realization that one is starting to be liberated, is quite exhilarating. Though the details may be somewhat murky and hard to understand, the basic feeling that you are advancing forward toward a greater and more glorious freedom, perhaps that you never even knew existed, leaves you wanting more and more.

Even if that freedom is coming to you in the form of a rather distasteful commercial jet pilot who, while delivering his message of universal Truth, spews food particles directly into your face. After all, what price can be put on freedom? It's all worth it!

The Irony:

Rosenblatt continued, "Look around you. Everything you can see with your eyes comes and goes. Lives and dies. You ever noticed, the world around us is in a constant state of change?"

"True."

"However, there is one thing that never changes. You know what that is?"

"No," I said with sigh.

"The one thing that never changes in an ever-changing world, is the fact that it is *always* changing."

"Right." I said.

"It's permanently ironic. Written right into the fabric of creation."

"What is ironic?" I asked.

"That the nature of an ever-changing world is changelessness. Don't you see that?"

"Hmm. Yeah I guess so."

"The changing nature of Creation never changes," said Rosenblatt.

"Yeah. But that's a contradiction," I said.

"Exactly. But so it is. Change is all around us. But in a changing universe, still, there is one thing that never changes. Change."

"The state of changelessness never changes." I said.

"Hey, you're starting to sound like me," he laughed.

"I see what you are saying. But, c'mon, what's the point?"

"The point is the irony," answered Rosenblatt. The universe is ironic."

"Okay."

"God is infinite, right?"

"The same yesterday, today, and forever," I said, proudly quoting Hebrews, 13:8.

"But the universe which God created is perpetually changing."

"Right."

"So, when you can walk with infinity in the midst of a finite world, then you are on the iPath."

"The what?" I said.

"The iPath," repeated Rosenblatt.

"You're gonna have to explain that one," I said.

Being on the iPath:

That was the first time I'd ever heard the iPath referred to by name. Rosenblatt took a moment to stretch out in his chair, as if he was winding up, before he continued.

"The iPath is the path of "I.""

"Uh-huh," I said.

"Being on the iPath is living as the "I" which is the image of God in which all people were created," he said.

"You mean, like in the Garden of Eden."

"Yes. That was the iPath. Mankind walked with God in the garden. In perfect communion. But it was interrupted when we lost touch with the image of God that is our true Selfhood. We began to see ourselves as having a selfhood apart from the Creator who created us in his own image. The Rabbi came to invite us back to the Eden experience. He taught, suffered, gave his life, and rose, so that his followers might be restored to our true, original Selfhood. That is the iPath my friend.

"But, instead, the world made the Rabbi into a religious icon. Totally distinct, unapproachable, and separated from us. He taught us plainly, he is with us always. And we have oneness with the Father thru the Son. The Son came for all eyes to see, as a Jewish Rabbi, rejected by the religious establishment, heralded by the common people. And now the

Son is presently invisible. Which leaves mankind to wait till Yeshua returns. Oh, the Rabbi will return. Make no mistake about that. And when he sits on David's throne in Jerusalem, the whole world will be filled with knowledge of the Lord. But for the meantime, it is possible that individual persons, like you and me, pal, can walk along the iPath. In oneness with the Father, thru the Son, along the iPath we can see the glory of the Kingdom. And journey through this creation in peace, joy, and ever-increasing happiness. This is the messianic life. The Life Messiah brought to the world."

"Wow," I said. I was floored. I really didn't have anything else to say.

"Just remember, that Life is a journey. It is not a destination. The Rabbi suffered and died so that his followers might be restored to the Kingdom of God. He said that Kingdom is right here in the midst of you. The iPath is the journey that the Messiah, which is the Life of the universe, has been living since the beginning of creation. The Life is the light of mankind, and we are invited to walk together on this same messianic journey. That's the iPath."

Servant or Friend:

Rosenblatt reached for my bible, flipped the pages, slapped it down and pointed to a verse. A few crumbs issued from his mouth and landed on my bible, as he continued.

"Just look at what it says right here. Go on read it," he said, with a finger on John 15:15. So I read it out loud:

> *"I am no longer calling you servants, for the servant does not know what his master is doing. Now I have called you friends, because everything I have heard from My Father I have made known to you."*

He looked directly into my eyes. Raised his eyebrows.
"So which one are you?"
"What?" I asked.

"Servant or friend?"

I paused. I'd never really thought about this question. Servant or friend? What a question.

So, with a gesture of palms up and a shrug of the shoulders, I expressed what Captain Rosenblatt already seemed to know. That even though I was teaching about this God in whom I most ardently believed and about whom I had acquired so much information, maybe I really didn't know the very God whom I thought I was serving and about whom I was teaching others.

Certainly, I couldn't lead others to a God whom I was seeking and serving, but whom I was not personally walking with myself. I was on a path to that God. And was attempting to lead others in that path which I was on.

But because of being on a path *to* God, I was not on the path *of* God. Which is the iPath.

You have to understand, that for a professional minister–whether Rabbi, Pastor, Priest, or Medicine Man– to accept this idea that you don't really know God, would be like whacking yourself over the head with a sledge hammer. It's the death knell. But I was already past that point. I'd already done it.

Deny Yourself? Really?:

And right then, Rosenblatt flipped open my bible, pointed to a verse, and continued shoveling in food while I read the verse to which he had pointed:

"If anyone wants to follow after Me, he must deny himself, take up his cross, and follow Me. For whoever wants to save his life will lose it, but whoever loses his life for My sake will find it. (Mat. 16:24,25).

Now this is a huge point. Because I have always been suspicious of teachers who tell their followers "deny yourself." That is a dangerous message. One that we must all be careful about. It can set the stage for abuses by individuals with ill motives to take advantage of people.

On the other hand, the scripture does say plainly that Yeshua taught this principle of "deny yourself" to his followers. And it was no small teaching. It was core. So it obviously has some meaning.

But I think it's been misunderstood. I think that religious bodies have encouraged their people to submerge their identity to the religious authority, or organization, or church, or whatever. In that manner, you are trading one false identity for another. This is wrong. We are all created in God's image. And the goal must be to be restored to that image.

Hence, for me, when Yeshua said you must "deny yourself" or "take up your cross and follow me," what it means is simply that you are not who you think you are. Not to deny yourself outright, as if "you" are nothing. You are not nothing. We are created in the image of God. We are definitely a something. Not a nothing. The problem is that we are out of touch with the reality of what we are. Our Selfhood. Because we believe ourselves to be something other than what God made us to be. That delusion is what needs to be denied. Not the self, but the delusion of self.

So, I am adamant in stating my belief that one must be careful not to submerge their identity into something else. But "deny yourself" means to deny the false image. Accept the simple truth that you are not who you think you are. Because things are not as they appear to be.

As I discovered it, therefore, when you recognize that you are not who you think you are, the door is open so that you can discover who you really are. Your true selfhood. The "I" that I am. Truly. And eternally.

Not that I ever ceased to be that. But I lost touch with it, as the whole of the human race has. But the good news is that Messiah Yeshua came to redeem us from this situation. And to restore us to consciousness of eternity, and of the Kingdom of God.

Until my transformation came, until I started walking on the iPath, I knew a lot. But I didn't know anything. And now I suddenly knew it.

And, so it was, in that moment, in the Salt Lake City airport Starbucks, as I watched the world's heaviest commercial airplane pilot go to work on a blueberry scone, which he really didn't need, that something pivotal happened in my life. And I would never be the same from that time forward.

Because on that day I came to know that I did not know. And in knowing that I did not know, I was able to come to know the most important thing I could ever know. And I've known it ever since.

What an epiphany! When you know that you don't know—then you know.

And, now I knew it. I didn't know much—yet. But at least, for now, I knew that I did not know.

I had begun the journey. I denied myself, that I might find myself. I took up my proverbial "cross" and followed the Master. No, I am not talking about self-denial in the sense of becoming miserable and deprived. Nor self-sacrifice, nor taking up a life of asceticism. I simply accepted that I was not who I thought I was.

It was liberating. And this was just the first step. It was the early phase. The beginning of the metamorphosis in me. I was on the iPath. And when you're on the iPath, you are walking with God.

Being Restored to Gan Eden (Garden of Eden):

Why didn't I see before? You see, we are dealing with a mystery. God, the one Reality of the universe, is invisible. How do we learn about something that is invisible? Nobody seems to know. Which is how we end up instead with ideas and concepts about God. But the invisible God can't be known in that way. We need real-time contact.

If the human race knew God, we wouldn't have any problems. We'd be living in something like Eden all over again, wherein there were no problems. No war, no famine, no depression, no hatred, no death. Gan Eden (Garden of Eden) is overflowing with peace, abundance, infinite joy, love, and eternal life.

No one can be restored to the Gan Eden experience by learning principles and practices. What we all need to know is God. And yet, God is Spirit. And Spirit is invisible. So, how can we know God, when we can't see or feel or hear God?

This is the whole challenge. And this is the very reason why the race of beings known as "humanity" has become like the blind, poking around in a darkness, trying to find our way home.

But if there are some inner faculties, that might enable us to apprehend and comprehend the Creator of the universe, in spite of the fact that He is hidden from our ordinary senses, then obviously, the subject matter of spiritual learning ought to be how to use those faculties. Not for learning principles and practices to be applied to life. But for experiencing real-time contact with God.

I can tell someone "love your neighbor" until we are both blue in the face. They already know the bible says that. The problem is, they don't know how to do it. And I could not give them the means to do that.

Yeshua's teaching was not life-application. Yeshua's teaching was life-*giving*. Shouldn't Yeshua's teaching be the teaching that I teach? Yes. Absolutely.

But you can't get those teachings from a book. Yes, they are recorded there. But you can read those teachings a million times, and still come away with nothing.

Because the teaching of Yeshua the Messiah is Spirit and Life. It is bread that comes down from heaven. But you can't see it. It is a river of water that gushes forth from your innermost parts, but you can't hear it. It is a teaching that can't be learned. It has to be given. I guarantee you that if and/or when it is given, it happens secretly, sacredly, and invisibly. Because it can only happen through an inner communion.

For years and years, I had been teaching *about* Yeshua all along. And I had been teaching what Yeshua taught. But I had not been teaching Yeshua's teaching. Because I had not personally ascertained it. I did not know that teaching. I wasn't privy to it. It had not yet been given to me to know it. Moreover, the stumbling block was that I thought I knew it already. That presumption became the barrier between me and the Lord.

My Teaching Is Not Mine:

As I was sitting there, thinking all these things, I felt a tremendous sense of gratitude come over me. It was a feeling of warmth and satisfaction. Even though I was kinda grossed out with this rather unseemly character that sat before me stuffing his face, I was nonetheless thankful.

"Hey, I just want to thank you for sharing all this with me," I said. "You know, I never—"

At that, Rosenblatt interrupted me, and blurted out, "My teaching is not mine. But from him who sent me."

That remark struck a chord in me. Unlike Rosenblatt, I could not in earnest say, as Rosenblatt said, quoting the Rabbi of Rabbis, '*My teaching is not mine,*' for indeed, my teaching was mine. And that was the problem. How could I make it not mine—but his? I didn't know how. But I knew that I needed to know. And I know that my recognition of this need is the reason why I became able to know.

In this respect I wish to be clear. I was no different than anybody else. I, just like everyone else, had believed in a God whom I did not really know, all the while believing myself to be one who knew. The difference was that I suddenly came to know that I did not know.

I, like so many others, previously referred to myself as a "believer," and to others as "not a believer." But we who were the "believers" knew nothing. Just like the "non-believers," who also know nothing. The only difference between us, "the believers," and them the "non-believers," was that we "believers" thought we knew everything. But we didn't. We knew nothing. Just like the non-believers, who also knew nothing. We were the same. Except that we believers thought we knew, and them the non-believers didn't care one way or the other. We both knew nothing. And, well, now I knew it. Baruch Hashem!

I'd come full circle – from not knowing, to thinking I knew, even though I still didn't, to finally realizing the great truth, as we say in Hebrew: Ani lo yode-ah (I don't know).

Consequently, from now on, I was not only different from those who know nothing, but also different from those who think they know everything, yet who also know nothing. I knew nothing and I knew it. And that was just fine with me. Because there's no way to be on the iPath and stay there, unless this happens.

The Life:

Rosenblatt went on:

"You may think you are living a life for God. But I tell you, there are no lives lived for God. God IS the life."

This blew me away. The dread Captain was spot on. Wow. Indeed, I had been one of the walking dead. Who don't know they are dead. But I was becoming undead. I was being drawn into the part of humanity which the bible refers to as *"ha-Chayim"* or *"the living."*

I would no longer be one of the walking dead. I still would walk among them, of course, how can you not? But I was not going to be one of them anymore. I would only be there to help them to become what I have become – undead. Even as I was helped to become alive, I would help others to do same. For freely I received, and freely I would give back.

I was just a novice at this point. I certainly didn't know what I was doing, what I was going to do, or how I would help anybody else to do it too. But I didn't care. I was exuberant that day. Because even though I might not be an expert at living, I was at least sure that I was no longer one of the walking dead.

81

As King Solomon said: *"For the one who is joined to the living has hope. And a living dog is better than a dead lion."* (Eccl. 9:4).

That is what happens when you get on the iPath. You start living. It is the journey of the living. I was getting off my path to God. And getting onto the journey with God. The iPath. I was walking with the Lord.

"The friend sees everything *I* am doing. He is right there with *me*," said Rosenblatt. The Truth of who you are is who *I* am. In whom you live and move and have being."

As he continued, each time Captain Rosenblatt said "I" or "me" he pointed with his index finger to the air.

"*I* am the one you are looking for. *I* am the timeless, soul-traveler Self. There is no Self-hood apart from *me*."

He took a long sip of his coffee.

"*I* am with you always. Right there in the midst of you. As long as you are looking for *me*, you can't see *me*. Stop looking and start traveling with *me*.

"*I* am in you and you are in *me*. *I* am all, and *I* am in all. And *I* am the timeless Truth of who you truly are."

Dessert Time:

Apparently it was dessert time. Rosenblatt shoved a big piece of scone into the scone hole hidden somewhere in that coffee-soaked, crumb infested beard of his. He took a few chews, and continued.

"You believe in *me*. You know all about *me*. The history. The facts. Everything that's been written, you've read it. You are very well-read, it's well-known. But you have not understood."

I opened my mouth to speak, but nothing came out. He went on:

"From now on, we are traveling on this path, the one *I* am on. We are traveling together. And there are others. Some have been gathered already. Others will be gathered. No one comes to this path unless the Father draws them. You have been drawn."

He took a long sip of coffee, which must've been cold by this point.

"Travel with me, pal. Because you see, there are no paths to God—"

"God *is* the path." I said, finishing the line for him.

Capt. Rosenblatt slapped me on the back of the shoulder.

"Ya see. You're getting it, pal. You're definitely getting it."

Rosenblatt let out a huge belch, and several people across the café turned in disgust. Unconcerned, he shoved in the last piece of scone. Then he continued:

"You can't help anyone become free until you are set free yourself."

"Okay."

"Like it says right there," he said, pointing to the TLV bible. *"Know the Truth and the Truth will set you free. Right?"*

"Yeah." I said. "But what is Truth?"

To that Rosenblatt let out a huge belly laugh, like Santa Claus, he was laughing so hard, he nearly choked on that last piece of scone that he was devouring.

"Ha!" he said, performing what looked like the Heimlich maneuver upon himself. "That's what Pilate said. Remember? What is truth?"

As he continued both laughing, choking, and pressing one fist onto his sternum, Capt. Rosenblatt balled up the paper and the plastic, took his tray over to the trash can, and waved to the group of flight attendants, who likewise starting packing up their stuff.

"Wait a minute!" I exclaimed. "Aren't you gonna answer?"

"Answer what?" he replied.

"What is truth?"

He walked over to me, got right up in my face, so I could smell his stinky breath (which I would've greatly preferred not to), and he pressed his index finger pointedly into my chest. And as he prodded me right in the center of the sternum with that short, pudgy, sticky, finger of his, the dread Captain Rosenblatt said:

"*I* am the Truth."

He then abruptly exited and walked on with his flight attendants, off to his next destination.

It was time to catch my shuttle. So, off I went, deep into the Rocky Mountains, feeling inspired by hope for even greater things still to come.

3

The Mountain

Fresh Manna:

It was early morning. The slopes on the mountain were covered with fresh snow. Manna from heaven. Fresh manna.

There is nothing more refreshing than crisp, cool, Rocky Mountain air. As I stopped to take a quick breather before skiing down to the chairlift, I was thinking about Lewis and Clark.

Those guys must've freaked when they saw the Rockies for the first time. Nothing like this back East, that's for sure. I've been hiking in the Appalachians lots of times. They are beautiful in their own right, and I actually prefer them for hiking. But the Rockies are in another league.

For one thing, the Rockies are about triple the height of the Appalachians, which peak typically around 3500-4000 feet. It can be a little tough to breathe in the Rockies. When you come from Florida, right at Sea Level, and suddenly your up over 8,000 feet at the base, and 11,000 or more at the peaks, it takes a couple of days to adjust to the altitude.

But when it comes to skiing, the Rockies are worth every bit of oxygen given up. They are simply a whole different ball park then the East. Majestic peaks, ski runs that go on for miles, unbelievable amounts of snow fall, and the lightest powder you can find anywhere on the planet.

In Utah, the sun is strong. You have to wear UV protection even in the dead of Winter, or you'll have a "squirrel face." That's when everything on your face gets burned, except for the part around your eyes covered by your ski goggles. Owing to the dry, desert air, the snow in Utah is as light as talcum powder, and it falls in massive quantities.

Also, the desert-mountain air, plus the sun, creates an environment where it really doesn't feel all that cold. I skied Vermont and New Hampshire before. You freeze your butt off, and the snow comes down heavy and wet, which becomes like frozen cement on the slopes. When you fall on that, it's like hitting the sidewalk. Utah snow is like falling onto a feather pillow. It is truly a skier's paradise.

Another thing about the ski resorts out West, they are so big, so vast, it feels like being on the moon. There are huge parts of the resort where you can be alone. I mean totally alone. Just you and God, in the midst of a massive mountain range. This is especially the case in early season, before the vacationers start coming.

It's an amazing feeling to be up over ten thousand feet, alone, in the midst of a snow-covered mountain. It truly puts a different perspective on life. Things that seem so important, suddenly are nothing before the awesome presence of the age-old mountain, which has seen it all come and go ten thousand times before.

So there I was in "paradise." It was a perfect day in the Rockies. A blueberry powder day, as the locals call it. That's a day, after a huge powder dump, immediately followed by perfect, sunny, blueberry skies.

And there I was, at the top of the mountain, somewhere in the neighborhood of about 11,000 feet. It was morning. And it was early. So hardly anyone was out skiing yet. I skied along a cat track, which is a narrow path, just about 6 feet wide, which traverses across from one part of the mountain over to another. This cat track lead me over to a spot where I knew nobody else would be.

I like to ski in basins. A basin is a giant bowl formed by tall peaks aligned next to one another, forming a kind of semi-circle. Mineral Basin, at Snowbird, Utah, is what they call a "back bowl." That's a spot on the back end of a ski resort where less people tend to ski, because it doesn't lead to the resort base at the bottom, nor to any mid-mountain restaurants. It's not in the main area of traffic, so very few people are there, especially not first thing in the morning.

The straight and narrow path on the "cat track," gives you little room to move back and forth. You have to turn your skis inward to create a snowplow effect, otherwise, you'll go too fast, and get into trouble. I was glad when the cat track ended.

When the track ended, now, before me, or I should say, beneath me, was a long, very steep, snow-covered slope. A cliff, really, which I would have to ski down before getting to some flatter, easier runs down toward the bottom of this giant bowl. My adrenaline was pumping as I looked down at it, and plotted my course.

There I was, stopped on the edge, preparing myself, as I was just staring down into the vast whiteness of this giant bowl. I put my poles into the ground, and took a deep breath of the fresh, cool air. It was a morning pause, to just take in the view and get ready to make my descent. I was all alone in that place, looking up at giant peaks, and looking down into white nothingness.

I took a few quick, deep breaths. It is really hard to breathe up there when you're not used to the altitude. I was panting for air. But something about that is exhilarating. Especially first thing in the morning. I felt the cool, crisp, dry air going in and out of me.

The First and the Last:

Then, as I settled in, a voice suddenly, unexpectedly, popped into my mind. I did not know from where it came. But it definitely was not me thinking it. It was a silent voice, more like a thought, but not my thought. It was a voice, not audible, but a voice nonetheless. A voice which said:

"I am the first and the last. The beginning and the end."[29]

---

[29] Is. 44:6, Rev. 22:13.

Wow. This little saying flowed through me, like the cool, refreshing, Rocky Mountain air. And it did not stop there. Inspired by the amazing natural surroundings, and ignited by the still, small voice that said to me those simple words: "*I am the first and the last. The beginning and the end,*" many things started to roll thru my mind.

First, I realized most clearly that I was not alone in this place. Even though no one was in sight, there was a presence. There was a witness, who was there when these gorgeous mountains and cliffs, were created.

In fact, I thought, this witness was the one who created it all to begin with. And as old as these rugged mountains may be, there is someone, out there, who is before all that I could see. One who is beyond the passage of time.

The timeless son of God, by whom and through whom all things were made, was in the world from the beginning and all things have come forth through him. And he was right there in the midst of me. No doubt.

I find it very difficult to describe what was happening. In essence, a symphony of thought began to erupt in me. More like realizations, than thoughts. Because I was thinking about God, but it was as if I was not doing the thinking. God was pouring into me like oil poured from a jar.

Set off by this one spark, accelerated by the awesomeness of the environment, a harmonious explosion of creative intelligence began to go off in my mind. And in the midst of this symphony of expression that was bursting in my mind, suddenly, out of that sprang forth again this voice, which popped up, unprovoked, into my awareness:

"*I am with you always. Even to the end of the age.*"[30]

I recognized that statement right away. It was the final word of Yeshua, in which he spoke to his followers, just before he departed and ascended up into the heavens.

---

[30] Mat. 28:20.

I was sure in that moment, not only that a presence was there with me, as I said. But moreover, that the same presence that was there with me, in those mountains, had *always* been with me. And, in fact, this presence was the very presence which brought me into the world to begin with.

I saw that the Spirit of God that was present in this awesome place, was the same Spirit dwelling in me. Which brought me back to the question—*Who am I?* In other words, what is the true soul of my being. Surely, nothing is infinite except the Lord. So, if there is such a thing as eternal Life, which I know there is, then it can't be independent of the infinite God. Because there is only one God. One infinite being in the universe.

When you look up at the surrounding mountains, it's hard not to worry just a little about an avalanche. The groomers take great care to make sure such things don't happen at least not where the people are skiing. But, like an avalanche, it was as if a wall came down in me. What wall? The wall between me and God.

I suddenly remembered, when Moses said, "*Mi Anokhi? Who am I?*" that God responded to Moses:

"I will surely be with you. So that will be the sign to you that it is I who have sent you."[31]

So there I stood, at the top of the slope, surrounded by the panorama of giant mountains which dwarfed me. And I just continued taking it all in. My mind continued to be flooded with more thoughts from the scriptures.

Suddenly, my thoughts raced back to the story of Elijah.[32] I remembered how Elijah ran for his life when Jezebel sought to have him put to death. I recalled how Elijah sat down under the juniper tree, and gave up. The juniper tree,

---

[31] Ex. 3;12.
[32] 1 Kings 19.

or broom bush, is the only tree where one can find shade in the desert.

But Elijah was alone. He was hungry, tired, and had no chance of escape from Jezebel. I recalled how he laid down under the juniper tree, and gave up. He actually prayed that he might die, saying "*It's too much.*" And suddenly, a malakh or messenger came, and touched him, and told him to get up and eat and drink. Somehow there was food and water there.

Elijah ate the food of angels, and drank living water, and went on for 40 days journey in the strength of that one meal. And then while he was hiding out at Mt. Sinai, in a cave, God was revealed to Elijah. I remembered how God spoke to him, as it says: "*In a still, small voice.*"[33]

I wondered—was that the same still, small voice that was speaking to me now? The voice which spoke to me on the airplane and which spoke to me in these snowy mountains of Utah? Was the same voice that was with Elijah with me too?

Now, don't get me wrong. This was not the first time that I had ever experienced a touch, or a voice, or this thing which I call the "Presence" of the Lord. I had experienced the divine Presence many, many times in the past. I was no stranger to the outpouring of the Ruakh HaKodesh or Holy Spirit of God. But this was different. Why?

It is not easy to explain. But I will try:

Did it Stick?:

Whenever Yeshua healed a paralyzed man, opened the eyes of the blind, cleansed a leper, raised the dead, or whatever, there were always some religious folk among the scribes and Pharisees who insisted it was either a fake or a work of the devil. Meanwhile, others saw and believed, and they rejoiced and sang praises to his name, and hoped to make him King.

---

[33] 1 Kings 19:12.

But, I wonder, either way, how many people were personally renewed, reborn or transformed by what they saw?

Whether they were believers who rejoiced, or unbelievers who crossed their arms and shouted, "Faker!" the end result was the same—unless some inner transformation occurred.

Let's face it, an experience that is here today, gone tomorrow, no matter how great, doesn't amount to much, unless something happens within. To see a great sight, even a sight done by the Lord, doesn't necessarily change a person for the better.

Take for example, Mt. Sinai, the whole nation of Israel heard and saw the divine presence descend upon the peak and speak from the midst of a dark cloud, with lightning, fire, and the sound of the shofar. But they were not changed. They went right on in their ignorance, in spite of what they witnessed, and just weeks later built a golden calf idol, and said *"This is your God, O' Israel, that brought you up out of the land of Egypt."*[34]

And by my estimation, many of the multitudes who ate the bread and the fish when they were multiplied, or who saw Lazarus come forth from the tomb, or lepers cleansed, or whatever, may have shouted and cheered, danced and sung, but were not necessarily changed any more than if they'd seen their hometown team win the Superbowl.

What I've observed, is that great events point the way, but nobody is changed personally or in any kind of deep way by public demonstrations—even when they are done by the Lord.

It is only through the inner work of God's Spirit that new birth is brought about personally and individually. This is the work of the Messiah, who transcends time and space, and is the very eternal life that created the universe. But it has to happen within each of us personally, or not at all.

As I said, like millions upon millions of other people in the world, I was no stranger to the divine Presence or Spirit

[34] Ex. 32:8.

of God. The outpouring of the Spirit is something which is stressed and emphasized in the messianic Jewish faith. The end-time revival of Israel is prophetic, and it is written about in the scriptures. And I am very much a part of that move of God, and have attended many public events where the Spirit was clearly being poured out, and oftentimes accompanied by wonderful things. And we see it quite regularly in my own congregation as well.

I cannot begin to detail all that here and now, and though vastly significant, it's not really relevant to this particular story. I just want it to be clear that I am not discounting it in any way. The difference is that what takes place in a corporate, public setting, no matter how revivalistic and wonderful it may be, and no matter how much I do appreciate and hunger for such things, still, the bottom line is this—has there been personal transformation to come of it?

Without inner transformation, then it is just another great time. Here today. Gone tomorrow. The question is, did it stick? But it doesn't stick unless something happens within. And that "something" is personal and individual in each one of us. Without which we shrivel up, spiritually.

I had experienced the outpouring of the Spirit countless times in public settings. I still do. And I yearn for it, as much as ever before. But the iPath is different. What was happening to me was that the Spirit was beginning to pour out, not upon me from without, but as a stream flowing forth from within me.

It was becoming something quite personal. Something which was not forensic, but intrinsic. Not for the world to see, but for me to see. Even though the world would be touched by it, it is in a much simpler, quieter way.

This was something not experiential, in the sense of here today, wasn't it awesome? Then gone tomorrow. No, this was sticking. And accumulating. Like the snowfall on the mountains. And it was not just another great time. It was more like a metamorphosis, that is, spiritual transformation.

Believe me when I tell you, that no amount of witnessing great miracles, signs or wonders, nor having amazing spiritual experiences will necessarily bring about an inner change.

You might be one of the doubting Pharisees with your arms crossed in rejection, or you might be one who rightly believes that what you just saw was a work of God. Either way, whether believer or non-believer, unless and until the inner-work of personal transformation comes to pass, being a believer or non-believer won't matter all that much. Because you can believe in what you saw yesterday, or what happened yesterday that you heard about from someone else—but whatever is happening out there does not necessarily change you inside.

Those who saw the Shekhina at Mt. Sinai or who saw Yeshua transfigured on Mt. Hermon, did not long afterwards call for Moses to be stoned (as Israel did), or deny ever knowing Yeshua (as Peter did). This happens just as soon as it is discovered that God is not conforming to human expectations. That's how it was in those generations, and that's how it is for our generation as well. Because after all, we are only human. And that is the basic problem.

In the past, when the Spirit of God fell upon me, innumerable times, maybe more, it was just like snowfall that doesn't accumulate. It hits the pavement, maybe makes a light coating, but by the end of the day it's gone. I guess the conditions were not right.

I know that some people want to grow in the Spirit of God so badly. Earnestly desiring it. But desire has nothing to do with it. Some of them go from one gathering to the next, always chasing the opportunity for another encounter with God's presence. Maybe they find something. Maybe they don't. It doesn't matter. What matters is, did it stick? Did it accumulate? Yeshua used to say that the eternal Kingdom is not "look here" or "look there", but, behold, it's right in the midst of each you.[35]

---

[35] Luke 17:21.

You Can't Chase God:

God is not a storm to be chased like those guys on TV that go off to Kansas or somewhere in the Great Plains, to chase tornadoes. The storm chasers. Cool show. They find the storms. They see the storms. It's all pretty amazing to see. And it makes good TV shows.

But you can't do that with the Lord. What is the point of chasing God? What I'm saying is that there is no point. Being a God-chaser is pointless. It's a dead-end. Because you can't chase God. God chases you. And you can't catch God. If anything, God catches you.

As the scripture says, *"Be still and know that I am God."* (Ps. 46:10).

There were multitudes that followed Yeshua around in the wilderness of Israel. They witnessed and marveled at the great works that were being done. But they missed the message of his coming, the works that he did, and of his teaching.

Many of the same people who hailed him as Messiah when he entered Jerusalem on Passover, were just days later calling for Barabbas to be released and Yeshua to be crucified. What was their problem? They saw his mighty works, they heard him teach and were amazed. There was no inner transformation.

It was only later, after Yeshua rose from the dead, and then ascended up into the heavens, that the spiritual outpouring came upon 120 of his Jewish followers gathered in the Temple for Shavuot in Jerusalem.[36] It was only through the Spirit which Yeshua promised would be sent to them after he was gone from their sight that something would happen in which they would be transformed into sons and daughters of the Lord. And by this transformative work, thus able to carry on Yeshua's work, imparting the same Spirit unto others.

---

[36] *See,* Acts 2.

What I have found is that there is a transformative, inner work of grace that takes hold of you, and starts to pour out from within. Until that happens, the seeds are cast but few of them ever take root. They just lay there in the ground, and eventually they are eaten by birds or get swept away by wind or rain or whatever.

I think it was there on the white slopes of the enormous Rocky Mountains, that I first realized I was being changed. I was a novice, did not understand much, and still had plenty to learn. But I understood that I was becoming something new. Something other than what I was. And yet, I saw that the thing I was becoming was not really. Because it was what I was all along...even though I was unaware of it.

I had started by asking the question—"*Who am I*"? In this manner I was becoming aware of what I am. I really was on a journey to myself, as I discovered the true spiritual center of my being. And as I made this discovery, the thing which was uncovered in me, which was older than the mountains before me, became the governing authority of the life being lived in and through me. And it was not metaphorical. It was real. When you become what you are, then you become a child of the living God, just as scripture says:

> *"But whoever did receive Him, those trusting in His name, to these He gave the right to become children of God. They were born not of a bloodline, nor of human desire, nor of man's will, but of God."*[37]

Born of God:

Of course, I may have called myself "a child of God" before. But it wasn't true. For what I discovered was that unless and until there is a transformative work, the spiritual life is just a path to God. It is the occupation of a spectator. Not a participant. The life of a servant. Not a son. The

---

[37] John 1:12,13.

servant stays outside in the servant's quarters. The son eats, sleeps, and lives in the house of the Master.

To go from servant to son is based on this principle, that unless a person is reborn, and becomes born from above, they cannot see the Kingdom of God.[38] And to be born again, one must first experience a sort of "death." After all, no one can go back into the mother's womb.

But the principle is clear. It is a universal law: The one who will save his life in this world will lose it.[39] New birth, the new Self, the new man, the true Self–whatever you want to call it–can only come about through a figurative kind of "death." But the good news is that it's the death of what you are not. Followed by the new birth. That is, the emergence of what you are.

As the verse above says, the new birth is: "*Born not of a bloodline, nor of human desire, nor of man's will, but of God.*"

As I stood on that mountain, fixated on the glory of the scene which I beheld, and exhilarated by all that was happening in the moment, the Spirit of the Lord was upon me. Because the Lord had anointed me to preach good news.

What good news? The same good news that was given to Moses at the burning bush. And which Yeshua gave to his inner circle of followers. That news, stated in the simplest way, is this: "*I am with you always.*"[40] That's the good news.

It can be stated, explained it, described in ten thousand different ways. But the message is straight and simple, and always the same: The message is, I-manu-el. That is Hebrew for, God is with us.

As I stood there on the mountain, alone upon a vast white sea, I knew that God was with me. And I suddenly remembered the words of Moses, who said unto the Lord:

---

[38] John 3:3.
[39] Mat. 16:25, John 12:25.
[40] Mat. 28:20.

If Your presence does not go with me, don't let us go up from here! For how would it be known that I or your people have found favor in Your sight? Isn't it because You go with us, that distinguishes us from all the people on the face of the earth?"[41] .

Like Moses, I wouldn't have wanted to go on another day without the Presence, that very same Presence of which Moses spoke.

I knew that there is an eternal life living in me, a timeless soul, a true Self, which is the Son of God, in whose image I was made, and which Yeshua was in fullness, as a human being, walking the earth.

The same Ruakh (Spirit) that worked miracles through him, the same Spirit that raised him from the dead, was alive in me. I remembered another verse of scripture:

And if the Ruakh of the One who raised Yeshua from the dead dwells in you, the One who raised Messiah Yeshua from the dead will also give life to your mortal bodies through His Ruakh who dwells in you.[42]

It was exactly as Yeshua had said it would be: "*I am with you always.*" I had come into contact with the timeless, soul-traveler Self. The Ruakh. The Spirit. The Messiah in me. The ageless timeless, Son of God which dwelt in me.

I am talking about the soul of my being, the same soul unto whom David spoke when he said, "*Bless the Lord, O' my soul, and all that is within me.*" (Ps. 103:1).

The soul of my being, the eternal Self, the original image in which I was fashioned, like every man, my true and everlasting Selfhood, was always there, but was now beginning to rise up into my awareness. I did not have to die physically for this to happen. But an old "self" was passing away.

---

[41] Ex. 33:15,16.
[42] Romans 8:11.

Something was happening. I did not know what it was, because I did not understand it. To this day, I can't really tell you how it happened or why it happened. I can only tell *what* happened. And what happened was just like that old Hank Williams, Sr. song says, "Praise the Lord, I saw the Light" And doggone it, who cares how it happened. All that matters is it happened. And that's why I have a story to tell.

The Mind of the Lord:

I didn't know at that time. But looking back now, I know that what was happening is that I was becoming conscious. God-conscious. Some might call that Christ-consciousness. I prefer messianic-consciousness. In any case, it's a mystery, that Paul tried to explain in this way:

"Who has known the mind of the Lord, that he will instruct Him? But we have the mind of Messiah."[43]

I was putting on that mind which is the "mind of Messiah." The messianic mind.

Sometimes in a moment, in the twinkling of an eye, amazing things can happen. Sometimes, suddenly, mysteriously, there is a "click." And the fog lifts. Almost inexplicably, you see things entirely differently. You see things not as they appear, but as they are.

That day, on the slopes of the Rockies, there was a "click." I was logged in. I was on God's superhighway. There were messages waiting for me in my "Inbox." Some of those messages had been there for quite a long time. But I wasn't logged in, so I wasn't reading them. The problem was that I didn't know how to log in. But now I was logged in. Now I was on the iPath.

I skied down into the basin. Not hardly a single tree could be seen in it. One has to be very careful in such a spot,

---

[43] (1 Cor. 2:16)..

especially if snow is falling. You can get vertigo, because all you see is white everywhere.

The white-out effect, without any trees to guide your line of vision, can cause you to lose all sense of direction. With no direction, things start spinning. It's an optical illusion, but it seems quite real. I had it happen to me once before in a storm.

I was feeling just a slight touch of vertigo. So, after going down about 500 feet, I went over a small hill, that dropped down steep, about 15 or 20 feet, into a nice flat spot, just at the edge of another steep drop-off. I stopped there.

I looked up at the blue sky, then scanned across the peaks to try and get my bearings. It helped. I started to feel stabilized again.

On a sunny day, like this, you'd better have good eye protection, or the sun upon the white snow can be blinding. You start to see spots. The good pair of Italian-made Carrera ski googles reminded me of Laura, who had bought them for me as a birthday present a few years back. Not easy to find in Florida, she got them online through Amazon.com. But that sun still made me blink as I looked upward at the ski.

Having got my bearings back, I looked back down into the bottom of the basin, and then all around me at the walls of the great bowl in which I was now immersed.

I was a tiny speck of nothing inside of a vast eternity of white-out. I was staring into the vacuum of a giant crater of white nothingness.

Then, suddenly, I heard a swooshing sound coming near to me. I looked back at the small hill behind me, and a snowboarder shot up in the air, over the hill behind me, and was headed straight at me. If I had not stepped aside, he would've landed on me for sure.

"Out of my way!" said the snowboarder, as he carried on down the slope.

Damn snowboarders. I didn't much care for them. A bunch of hot shots. Surfers on snow, basically. Cocky, always goofing around, and often reckless and out-of-control.

"Woo-hoo!" I heard him holler on his way down.

He was wearing one of those ridiculous hats, with green fabric spikes sticking out of it. The kind that only snowboarders wear.

With the snowboarder out of sight, it was just me and the mountain again. My heart, which was racing, on account of the near collision, started to settle down. But I felt a slight touch of vertigo again.

In such a place, one realizes just how small that you are in the grand scheme. And in realizing how small you are, you realize how big you are. Because, when you realize your nothingness, then you realize your everything-ness.

I was alone. To these mountains, I was a complete unknown. Struggling with my sense of direction, I didn't know how I would proceed from here. I stared into the white-out vacuum of this great crater, and skied on.

The Eagle:

Soon I was at the bottom of the basin, where I got onto the chairlift, and headed up the mountain, for another journey down.

I had a little pocket bible, just Psalms and the New Testament, that I carried with me in the chest pocket of my ski jacket.

As the lift went up, right then I saw an eagle flying overhead. It was a bald eagle. If you've never seen a bald eagle, it's hard to put into words. If I had to put it in one word, the best I can say is "Majestic!"

Apparently, hundreds of bald eagles fly into Utah beginning in November, and they leave in March. That's not very many, and the sightings are rare. They come down from Alaska, Canada, and the northern States to spend the winter. There are only about 1000 of them in Utah each Winter, and here it is I saw one of them. Wow!

There is something special and mysterious about these creatures. They live on the lofty tops of mountains, amidst the solitary grandeur of nature. It's majestic beauty sets it apart from all other birds.

There's something about the bald eagle that just seems to signify Freedom. I don't know if perhaps that's because it's the national emblem of the USA, or maybe because of the way it goes where it wants, soars to the highest heights, swoops into the valley below, and seems to be unbounded by the ordinary parameters of natural life.

Those bald eagles are so few in number. It's a wonder that we even know about them. And, yet, they have made their presence known. It makes you wonder, how can such a small number of them make such a great impact?

I thought to myself, Jews are like that. A tiny people in the world. Just 15 million of us, in a world of over 7 billion. It's a wonder anyone has ever heard of us. But Jewish people have definitely made our presence known in the world. And, like the bald eagle, Jews also tend to go south in the Winter. Although, not to the Rockies, more likely to Florida. Being a Jewish resident of Florida, I am an exception in this regard.

The Secret Place:

As the lift continued going up, I took my glove off, and sat on it to make sure it didn't fall off. I took the pocket bible out of my ski jacket pocket. I needed to do something other than look at the white cliffs. So I read. And it was opened to a verse from Psalm 91:1:

"He who dwells in the secret place of the Most High, shall abide under the shadow of the Almighty."

Sure enough, I was in the secret place. Here in the Rockies, except for one stupid snowboarder, I was hidden away and cut off from the whole world. What an amazing feeling.

The sun was shining bright, the light reflecting everywhere. I could sense the presence of the all-Mighty, all-knowing, God, who seemed clearly to occupy all space in this vast location. And it seemed that I was altogether with Him. Joined to Him in this place.

As I continued up the mountain on the lift, indeed, there was a presence. I could feel it. Tangible. It was creamy. Like balm. It was mushy. And I was in it. Like being in vat of butter.

The Spirit of God continued to download revelation into my mind. I closed the pocket bible, and as I reached back into the chest pocket on my ski jacket, I found my acupressure bands, which Laura had inserted into my jacket pockets. Thank God for wives. She was always looking out for me.

I had actually obtained the acupressure bands a year earlier when Laura and I had gone on a cruise. By applying pressure about two inches above the wrist, they seem to do away with motion sickness. And with vertigo.

Laura had placed them in my jacket pocket, knowing that I had a problem once before with vertigo. So that was the end of that.

Upon reaching the top, I skied off the lift, down the cat track, and back to the original spot where I'd started the morning. Again, staring down into the basin, I stopped and took a pause.

Now the Ruakh HaKodesh, or Holy Spirit of God, continued to flow in me in a most extraordinary way, bringing me great comfort and a deep sense of joy.

So, I skied down the mountain, deeper and deeper to the bottom of the basin. I was gliding down the mountain on my skis, along the powdery snow, under blue skies, on a cold day that didn't seem cold, because of the magnificent sunlight of the gorgeous Rocky Mountains.

Captain Rosenblatt was right. There are no paths to God. God IS the path. He is the Life, and the length of my days. I was now on the infinite journey. One without beginning. Without end. The iPath.

Unbeknownst to me, I had come to this snow covered crater, dwarfed by its giant presence, for this very purpose, to be joined in fellowship with the Spirit of the Lord. It was not my work, but the work of the Spirit of the Lord, within me, drawing me closer. For what cause? I think, as Yeshua said,

"I have come that they might have life, and have it abundantly."[44]

I stress, I wasn't doing anything special to bring this about. Does every person who goes skiing in Utah have this same amazing experience which I had? Clearly not.

I was just skiing in Utah. Something was happening. And it was not the work of Gary Goldman. It was the work of an "other."

I paused from skiing for a moment, to catch my breath. I closed my eyes, and immediately, I was being filled with God's presence. I just stood there, eyes closed, and as the Spirit of the Lord moved in me, I just let it happen. Secretly, silently, and sacredly.

And right then, again, a voice popped into my mind. It wasn't audible, and yet, it seemed like someone speaking to me. Because it was a "voice" which I heard, but I heard it with my inner ear. And what it said to me was this: *"Stop praying to God. Let God pray in you."*

Mission accomplished. I had done exactly that. God was praying in me. For sure. But I didn't know how I'd done it. Nor how I might ever do it again. Because I really didn't do anything.

And yet, I wondered, maybe I actually did do something—by not doing anything. I was dwelling in the irony. By doing nothing, I had done everything. At least, everything that needed to be done, in order to do what God would have me do. Which is nothing. Just to be still. Yes, be still and know that God is God. That is what I had done.

I can tell you this: Doing nothing is a lot harder than one might think. Just try some time to do nothing. Even for just a moment. It's easy to still your body. But even if you still your body, you can't quiet your mind. Because it's always racing and racing. And if you try too hard to still your mind, then you're thinking about not thinking. And that's just more thinking, which only adds to it.

---

[44] John 10:10.

Not that I suggest trying to stop your mind. What I'm saying is that you cannot stop thought. If someone ever tells you to "still your mind" or "quiet your mind" or anything like that, don't believe it. You can't do it if you tried.

But what I can do is change my way of thinking. I can switch the stream of thought flowing from my brain—replete with all of its anxieties, fears, opinions, conclusions, and concepts—and log into the Spirit of God. It's not stopping thought. It's more like changing the channel. But at this point, I didn't know much about that. That came later.

The scripture says we have the mind of Messiah. But trust me, if we can learn to put on that messianic Mind, then the thought-stream of God is broadcast in us. It is livestreamed into our own personal consciousness. This is what it means to be conformed to the image and likeness of the Messiah, and to be children of the Lord. Our thought stream is fallen, decadent, polluted and selfish. The Spirit of God is pure and crystal clear stream of living water.

It was starting to happen to me. I couldn't describe it, like I can now. Nor did I know at that time how to tune in to it. But I'll just say for now that it happens if we can learn to do what the scripture says: *"Be still and know that I am God."*[45] How that is done, I would learn later on, and I will share it when I get to that part of my story.

For now, I pushed off, and skied down into that bowl, all the way to the bottom, hooting and hollering all the way down. Then, I got in line for the chairlift, to go back up.

Unwritten Rules:

Now, as the day progressed, there were just a few others skiing the mountain. There was maybe three or four people ahead of me waiting to get on the chairlift. And then one guy pulled in behind me. All of them were snowboarders.

As I've said, I don't like being around snowboarders. A lot of them are reckless. They fly by you at 100 mph, and

---

[45] Ps. 46:10.

they'll run right into you if you don't move. I like to ski—not surf—down the mountain. To each his own, but I generally keep my distance from snowboarders.

I enjoy the chair rides up the mountain. Especially when I have my own chair. Even though each chair on the lift has seats for four people, typically, when things are that slow, it means singles get their own chair and ride up alone. That's just kinda the unwritten rule for singles, when no one else is waiting in line.

So I let each of the snowboarders in front me get on their own chair, before I positioned myself to catch my own chair. I respected the unwritten rule. Admittedly, in any case, I had no desire to ride with anyone else. Not just because of my introverted tendencies. But also, because I don't like to be around snowboarders.

But as I was about to move forward and catch my chair, the snowboarder behind me pulled in next to me, to my left, and positioned himself to get on the chair with me. As far as the look I gave him, either he didn't care, or it was too late. He plopped into the chair, and up we went. Like it or not, I'd have to deal with company on this trip up.

He had jet black hair, from what I could see coming out of his snow cap. It seemed rather long in the back. He was young. By his face, he looked to be maybe mid or late twenties.

As we began our ride up, immediately, I noticed that goofy snow hat he was wearing, with the green spikes sticking out.

"Hey you're the snowboarder that almost ran me over earlier."

"Oh, wow, that was you, man?"

"You said, 'out of my way!' after you nearly killed me," I reminded him.

"Hey, I'm sorry, man. Coming off that hill, I couldn't see you."

So as I began the ride up with my would-be killer, I was feeling pretty uncomfortable already. But as I've learned, it's always better to forgive an offender, especially when you're stuck with them, riding up a mountain on a chairlift.

"That's alright. Honest mistake," I said.

After we got past that, as expected the ride up then began with the inevitable questions.

"So, where you from?" said the snowboarder, as we started our journey upwards.

I noticed a very slight accent of some kind, which sounded familiar, but I couldn't quite recognize.

"Florida," I said. "Tampa Bay area. How 'bout you?"

"Me, I'm from forever."

"Oh really?" I said.

"That's right. When you come from forever, you can be everywhere. Ya know?"

I was unimpressed. And made no effort to hide it. I'm sure he could tell.

"I'm Shlomo," he said.

Now, I knew, of course, that Shlomo is Hebrew for Solomon. From the root, "Shalom," it means peace. Or "his peace" to be exact. And now I recognized the accent, it was definitely Israeli.

Jews in the U.S. are usually pretty subtle about revealing to one another that we are Jewish. It's sort of a game we play. Per the unwritten rules, It isn't considered good form to just come right out and ask someone, "Are you Jewish?" We are all pretty good at identifying one another after some light conversation.

My last name is a dead give-away, so I don't usually reveal it up front. That would violate the rules. But when you meet a guy named, Shlomo, there's no further need for subtlety. He's obviously Jewish. So, I might as well give up my name as well.

"Gary Goldman," I responded, extending a gloved hand, to which Shlomo responded by putting forth a gloved fist. I obliged, and gave him a fist bump.

"Jewish?" said Shlomo.

"That's right."

"Maybe we're same tribe or something," he laughed.

"You're Israeli?"

"I am," he said.

"Nice," I said.

The Journey:

"So, what brings you here from Florida, Goldman?" Shlomo asked.

"I don't know," I said, "I guess I came here seeking inspiration."

"Cool. For what?"

"I'm trying to write a book. But I don't know what to say yet."

"I see," said Shlomo. "Gonna paint your masterpiece, huh?"

"You could say that."

"Well, if you need inspiration," he said, looking around, "I'd say you're in the right place."

"Most definitely," I said.

We were both quiet for a moment, and then Shlomo continued.

"So, how is the surfing over there in the Sunshine State?" said Shlomo.

"The Atlantic is pretty good. But I'm on the Gulf. You can't really surf the Gulf."

"Too bad."

"I guess," I said.

"You don't surf, then I take it?" he remarked.

"Nah. Not my thing," I said.

"Too bad. Surfing is good medicine."

"So, where do you surf?" I asked.

"Right now, in California. I've been staying in L.A. Malibu actually. Before that, India. Great waves there."

"You were in India?"

"After my service in the army, I went to India."

"Yeah, I am familiar with that tradition." I said.

It is quite a common practice for young Israelis, after finishing their military service, to go off to India for a few months, usually seeking some kind of spiritual adventure.

"I went with a group of friends, but then I went off on my own. I trekked up into the Himalayas. Met this old man who lived in a cave. I stayed there for a while. Studied with the old man. Then after that, I stayed on the coast and learned how to surf."

"Awesome," I said. "So, what are you doing here in Utah?"

"I'm on a journey," Shlomo said.

I paused, and thought about that for a moment.

"Where are you headed?" I asked.

"What do you mean by that?"

"I mean, what's your destination?"

"The journey," he said.

"Huh?" I said.

"The journey IS my destination."

Right then, the chairlift suddenly stopped. We were up high, suspended over the basin. They do that sometimes. Usually, it's because somebody fell getting on the lift down below. If no one is hurt, once they get that person out of the way, and back on their feet, it'll usually run again. Meanwhile, I was not thrilled about dangling over the great abyss.

To Wait Upon the Lord:

"So, what do you think?" Shlomo said.

"Of what?"

"The mountains?"

"Incredible," I said. "I saw a bald eagle earlier this morning."

"No kidding," he said. He took a deep breath, closed his eyes, stretched out his hands, with both palms to the sky, and said, in English: *"But those who wait upon the Lord shall renew their strength. They shall mount up with wings like eagles, they shall run and not be weary, they shall walk and not faint."*[46].

"Hey, that's pretty good," I said.

Actually I was impressed. Actually I was shocked. I did not expect this guy to be quoting scripture. Then Shlomo continued.

"What do you think it means to 'wait upon the Lord?" he asked me.

"I think it has to do with being patient."

"You mean like you're waiting for God to show up?" he said.

"Something like that," I responded.

"But God doesn't show up. God is already here," he said.

"Yeah. True."

"I think it's you and me, that need to show up. Not God."

"I see your point," I said. But how do you suggest doing that?"

"I learned something from this old man I met in India, this guy who lived in a cave up in the Himalayas. You know what we used to study?"

"Tell me."

"The scriptures."

"Vedic?" I asked.

"No, Goldman. The Jewish scriptures." he said.

"Really? The old man knew them?"

"Better than anyone I've ever met," said Shlomo.

"Wow."

"He taught me that to wait on the Lord, means to wait *in* the Lord. Do you see the difference?"

"Not really."

"When you are *in* the Lord, waiting, there is a connection. You're not waiting for anything to happen, because it's already happening. As long as you wait *on* the Lord, nothing is happening. It's like you and God are separated, and you're wanting him to cross over something

---

[46] *NKJV* Isaiah 40:31

like that big chasm down there," said Shlomo, pointing to the white abyss in the basin below us.

Shlomo took a tube of #30 UV protection out of his jacket pocket. With a hand gesture, I declined.

"I think you need some," said Shlomo. "On your nose."

I reconsidered and accepted his offer. Removing a glove, I put out my index finger. As I started to smear it on my nose.

Shlomo said, "Yeshua used to say, '*Anokhi ha-Gefen, gefen ha-Emet.*' You know what that means?"[47]

"I am the true vine," I said.

"Hey, that's pretty good, Goldman," said Shlomo. "So you know who Yeshua is?'

"Sure," I said.

"That's Jesus, you know? It doesn't offend you if I talk about Yeshua."

"Nah, I'm cool with that."

"Well, good," said Shlomo. "A lot of our people are not, as you know."

"Well I am," I said.

I balked at telling Shlomo more details about the fact that I am a messianic Jew, and a Rabbi, etc. There wouldn't be time. And it would just raise more questions. Questions I didn't want to get into. This young man obviously had some wisdom. And I could just anticipate him saying to me something like: "*You are a teacher of Israel and you don't know these things?*"[48]

I didn't want to deal with that. I was intrigued by this young Israeli who, although at least 20 years my junior, seemed to know something worth knowing, something I did not know. This had divine appointment written all over it. So I let him continue.

"So Yeshua used to say to his talmidim, "Anokhi ha-Gefen and then he would tell them 'abide in me.'[49] You know what he was talking about?"

---

[47] John 15:1.
[48] John 3:10.

"Prayer, I guess."

"Yeah, but what kind of prayer?" he said.

"I wish I knew."

"I can tell you this, Goldman. If you knew how to pray like that, I mean the way Yeshua taught his talmidim, if you knew how to 'abide in me,' then things would be different. Then you'd have your inspiration. You'd paint your masterpiece."

This Bread:

At that moment, the chairlift started moving again. We still had a ways to go, but I was glad to be moving up the mountain again. It was a beautiful sunny day, but there was still lots of fresh powder to ski from the storm the night before.

Shlomo pointed down toward the giant, snow-dusted bowl below.

"You see that?" he said.

"Yeah," I responded. "It's beautiful."

"When the snow falls, it's like manna falling from heaven. And there's not an inch of ground that doesn't get covered by it."

"Yeah, it really came down last night. I was watching from the window in my room," I said.

Shlomo was pretty intense. This ride was not over, and I sensed that he wasn't going to let up. He wasn't.

"Our fathers ate manna in the wilderness, and perished," said Shlomo.

"They sure did."

"But there is another kind of bread, Goldman. You know what 'Khayei Olam' is?" he said.

"Life eternal," I responded.

"Yeshua said there is a bread that falls down from heaven. This bread is the bread of life. So that we can eat it and have Khayei Olam.[50] You've heard of this bread?"

---

49 John 15:4.

"I have."

"Where do you get it?" said Shlomo.

"From Yeshua," I said.

"Okay. But where do you go to be with Yeshua, so that you have this bread?"

I paused for a moment. I didn't really have a response. I scratched my chin and thought about it.

"Anokhi lekhem ha-khayim," Shlomo said.

"I am the bread of life," I translated out loud.

"Your Hebrew is pretty good, Goldman. Do you know what Yeshua was talking about?"

"The bread of life," I said.

"True," he said. "But what is it? Where do you get it?"

"Well, good question. You have to go to God to get it," I said.

"Now, how does anyone do that?" he said.

I didn't respond. He nodded, as if he'd scored some kind of goal with that last remark.

Then he said, "You know, Goldman, I hiked all the way up into the Himalayas. Just to discover that everything I could ever need is right here in the midst of me. Always." He pointed to his chest. "Hidden away, here, in the storehouse. That's where this bread is, of which the Rabbi spoke."

"But Yeshua said that he is the bread of life," I said.

"No. Yeshua said, 'Anokhi.' I."

"I, what?"

"I am the bread of life. Not he is. I am."

"You are?" I said.

"No," said Shlomo.

"Who is?"

"I am," he said. "*I* am the bread of Life."

"But—"

"Right there in the midst of you, more vast than this gigantic bowl down below, is a storehouse of infinite supply," Shlomo said. "Health, harmony, wealth, righteousness,

---

[50] John 6:51 and 58.

wisdom, joy, victory, deliverance, peace, justice, love. It's all there."

"Yeah. I guess you're right."

"The Rabbi said you will ask whatever you wish and it shall be done for you."[51] If you knew who it was who is speaking to you now, then you'd ask whatever you wish, and it would be given to you."[52]

"Well, I know who it was that said to me 'get out of my way' " I joked.

"I hope you do," said Shlomo. "I sure hope you do."

At that we both had a laugh.

Shoving Off:

As our chair pulled up to the top of the mountain, I skied off the chair, and Shlomo boarded off too. I skied over to a spot at the top of a huge drop-off, and he pulled up right next to me. My tips hung over the steep edge, which I looked forward to skiing down, but I would not push forward and ski down until I was ready.

I could have shoved-off right there and gone my separate way, but I sensed that Shlomo wasn't done. And I guess, knowing I might never see him again, I just wanted to hear him out. He continued.

"I guess this is it, huh, Goldman?"

"Yeah. Great meeting you," I said. "Probably never see each other again, so, hey, have a good journey."

"But *I* am with you always," he said, pointing to the sky and all around toward the mountains. He stressed the word "I" when he spoke here.

"I'll have to remember that," I said.

"But I don't think you know who *I* am."

"Well, I just met you," I said.

---

[51] John 15:7

[52] See, John 4:10 – *"If you knew the gift of God, and who it is who is saying to you, 'Give Me a drink,' you would have asked Him, and He would have given you living water."*

113

"*I* am in my Father, you are in *me*, and *I* am in you," he said.

"From John 14:20, right?"

"You know the verse, but do you who *I* am?" said Shlomo.

"I know who I is there in that verse. But you, I don't know very well," I said. "Glad to have met you, though."

"If you knew *me*, then you would know my Father also.[53]"

"Why can't you just say what you mean?" I said.

"What do you mean by that?" said Shlomo.

"Say who you are, and who I am, and who the Father is."

"What? You don't know?" he said.

"I'm confused," I said.

"Exactly."

"Impossible," I said.

I took a deep breath. Adjusted my goggles.

"Look, I'm going to shove off here, okay?" I said.

"He who has seen *me* has seen the Father,"[54] he said.

"All I see is you."

"No, Goldman. You don't see *me*."

"Who are you then?"

"If you knew who *I* am, then you would know who you are," said Shlomo. "But because you don't know who you are, you don't know who I am either."

I stuck my poles in, and looked toward the downhill slope.

"I think I'm gonna do some skiing now," I said.

I could've probably learned a lot more from this young Israeli who was wise beyond his years. But I guess I'd just heard about enough at that point. It was all that I could process at that time.

I gave a thumbs up, took a deep breath. And planted my poles. Shlomo smiled. He had that same Mona Lisa smile, just like Marley. A smirky look which said that he knew something. Something which I did not know, but which he

---

[53] John 8:19.
[54] John 14:9.

couldn't tell me either. Presumably, because I wouldn't understand it. But it was something which I needed to know.

"Onward in the journey, Goldman. You'll see. To be on the iPath is about living in both worlds."

"Wait," I said as I was about to shove off. You've heard of the iPath?"

"Of course," he said.

"I'm on the iPath too," I said. "At least, I think I am."

"If it is so, then we are brothers, Goldman. Not only by blood, but more important, in the Spirit of God. Because we are on the iPath. The path of I. We are on the journey, of which Yeshua was the first. He has gone ahead of us, to call for his own, to follow him along this path of Life. And there are others. All around the world. I have met many of them!"

"Cool!" I exclaimed. "But what is the iPath, exactly?"

"We are living in the nexus between two worlds. Between heaven and earth. The imperishable Life, Goldman. The Life which no eye can see, is brought forth into this world. It's the imperishable, lived in the perishable. The deepest valley lived upon the highest peak. The "I" in the "you..."

Shlomo paused, and at this point I noticed that he had joined his hands together, each of his ten fingers interlocking. He went on:

"...the changeless in the changing, the infinite in the finite, joined together, and integrated as one."

"Awesome!" I said. "Tell me more."

"We are all together, Goldman. One family. One God. I in you. You in me."

Right then a group of snowboarders who had just gotten off the chairlift, came flying in our direction. As the snowboarders came dangerously close to me, I shoved off, down the steep hill, and did not look back. Shlomo did the same. It was the only way to avoid getting slammed by this group of reckless youth.

I pushed off with my poles and skied away, not daring to look back. And as I sped down into this giant void, covered in an abyss of white powder, under perfect blueberry skies, I heard Shlomo's voice continuing behind me:

"Stay on the iPath, Goldman."

I skied all the rest of that day and two more days after. I did not see Shlomo again there.

The Down Low:

At this point in my Sabbatical, some amazing things were happening to me. I didn't understand what was happening. But one thing I knew about it was that I needed to keep it on the down low. I mean keep it to myself. At least for now.

Before I came to Utah, when I had met Marley at Starbucks, do you think I ran home and told Laura? No way. Do you think when I got on the shuttle from the airport that I got on the cell phone to tell my wife about the amazing, overweight, Jewish airplane pilot who told me everything I needed to know about God and the universe? Not a chance. Nor was I going to tell her about the sayings of Shlomo the Israeli surfer who trekked up to the Himalayas and learned the secret of life from some bible-reading old man in a cave.

Laura and I have no secrets. But this was going to have to be a first for us. At least for a while. Because this was something happening within myself. I couldn't explain it. Not even to her. And if I couldn't explain to her, I definitely couldn't tell anyone else. I knew this. And I accepted it. I had much more to learn about this new—whatever it was.

Another thing that I didn't realize yet, but I later discovered, was that being on the iPath is not something that happens all at once. You get on it. But then you meander off. You drift between two worlds. Between this world and that world.

This perishing, corruptible world, is always pulling. Like a maelstrom. It sucks you down into the land of the lost. But there is another pull, a stronger pull, that pulls you back to the eternal, incorruptible world. The land of the found.

Like the Jews returning to the homeland. After two thousand years in exile, no one can really explain how it happened. It just happened. So, too, the world is pulling all humankind into oblivion, but there's a pull home, going against the grain of the world. It's only by the grace of God that I was ever able to get into the right current.

But sometimes you can drift off course, and you don't even know it. It sneaks up on you. And at this point in my journey, I didn't know how to deal with that. Shlomo was trying to explain to me, but I didn't totally get it. Marley and Rosenblatt helped me along the way, but staying firmly on the iPath, and not drifting, is an art that I would have to learn as time went by.

When the trip was over, I returned feeling refreshed, inspired. But as soon I was immersed in life back home, I quickly forgot much of what had happened in Utah. I was faced with new challenges. And it was like ice upon the fire.

4

The Victory

Thirty Seconds to Half Time:

Thirty seconds were left until halftime, and we were down 14-0. I had one time out left, but I was thinking I might opt not to use it, and just run the clock out instead.

Skywalker, our wide receiver, was running to the sidelines, with his hand to his throat. This was his signal to his mom, that he needed his puffer.

This routine only seemed to happen when Skywalker made a mistake on the field. The boy had just dropped a pass. Which is what happened practically every time we tried to throw to him.

I didn't like throwing the ball. But if we had a decent receiver, I would have thrown anyway. It's part of the game. Plus, not much else had been working for us in recent weeks. But we didn't have a decent receiver.

We called the boy "Skywalker" for two reasons. One, because his first name was Luke. Second, because he was the fastest 12-year old ever to run upon the face of the earth.

Skywalker came to Florida from some farm in Iowa, where there were like ten kids in his school, and the only sport they may have played was chicken chasing.

As a coach, as much as we all prided ourselves in teaching kids how to play football, we all conceded there is one thing in this sport that can't be taught—speed.

Speed was God-given, and if a kid had it, you knew that it was from God. Because it could come from no other source. So whether you loved God or not, as a coach, you definitely loved that kid. Because nothing is more valuable to a football team than a kid with speed.

Before this year, Skywalker had never played tackle football in his life. And as God-gifted as he was with speed, God didn't give him any toughness. The kid was a mama's boy if there ever was one. Toughness, unlike speed, can be learned. But it's not easy to teach to a 12 year-old.

Skywalker didn't like to get hit. I was experimenting with using him at running back, but every time he got tackled, he got upset, and started crying. And then we'd have to get his puffer from mom, so he could breathe steadily.

Furthermore, Skywalker had rock hands. Although no natural-born human could cover him, it was of no use to us. I could send him on a deep post, or a go route, and it was a guarantee that he'd be wide open every time. But equally certain was the fact that the pass would bounce right off his hands. Or his head. Or some other body part. And then he'd start crying. And then we'd have to get him his puffer.

So, unfortunately, although he was the fastest kid on planet earth, Skywalker was of little use to us. Except as a decoy.

I motioned to my knee, which told Bobby Thompson, our QB, to just take a knee. That's how I wanted to end the half, rather than doing something risky.

Bobby didn't like it. He looked over to the stands at his mom and dad, and he shook his head. But I held my ground. We were taking a knee, and I didn't care what Bobby or his parents or anyone else thought about it. That's what we were doing. We'd have the ball to start the 2nd half. And I wasn't taking chances right now.

I could hear the grumbling coming from our stands. I not only could hear it, I could feel it. Heck, I could smell it.

The Religion of the South:

This is the deep south. The State of Florida. Football is the official state-sponsored religion. It's popularity is second only to christianity. A close second. Maybe not even second.

We start them when they are little kids, playing flag at age five. Every male child is expected to play football in Florida. Check any poll, and you'll see that the largest percentage of elite college and NFL football players come from Florida. Even more than Texas and California, which are both close to double the population size of Florida.

Parks and recreation are a major part of life in the Sunshine State. We have warm weather and sunshine year-round, so the climate is conducive to outdoor sports. Especially football. We not only play it in the Fall, like the rest of the country. But we have Spring football from February to April as well. Florida is known as the Sunshine State. But they could've just as well dubbed it the football state.

In our neighborhood, the parents were not only football fanatics like every other neighborhood which we played against. But ours were the type that had high expectations that often were not realistic.

The fact that our team was a bunch of smart, but privileged, kids from suburbia, with limited talent, and major entitlement issues, didn't matter to our parents. Nor did it matter to them that we were playing against speedy, athletic, tough, fearless, mega-talented inner city kids, many of whom quite realistically saw football as a ticket to college and even a potential career for the future.

We were losing. And ours were the kind of parents that expected absolute excellence from their kids in all activities, even the activities for which they had little or no talent—like football.

But whether they were playing football, competing in the science fair, or throwing horseshoes at the beach, it was expected that our kids would excel—and win. Because anything less than excellence, was unacceptable to these kind of parents.

And, of course, if their kid's team wasn't excelling, it couldn't be due to the fact that their kids have little or no athletic ability. No, any lack of excellence on their kids' team could only be attributable to one factor—the coach. It was always the coach's fault.

The True Heroes:

I understood this and I accepted it. I was the head coach of a team of privileged, entitled kids from a neighborhood that considers renters to be suspicious characters. I was also the offensive coordinator. If we didn't win, I knew they would blame me. It's part of the job.

They wouldn't blame any of my assistant coaches. No, and as the half ended, my chief assistant, defensive co-ordinator Bill Parker, who was an assistant Pastor at Sunny Lake Community megachurch, was quick to mozy on over to the stands to schmooze with some of the grumbling parents. It's never the assistant coach's fault. It's always the head coach.

Why was I doing it? First of all, I love football. I played football from age seven, all the way through my senior year of high school. Many of life's great lessons are learned through football. Secondly, my own son, Daniel was a player on my team of 12 and 13 year-olds.

Fortunately for me, Daniel was a lineman. He was our best lineman, hands down. Nobody would dispute that. Daniel played both ways—offense and defense. But as long as I kept Daniel on the line, and didn't dare to play him in one of the skill positions, like quarterback, running back, or receiver, then nobody would try to accuse me of favoring my son over theirs.

In my philosophy of football, I used to say to our linemen, "It all starts up front." That means that the linemen are the ones who make or break the team. Games are won or lost at the line of scrimmage. You win the line, on both sides of the ball, you win the game. That's the way I saw it. And believe me, it's true.

But the guys in the trenches, who are hitting and smashing bodies on each and every play, go unnoticed most of the game. Nobody celebrates when a big block is made to open a hole in the interior. They celebrate when the running back runs through the hole unscathed and scores a touchdown.

It is a great life principle. Things are not the way they seem. True heroes go unnoticed, while the selfish are exalted as heroes. Regarding this, I always remember the bible verse that says, *"For they loved the praise of men more than the praise of God."*[55] Well, linemen must know they have their reward, so that nobody needs to praise their name.

Daniel understood this. He never complained, never asked me to put him in the backfield. Which was good for me. Because when a dad-coach puts his own son in the backfield, to carry the ball, there will be friction. They will always accuse the coach of trying to steal the glory.

Of course, lots of dad-coaches do it anyway. They are going to elevate their own kids to glory and do not care what anyone has to say about it. I wasn't the type.

But either way, if I was the type or not, there is only one way you can get away with such things. For there is another great principle in the game of football, which parallels life. I'm not necessarily saying it is right or wrong. I'm just saying that it's how the world works. It is one of the key principles upon which the world operates. And that principle is this: Winning is the great panacea.

In fact, no matter what wrongs might be committed by the coach, players, the league, the referees, or even the weather, so long as the team is winning, it's all good. Winning means that all ills are cured.

Conversely, if you're not winning, then it doesn't even matter how much good you have done as a coach. Winning is

---

[55] *NKJV*, John 12:43

the bottom line. Otherwise, eventually, inevitably, they will come after you with noose in hand.

Not that we weren't having a good season. Our team was 6-3. We had won the opening six games of the season, and at 6-0 initially, a berth in the playoffs seemed to be a guarantee. There were even some whispers about "Superbowl," which is the County Championship. And as much as I, admittedly, enjoyed all the praise, I knew it might be short-lived.

For I knew, while it was happening, that our schedule was light at the beginning, tough at the end. We'd find out what we're made of in the last four games of the season, where we faced our toughest opponents. And just because they loved me today, didn't mean they wouldn't hate me tomorrow. The truth is, everybody loves a winner. Especially in the neighborhood where I lived.

Everyone Loves a Winner:

Let me try to further explain the operative law that applies here:

In coaching youth football, if you're not a winner, the people will not love you. No exceptions. But they may not hate you either. If you are not a winner, though unloved, they will sometimes, under the right circumstances, give you a second chance, so that you can be worthy of their love.

The "right" circumstances, in which you might get the second chance, are when you lose from the very beginning. You see, this is one of the great laws of coaching. It's always better to lose early on, than to lose late. Why?

Because if they never expect much from you to begin with, you might survive. At least long enough to start winning. But the worst thing you can do as a coach, is to win a bunch of games early, and then lose. This is intolerable.

Why? Because when you win, they love you. No exceptions. You can try to make them stop loving you. But, believe me, you can't make them stop. Not as long as you are winning. And once they have placed their hope in you, there's no turning back.

123

You see, so long as they place no hope in you to begin with, you're safe. You're a loser, and you'll be on your way out soon. And everybody knows it.

But if you happen to turn it around and start winning, well, then the losing never happened. You never were a loser. You're sin is wiped away. They always knew you had it in you. It's only when people start believing in you that you are set up for disaster.

Nothing is more precious to people than their hope. And nothing is more fragile. If, for example, as a sign of their love for you, they were to put some priceless family heirloom in your care, you could always give it back if things did not work out. And, thus, all would be forgiven. But you cannot give people back their hope.

If you let them down, after they put hope in you, you might as well have walked across the street and tossed that priceless family heirloom to the alligators in the black, mucky lake.

So, believe me, as a football coach, unless you are no mere mortal, you don't want anyone to put their hope in you. It's the death knell. Because if they place hope in you, and you do not deliver, then they will wish you dead. They will forget all that you did in the past.

One of the parents will suggest that maybe they should take you across the street and throw you to the gators in the black, mucky lake. And other parents will laugh about it.

But they aren't kidding. If it was legal, they'd do it. Fortunately it isn't legal. But if it was, then you'd be gator bait for sure.

You might think that coaching youth sports is a community service. After all we are volunteers. Parents should be appreciative and thankful for the great amount of time that we put in. Right?

You might think that by this point in the season, they should have the team mom take up a collection to get the coach a nice plaque with the team photo laminated onto it that says, "Thanks, Coach Gary!", together with a $25 gift certificate for Beef O'Brady's so Coach Gary can take his family to dinner and only have to pay for like 2/3 of the bill out of my own pocket.

Well, I already got the laminated thank-you plaque with the team picture, and the Beef O'Brady's gift certificate too. But it doesn't mean they're thankful or appreciative. And it doesn't mean they don't still talk about throwing me into the black, mucky lake right across the street from the park, the one teeming with alligators.

Parents' relationship to those who serve as head coach in youth football is based on the principle of: "What have you done for me lately?" So, when you are winning, as I was at the beginning of the season, winning six in a row and getting the highest praise from our supportive parents, well, you'd just better keep winning.

Because when you fail to keep it going later on, the same people who loved you will be the ones shouting, "Toss him to the gators!"

Perhaps you find this phenomenon puzzling? You have to understand that when you win six in a row, they place their hope in you. The reason they hate you thereafter, when you lose, is because you betrayed them. You deceived them into thinking you were a winner. They gave you their most precious possession. Their hope. They put it in your hands because they trusted you. And you responded by losing. How dare you?!

And when their image of you is blown apart, they become angry and they start having thoughts about killing you. As I said, of course, they won't, because it is illegal. But *only* because it's illegal. And thank God for that.

Because if it wasn't illegal, you'd have to arm yourself. In fact, you'd have to show up at practice with armed men. Highly skilled and trained in the art of warfare. Because there'd be a posse waiting for you there for sure.

Not because you failed. But because you failed after you succeeded. You made them believe you were a success. And then betrayed them by not succeeding. So now there are people out there who are thinking about how nice it would be if you didn't exist anymore.

125

And nobody wants to be thought of that way. Do you? Of course not. It's discouraging. It keeps you up at night. You stress about it all day.

You'll be sitting at work, but you can't get anything done, because you're thinking to yourself, *what if we go heavy right out of the Fandango formation, pull the guard, drop the flanker onto the line of scrimmage, step back the tight end as an H-back, send the fullback in motion here to draw off the linebacker, and bam! We hit a trap to the weak side?*

High Expectations:

So don't let people put their hope in you. Let them hope in the Lord, but not in you. And hopefully they know the difference. Hopefully, they know that you're not him.

Because people have high expectations. Non-negotiable. And even the Lord doesn't meet their expectations. So, neither can any of us. As sure as sundown, those same people who praise you, will one day be cursing your name.

But as I said, it's hard. Because when you're winning, they love you. And you can't make them stop. Even though you might know it's a set up for disaster. And when disaster strikes, when you lose three in a row, after winning six in a row, well, all hell breaks loose.

And believe me, when hell breaks loose, it's hard to forget about it. Going skiing in the mountains of Utah, might take it off your mind temporarily, but then it comes back. It's a hell hound on your trail. You can't make it disappear.

As much as you try to compartmentalize it, to get it out of your mind, as much as you try to be normal, going about your business as if nothing unusual is happening, you will nevertheless be up at night, sitting at the kitchen table, while your family sleeps. You'll walk into the room, with your pencil in your hand, drawing up X's and O's on a napkin.

You feel so all alone. People are murmuring against you. And in the dark, you sit there, and it seems you can hear them. Feel them. You may try to pray the voices away. You come against them. You rebuke them. You declare they have no authority. They will not prosper against you. Your O's will show those X's who's boss. And, yet, the more you try, the worse it gets. You can't make it go away. But you can't ignore it either.

So, when morning comes, you go to Starbucks to drink coffee. And Becky Thompson is there, with God's Awesome Ladies. And Pastor Buddy walks in. How everybody loves Buddy. Everyone praises him. But no one pays you any mind. Except to get you saved. Because you need it. Hell-hounds are on your trail.

You're in the corner, by the window, doodling football plays on your napkin, wondering what Evan the tattooed-Jew is saying. He mumbles something to Latasha, who's singing a song. It's moving, it's deep, it's the song of wounded people, people who are suffering, and Latasha, as she sings seems to be looking at you. Right at you.

Then suddenly you realize, as Latasha comes near, to change the garbage can liner, she's really just signing a song, it had nothing to do with anyone in particular. And Evan was just inquiring as to whose turn was it to change the garbage can liner.

But you get paranoid, ya see? And you start thinking the whole world is against you. Because there are voices out there in the dark, murmuring things. And you know that these murmurers had once put their hope in you. They loved you. And you loved the fact that they loved you. Even though you knew it might not work out. And now, you've let them down. And they are rising up against you. Angry.

In fact, if you got hit by a truck while crossing the road, or struck by lightning, or attacked by a Florida panther while hiking, they'd feel that it was God punishing you, to make things right in the universe. Even if they don't believe in God. Now they will. Because who ever heard of a panther attacking a hiker? It's quite rare.

So when it happens to the guy who won a bunch of youth football games, and then, God forbid, lost several in a row, then everyone acquainted with the situation will know that there is a God in heaven. And they will praise this God. For a youth football coach dared to take people's hope and then failed to deliver. So God sent the avenger. The panther.

When you are that coach, who lost a third game in a row, you'd better watch your back. Because I guarantee you, that while you're making your post-game speech to the kids, talking about how winning isn't everything, and how football is really supposed to be about developing values like character, perseverance, loyalty, commitment, teamwork, overcoming adversity, etc., you'll see the parents mocking you with their smirks and saying to one another, "If only he'd get mauled by a Florida panther while hiking ..."

I was that coach. I had won six straight. Then lost three. And now we were down 14-0 at the half in the final game of the season. And playoffs were on the line.

Even though I'd done all I could do to quell the high expectations early on, repeatedly saying things like, "It's a long season; we've got a lot of work still to do; and it's way too early to talk about playoffs or championships," etc, etc., the parents wouldn't hear any of that.

In fact, it only made them love me even more. Because they felt I was being humble in the face of unmitigated success. And people love humility in the face of unmitigated success. So, my attempts to temper their enthusiasm, only compounded the problem.

Now, it was the first week of November, half time of game 10, the last game of the regular season. At 6-3 on the season, and down by 14 points, we were in serious danger of being 6-4, and possibly not making the playoffs.

As the team mom passed out bags of fruit, I thought for a moment what I would say to my team on the sideline during half-time. As I prepared my thoughts, I could clearly see, not far off in the distance, the lynch mob forming by the stands. And my chief assistant coach Bill Parker, schmoozing in the midst of them.

Many of our parents were Sunny Lake Community megachurch regulars, and Parker, who was in charge of the youth ministry, was a very popular assistant Pastor. Unlike my three other assistants, all of whom were dads with sons that played on our team, Parker was coaching simply because of his alleged "passion for youth." And his passion for scamming families away from other churches.

Any child on our team whose family was not already a Sunny Lake Community megachurch member, would be "fair game" for Parker to invite to youth events at the church. This, in turn, would often put the hook in for the family to leave their church and join up at Sunny Lake.

After three losses, Parker's favor with our angry mob of parents was definitely on the rise. Many of them were saying that Parker should've been our head coach. These same parents who once spread their garments and laid down palm branches before me as I walked onto the field, were now crying out: "Crucify him!"

It was life or death for me. If I didn't give them what they wanted, if I did not at least get this team to the playoffs, Parker would get off scot-free, but as for me, they'd put a helmet of thorns upon my head, and march me from end zone to end zone, a condemned man, carrying a goal post upon my back.

Oklahoma:

Somewhere in that lynch mob, I heard a familiar voice cry out. A voice that said, "Throw the f---ing football!" Hearing that voice, it triggered something in my mind, and my thoughts suddenly raced back in time, a few months, to early August, pre-season practice. It was the voice of Tommy Thompson.

Tommy Thompson, whose son, Bobby, was our team's quarterback, was a member of our coaching staff at the beginning, before the season started. Thompson was serving as our defensive coordinator.

Unbeknownst to me when I agreed to the suggestion by the league Athletic Director to include Thompson on my coaching staff, Thompson had some personal issues that greatly hampered his ability to coach youth sports.

During one grueling, summer, pre-season practice, in the treacherous Florida heat, as we were doing Oklahoma drills, Thompson got out of control.

He was drunk. He reeked of alcohol and was stumbling around, yelling at the kids. I suggested to Thompson to go home, but he declined. And he was quite animated about his objection to my suggestion.

"Just do your f---ing job, and stop worrying about me," he said.

During the Oklahoma drill, Thompson was grabbing kids by the facemask, getting right up in their grill, and yelling at them like a madman. He was trying to get the kids fired up. Trying to teach them to hit harder.

I took Thompson aside privately and asked him politely to calm down. But he'd have none of it.

"This is football, not ballet, dammit." he said.

Andy Feingold was next up. Andy was clearly the smartest player on our team. But Andy belonged in a physics lab, not on a football field. He was scrawny, had terrible technique, and he was the weakest player on our team.

Andy was an "MP." That stands for "minimum play." The league required that each kid played at least 6 plays per game. Not including special team plays like kick-offs and kick-returns. The MP's were basically kids that probably would not play at all, but for the minimum play rule.

If the game was a big win, it was easy. We could always get lots of playing time for the weaker players late in the game. But in close games, the issue of when to play the MP's was a true art form. It could make or break the game. Especially with Andy. He really didn't belong on the football field at all.

I made a practice of planning strategically when to play Andy. But whenever Andy was in the game, I'd be holding my breath. He was a major liability. So most of the time, we would put Andy at weakside guard and make sure to run a play to the other side.

Andy Feingold was the adopted son of Tiffany Feingold-Spiegelman, and her ex-husband Jay Feingold. Perhaps because Andy's dad was a lawyer, or just perhaps because he was such a smart kid, Andy seemed to understand that there was something not kosher about a drunk man grabbing 12 year-old kids by the facemask and shouting obscenities in their face.

So, when Andy's turn came up for the Oklahoma drill, Thompson was messing with the wrong kid. Andy was on the defensive side of the ball, and Thompson started by criticizing Andy's three-point stance.

"Get your butt up, Feingold! What's wrong with you boy?"

Andy tried to raise his tail, but he just couldn't get in a proper three-point stance, even though we had tried for weeks to work with him on it. Thompson was crouched down right next to Andy, his face up against Andy's ear hole.

"Feingold, you look like you're squatting in the outhouse on a cold January morning."

Thompson then proceeded to knock Andy over with a shove of his foot. Andy got up and re-positioned himself for the drill, in a three-point stance.

After Andy got totally run over by the blocker, as usual, in the Oklahoma drill, Thompson grabbed Andy by the facemask, as he lay flat on the ground. He lifted the boy up by the facemask. Thompson then got nose to nose with Andy, and yelled into his grill:

"Feingold, you're the sorriest excuse for a football player that I've ever seen!" Thompson jerked Andy's head side to side by the facemask. "Why don't you just ask your mama to get you a tutu and sign you up for ballet lessons?"

When Thompson finally let go, Andy waved his hand in front of his nose, and loudly remarked, so all the other kids heard it:

"Somebody get that man a breath mint."

Thompson went bananas. I had to get in between him and the Feingold boy, because the boy was laughing hysterically, as were most of the other players. I think Thompson was literally going to hurt one of them.

Thankfully, Thompson's wife, Becky, one of God's Awesome Ladies, came running from the stands, hollering at her husband that he needed to calm down. Thompson didn't take kindly to his wife's interference. In fact, he expressed his disapproval most vividly, by picking her up and body slamming her to the sod.

The cops came out, and it was big scene as they carried Thompson off in the patrol car.

A few days later, Thompson called me, and said he'd have to drop out of coaching. The restraining order obtained by his wife prohibited him from being on the field. In exchange for Thompson, the league replaced him with Asst. Pastor Bill Parker. I wasn't thrilled about it. But I was glad to be rid of Thompson.

Football Philosophy:

So, we wouldn't see Thompson for a while, at least not until his lawyer could straighten out this domestic "misunderstanding."

But before ending our phone call, I wished Thompson well. Then he said he had one word he wanted to leave with me. "Throw the f---ing football."

Of course, I knew what Thompson meant. This was not just a difference that he and I had in terms of football philosophy. True, I belonged to the "run-first" school of offensive thought. Especially with 7th and 8th grade kids.

And Thompson, as my chief assistant, was frustrated with me over this, as he belonged to the philosophy of air-attack. Which rarely is successful with 12 and 13 year-old kids. Not unless your team happens to be blessed with a sensational quarterback, and at least one really good receiver. We weren't. We had neither.

Nevertheless, Thompson had insisted all along that we should be a passing team, not a running team. Of course, Thompson's belief in the passing game was not about football philosophy. It was about showcasing his son, Bobby, our quarterback.

Thompson had been urging me in the pre-season practices to let Bobby throw more. The kid wasn't much of a runner, but he did have some football IQ, and could manage the offense pretty well. Sure, there was nothing glamorous about handing off to other players, but it was the best option we had.

An air attack for our team was out of the question. Bobby was at best a mediocre passer. And our talent at receiver was practically non-existent. Our best receiver, Skywalker, could get open, but he couldn't catch a cold, let alone a football. And nobody else had the speed or agility to get open. Our big tight end could catch a pass, but he was slow as molasses.

The Lynch Mob Forms:

So I was glad to be rid of Thompson. By the time we got to this, our last game of the season, I had not seen or heard much of Thompson. Between alcohol rehab, and the restraining order taken out by Becky, he was gone most of the season.

And there I was at half-time, watching bags of fruit being passed out by the team mom, as the lynch mob formed, and Asst. Pastor Parker pretended not to be loving it though he clearly was. And I was thinking about what I would say to my team at half time, to get us back into this game.

The last thing I needed right now, was to hear a drunk fool shouting at me from the stands: "Throw the f---ing football." And yet, to my astonishment, that is exactly what I heard.

It was Thompson. He'd been resurrected from the dead. Apparently, Becky Thompson had changed the way she felt about her husband body slamming her to the turf a couple of months earlier. I found out later, Thompson had faithfully attended weekly meetings of the alcoholism group at Sunny Lake Community megachurch.

In this manner, with the help of Tiffany Feingold-Spiegelman, and the prayerful support of God's Awesome Ladies, Mr. Thompson obtained not only his wife's forgiveness, but moreover, Tiffany's husband, Murray Spiegelman, took on Thompson's domestic violence case, pro bono. Apparently, the case was dismissed. Restraining order dissolved.

But Thompson was clearly drunk again.

"Throw the f---ing football!" shouted that inebriated voice from the stands.

"We need a coach out there who knows how to win football games!" shouted Becky Thompson.

Mrs. Thompson, in spite of being body-slammed to the sod in front of a bunch of 12 year-olds a few months earlier, apparently was now of the opinion that getting her son more opportunities to throw the football was a greater priority than dealing with her husband's alcoholism and tendency to physically abuse her in fits of rage. Amazing how hatred has the power to unite even the most divided people.

"Throw the football!" shouted Becky.

Becky's statement brought some applause, mixed with hoots and hollers from the lynch mob. That gang consisted mainly of angry dads, but also a few angry moms, standing with arms crossed, next to Thompson. A few of them were motioning for me to come over. I did my best to ignore them.

How I Became Head Coach:

Two key members of the lynch mob were Murray Spiegelman and Jay Feingold. As former law partners, it was no secret that Feingold and Spiegelman now hated each other. This hatred was on account of Feingold's former wife, Tiffany Feingold-Spiegelman, who had left Feingold to marry Spiegelman.

In spite of all this, Feingold, Spiegelman, and Feingold's new partner Steve Levine, were now a band of brothers, united together in a common cause – hatred of me. One should never underestimate the unifying power of hatred.

Needless to say, this entire situation did not bode well for me. Not only on account of the pressure I was under generally as head coach of a youth football team that might not make the playoffs, but, moreover, I was beginning to worry that the option to renew the lease on my home might be in jeopardy.

The option came up every year on January 1st, and it was by no means a guarantee that the landlord, Tiffany Feingold-Spiegelman, would offer it to me at the end of this year.

As it now appeared, most of the parents were against me—the Feingolds, the Spiegelmans, the Feingold-Spiegelmans, the Levines, the Thompsons. Not to mention Asst. Pastor Parker, as well as some notable members of God's Awesome Ladies. Good gosh, the whole world was against me.

I also note here that the law firm of Feingold and Levine, PA. was a major financial contributor to Sunny Lake Athletic Complex. Right under the scoreboard on our main field, is an ever-present reminder.

I am referring to the giant picture of Feingold and Levine, (who probably need to realize how non-photogenic they are), on our home field scoreboard. They stand there, stern-faced, with arms crossed, on either side of a photo-shopped montage of images, including a totally demolished vehicle, a woman in a neck brace wincing in pain, a kid getting bit by a dog, and a huge bold letter caption that runs across the top of the billboard saying: "Not in our house!"

Before the season began, Jay Feingold and Steve Levine had made a big stink with the board at Sunny Lake Athletic complex for appointing a "Jew for Jesus" as head coach of their son's football team.

This resulted in strained attempts on my part to try and explain to the board that I was not a Jew for Jesus, but a Messianic Jew. Of course, none of that made any sense to the board.

However, Pete Malone, the Athletic Director, and owner of Patriot Plumbing Company, apparently saw some danger in Feingold and Levine's complaint about me.

As it was reported to me by a friend on the board, Malone reminded Feingold and Levine that the Sunny Lake Athletic Complex had once been sued by Dr. Patel, who insisted he was passed up as head coach because of being a Hindu. Even though Patel had never coached football in his life, and even though being a Hindu had nothing to do with it, the matter was taken up in the newspapers. It was a huge embarrassment for the league, and had to be settled out of court.

So, apparently, at the board meeting, Malone said something about me like: "The guy has been coaching here for years, as an assistant. He's a good guy. We didn't know about this Jews for Jesus thing, but if we dismiss him now, we might be liable for another discrimination suit."

Of course, I never mentioned suing anybody, and I would not have dreamed of it. But Malone didn't know that. Of course, neither did Feingold and Levine. All they knew was that such things can, and often do, result in lawsuits. So, they could not dispute Malone's concerns.

Therefore, in spite of Feingold and Levine's objections to me on account of my profession as a messianic Rabbi, thanks to Dr. Mahesh Patel, I was untouchable. I did, however, get a stern warning from Athletic Director, Malone.

"I don't want you talking to the players about your religion, got it?" said Malone to me, when he gave me the news that I was going to remain head coach.

"No problem."

"They're just kids, ya know. They'll believe anything."

"That's fine. Anyway, I don't really have a religion, exactly," I said.

"You're a Jew for Jesus, ain't ya?" Malone retorted.

"No, not really."

"Well, Feingold and Levine say you are."

"Messianic Jews are Jews who believe that Jesus is the Messiah. But we are not Jews for Jesus."

Of course, Malone was clearly confused.

"Hey, look," said Malone, "Feingold and Levine, they're decent fellas. And so are you. Now, I'm Catholic. But I got nothing against you people. As far as I'm concerned, Jews are good people."

"Thanks," I said.

"The truth is, I respect people that are different. Because that's just how I was raised. Ya see? I respect you, as a Jew, because that's what I was taught to do. And as long as I'm the Athletic Director, well, that's just the way we're gonna handle these things."

"I see," I said.

"Bottom line, I got nothing against you or Feingold or Levine. So, work it out. Because I'm not getting involved in you people's religious quarrels."

"I appreciate it." I put out a hand to shake on it, but before shaking, Malone added:

"Just don't be running around here trying to convert anyone. Ok?"

"No problem," I said. We shook on it.

Malone, in spite of his great compassion for the Jewish people, clearly didn't understand this situation. But what did I care? I remained head coach of the 12-13 year old team, and I pressed on.

Suddenly It Thundered:

So, during half-time of that final regular season game, as if in an instant, all of these things, were racing through my mind on the sideline. I was still trying to muster something to say to my team, as I watched our team mom distribute the bags of fruit to our discouraged players, and as Skywalker puffed on his puffer.

Then, suddenly, it thundered. I was startled by the sound. It was not raining, and I hadn't even noticed the dark clouds which had moved in. There were flashes of lightning off in the distance, and then a loud buzzer went off. It was the lightning detector.

Lightning is so common in Florida, and it can be quite dangerous to be outside during an electric storm. Every youth football complex is required to install a lightning detector. When that buzzer goes off, the field must be cleared until the detector shows that at least ten minutes go by without any sign of lightning.

Our team retreated to the equipment room, while the spectators either retreated to their cars or gathered under cover by the concession stand. Bill Parker left the lynch mob and rejoined our team in the equipment room. So, I decided to give the whiteboard to Parker, to talk about the defense.

Then, just as Parker began, quite unexpectedly, I felt a tap upon the back of my shoulder. It was Marley. This was the first time I'd seen him since that day in Starbucks, the one in my neighborhood.

"What are you doing here?" I said.

"I'm the videographer," said Marley. "I film the games for the league. Up there." He pointed up to the press box.

Getting my attention, Marley motioned to me to come with him. I obliged. We walked outside. It wasn't raining, and even though technically we were all supposed to remain under cover, I sat down with Marley, on the edge of the bench. No one else was on the field. It was private. Just Marley and me.

"I think you need some help, Coach."

"You're right about that."

The Victory Speech:

The ability of a coach to give a pep talk to the players is one of the true essentials of coaching. It's very much akin to standing at the pulpit and giving a sermon.

Some of those speeches can mean life or death to those who hear them. But sometimes the Rabbi needs to be ministered to. And sometimes the coach is the one who needs the pep talk. This was one of those times.

"Don't think that God will give you the victory," began Marley. "God IS the victory."

In the annals of sports history, I doubt whether there have been many pep talks like this one. Sensing that something great was about to happen, I clicked on the recorder on my cell phone, and put it in my shirt pocket. Marley didn't seem to mind. At this point, the way it happened, Marley talked. And I listened.

"I am going to tell you this, so that you will have peace. In this world you have tribulation. But be encouraged. I have overcome the world.[56] Lift up your eyes to the mountain. From where your help comes. [57]

"The loser now, is later to win; and the winner now is later to lose. But there are no winners and losers in God's house. It is a victory without beginning, without end. A victory which IS. A Glory that never fades. The Lord is one, and knows no opposite. A Light which does not dawn, nor set. It is a Light which only shines. Be in that Light. All who follow it, will not know darkness.[58] Nations will come unto you, and kings to the brilliance of your rising.[59] Whatever you ask in my name will be done, because whatever you permit or forbid on earth will have been permitted or forbidden already in heaven, and in this the Father is glorified in the Son.[60]

"The victory is yours, you will see it when your eyes are opened. It is hidden from the world. It is in the world but the world knows it not. Because it is not a victory over this or that. It is the victory from beginning to end. Because it is without beginning or end. The victory which IS. Even death itself is swallowed up in it. Mortals fear death, but the children of God do not. Because they know who I am, they have the Truth. They are imbued with eternal life. They are therefore alive. Because they see me, they see immortality within themselves. The nothing-ness of death was fully exposed by the empty tomb. But they not only see it, they have grasped onto the fringes of Resurrection's garment. That is the victory. Take hold of it!

"Lift up your eyes to the mountain. Where the unfading Glory is upon you. The Glory which the Son had with the Father before the world came to be.[61] The Glory rises upon

[56] John 16:33.
[57] Ps. 121:1,2.
[58] John 8:12
[59] Is. 60:3.
[60] Mat. 18:18, John 14:13,14.
[61] John 17:5.

you so that you may be one just as we are one.[62] I in them, and you in me, perfected in the love of God.[63]

"This world is a duality. It appears in pairs of opposites. It is the consciousness of good and evil.[64] But God is one. God is not in duality. So, do not judge by appearances. Do not believe them. They are not the reality. There is no path to Reality. I am the path. I am the Reality. I am the Life.[65] Nor is there a path to resurrection. I *am* the resurrection. And the Life. Not a path to eternal Life. I *am* eternal Life.[66]

"When you know who I am, my word which abides in you will become the government of your experience. I am the word, and the Life. And because my word abides in you, I am in you. Therefore, you will ask whatever you wish, and it shall be done for you.[67] You will stare any appearance right in the face, and know that is isn't true. Because I alone am true. I alone am the Reality. There is none beside me. And this glorifies the Father. That you bear much fruit, and so prove to be my talmidim.[68]

"The eternal Reality that abides in you is the first and the last. The beginning and the end. The one and the only. I am that. The only. I have no opposite. I am the Life. That which opposes me is nothing. It is illusion.

"Let the dead bury their own dead,[69] but as for you, walk in the Reality, which is the Kingdom of God. That Kingdom is an everlasting Kingdom[70] from before time, without beginning, without end. It is within you[71], it is the law upon your heart.[72]

---

[62] John 17:22, Is. 60:1.
[63] John 17:23.
[64] Gen. 2:17.
[65] John 14:6.
[66] John 11:25.
[67] John 15:7.
[68] John 15:8.
[69] Luke 9:60.
[70] Ps. 145:13.
[71] Luke 17:23
[72] Jer. 31:33, Heb. 8:10, Heb. 10:16.

"This world, as it appears, is an illusion. It is under condemnation, and passing away. An illusion of the mortal senses. But you hold the infinite in your hand. You hold the key to the kingdom of heaven, the Reality, and the truth of the way things are. When you know the Truth, you hold key, and even the gates of hell cannot prevail against you.[73]

"I am the true vine,[74] the image of God, the invisible Life, that is running through you, and in which you were created, and by whom all things came to be.[75] This is the only power. The Father loves the Son and has given everything into his hand.[76] All authority is in the Son, on heaven and on earth.[77] There is none else. No other god. Nor other power in the universe.

"The Life is living in you.[78] The Life is in the Father, you are in the Life, and the Life is in you.[79] Know this, and the weapons of this world will not touch you. A thousand may fall at your side, ten thousand at your right hand, but it will not come near to you.[80] For God is one. There is One God. And none else. One God and Father of all, who is over all, and through all, and in all.[81]

"Let nothing be nothing. Nothing will be nothing so long as you let it be what it is. It is a deception. You give it power over you only by believing it to be true. God is the only Truth. Let things be what they are, recognize the nothingness of that which is nothing, and in this manner, victory will be the law of your life.

"Don't be afraid. Don't let your heart be troubled. You believe in God. Believe also in me.[82] Your helper. The Father has sent the helper, that he may be with you forever. The

---

73 Mat. 16:18,19.
74 John 15:1
75 Col. 1:15,16; Gen. 1;27.
76 John 3:35.
77 Mat. 28:18.
78 Gal. 2:20, Col. 1:27.
79 John 14:20
80 Ps. 91:7.
81 Eph. 4:6.
82 John 14:1

world cannot see him. Or know him. But you know him. Because he abides with you. And will be in you.[83]

"God is one. There is one God. The human race accepted two gods—one good, one evil. And that's the problem. That's why there is winning and losing. It's a deception. The duality is not the Reality. It is deception. God is one. God is infinite. Mortality is brought on by a delusion of two gods. Loss is brought on by the same. There is no loss in the infinite God.

"Lift up your eyes. You will know the Truth and the Truth will set you free.[84] The usurper sought the inheritance. But the Father loves the Son and has placed everything in the Son's hand. Nothing can snatch it out of his hand.[85] What God has given, no one can take away.

"The Son came as a man, to lead humanity out of the illusion, back to the Reality. The Son suffered for them. Went to the tree. Paid the price for their debts. If the Son has set them free, they are free indeed.

"But they are not free. Because they believe the illusion over the reality. They believe their images. Idolators. They abide in their doctrines, but they do not abide in the Son. They speak of me with their lips, but their heart is far from me. In vain they worship me, teaching as doctrines the commandments of men.[86]

"The harvest is plentiful. But the laborers are few. The good Shepherd has laid down his life and will lead you to springs of living water. But who has believed my report? To whom has the arm of the Lord been revealed? I am the Life. I am the Reality. Unchangeable. Eternal. Abiding Truth. The one and only. I am that I am which went up to the tree, which rose from the dead, and which is the very Life living in the midst of you. If only you will see it. I am is he. Before Abraham was I am.[87] Beside I am, there is no Savior.

---

83 John 14:16-17.
84 John 8:32.
85 John 10:29.
86 Is. 29:3, Mat. 15:8,9.
87 John 8:58.

"The Spirit is poured out upon the earth. I piped to you and you didn't dance. I sang to you, but you wouldn't wake up. Let him who has ears to hear, hear what the Spirit is saying.

"A remnant is arising. A remnant is waking up. This present darkness is being removed. The arm of the Lord will return. To take the throne in Jerusalem. A remnant is being prepared. The streets of Jerusalem and the cities of Judah will rejoice. Israel will declare that the Lord is God. And all the nations will know it. The Lord, he is God. In the heavens above and on the earth below. The Lord will be King over all the earth. There will be one Lord. And his name will be one.[88] They will say from the grounds of the Temple, "Baruch haba b'shem Adonai!" And they will say it in all the earth.

"Death will be swallowed up in victory.[89] The duality removed. The Reality revealed. One God. Not two. The whole earth will be filled with the knowledge of the Lord. Like the waters cover the sea.[90] The set time has come. Now shall all Israel be saved. For this is the time appointed. The time to favor Zion is at hand.[91] The end is near. And the Spirit is saying 'Wake up, wake up, you daughter of Zion. Wake up, you sons of Jacob—"

Suddenly, there was a long buzzer. It was the all-clear sign from the lightning detector.

The scene quickly changed. Spectators came pouring out from their hiding places and back to the bleacher seats. Our team came out from the equipment room, and our opposing team came out from a trailer which was designated for their use.

Billy Parker said, "Where were you, Coach?"

I didn't respond. I don't know how much time had passed. I would guess about thirty minutes. Maybe more. I was still sitting on the sideline bench with Marley.

---

[88] Zech. 14:9.
[89] 1 Cor. 15:54, Is. 25:8.
[90] Hab. 2:14, Is. 11:9.
[91] Ps. 102:13.

Then, I heard a voice holler, "C'mon, coach, throw that football!" It was Mr. Thompson. He and the other members of the lynch mob were starting to assemble again by the bleachers.

A referee came over and said to me, "Coach, we're gonna give each team about five minutes to warm up, ok?"

I told one of my assistants to get them stretched out on the sidelines. As the kids started stretching, I stayed on the bench, with my clipboard in hand.

Astonished at what I had just heard from Marley, I looked for a moment over at the spot where the lynch mob was forming before. Yep. They were still there. All of them. Thompson, Parker, Feingold, Levine, Spiegelman, Feingold-Spiegelman, etc., and a host of other parents. They were caucusing amongst themselves, but they were all looking directly at me.

Becky Thompson flashed the "L" sign to me, formed by her index finger and thumb. Other than what Mr. Thompson had hollered out at me, I could not hear anything else that the parents were saying to one another. But I presumed it was something related to me encountering a Florida panther in the wild.

Marley was still sitting next to me. Marley redirected my attention.

"Coach," he said.

"Huh?" I responded.

"In the Messiah, the weapons of this world have no power. Abide in me, and I will abide in you. These weapons will have no power against you."

"God is omnipotent. Not the mightiest. The ALL mighty. The one and only. Not the greatest power. The only power. There is none beside him. Anokhi, Anokhi Adonai! I, I am the Lord. And there is no savior beside me.[92]

"You have the overcoming *I* living in you, working in you, the same I, which I am, which is Life from the dead. The I of me is the I of you, and if you abide in me, then I am

---

[92] Is. 43:11.

abiding in you. I and the Father are one.[93] And you are in me, if you abide in me.

"If the Spirit which raised Yeshua from the dead lives in you, then your mortal self will be quickened. It will be swallowed up in immortality.[94] And your eyes will be opened to the one God. Therefore all opposition is nothing. It is illusion.

Time to Play Ball:

Another buzzer sounded. It was the buzzer that indicated the end of half-time, time to play ball. I got up from the bench, and closed my jaw that had been hanging open. I looked back at Marley, still seated on the bench. I tried to speak. Cleared my throat. Sighed deeply. After a couple of false starts, at last I managed to say to Marley:

"I'm the one who is supposed to give the half-time speech."

He responded: "I thought you might need some help."

The referee blew a whistle. I glanced down at my laminated play sheet, which had been rolled up tightly in my right hand. I unrolled it. Took a few steps toward the sideline.

One of my assistant coaches shouted, "Kick return team," and out on the field they went. I began reviewing my play sheet, plotting what I'd do to start out the second half.

"Coach," said Marley, just before he returned to the press box, "the Kingdom of God is within you. It's not out there on field. It's in your heart. Use the eyes of your heart, and you will have the victory."

"Honestly, I don't even understand most of what you just said. And I've got a lot of questions about what just happened."

"There's no time for that, coach. Look within your heart. There will be an answer."

---

[93] John 10;30.
[94] Rom. 8:11.

To me, that just sounded too cliché to be true, and I wasn't in the mood for it. I was feeling the heat from the lynch mob. And as I watched the kicker place the ball on the tee and line up his team for the kick off, I was definitely still distracted.

The home team sideline was directly under the press box. Marley, up in his perch again in the press box, leaned over and got my attention one more time.

"Hey, Coach, my sheep hear my voice.[95]"

The referee blew his whistle, and the kicker raised his hand in the air, giving the sign to his team that he was ready. As he and the team started forward, toward the tee, a strong gust of wind blew the ball over, and it had to be reset. This was not unusual. It happened a lot on windy days. But it had not been windy that day at all.

So maybe I took it as a sign. I don't know. In any case, as the ball was being re-teed and the team re-aligned in kick formation, in spite of my reluctance, and doubts, I did what I thought that Marley was suggesting.

For a brief moment, I closed my eyes, and quietly, privately, looked within, to see what I could see, and hear what I could hear.

Indeed, I did see something. As I stood there on the sideline, quietly looking within myself, I suddenly saw what appeared as a golden lamp, filled with oil, and the oil was being poured out through the spout of the lamp. And the oil that was being poured out was being poured out upon my head.

The whole thing couldn't have lasted thirty seconds. Maybe less. But what I saw was vivid. It made a strong impression. I'll never forget it. I saw it most clearly.

I did not hear anything. At least, I didn't hear a "voice." But as I saw the vision, a thought rushed into my mind. It was clear that it was not my thought, but the thought of an "other."

---

[95] John 10:27.

And yet, at the same time, as much as I knew that I was not the one thinking the thought, and as much as I knew that the thought did not come from me, nevertheless, it was as much my thought as if I had thought the thought myself. Even though I knew for a certainty that I did not think it.

And the thought said: *"You are me."* Does that seem weird? Join the club. I felt the same way.

And yet, this little word that I received from the Spirit of God on that day, impacted my life in a tremendous way. I was already being impacted, a change was underway. I was on the iPath, but I still understood very little. So, that word, *"You are me,"* opened my eyes to better understand the change that was taking place. So that in understanding it, I could advance along the iPath, even more.

I will explain this more fully in the next chapter...for now, the game was on.

Foot to Leather:

Then I heard the sound of foot to leather. The second half had begun.

Not a great return of the opening kick-off, but at least it was our ball on our own 35 yard-line. I had already scripted the opening play of the second half. Unless we returned the kick past mid-field, which we didn't, the first play of the second half would be "Zoo, heavy right, 26 power," a basic off-tackle, power run play to the right.

"Zoo" means that the wingback, who is the "Z" back, would go in motion. By going "heavy" you shift to an unbalanced line, by moving the left guard to the right. This requires the defensive line to shift. But hopefully, the defense won't recognize the heavy formation, which they often do not. This might catch them out of position, and open a wider running lane.

On 26 power, you pull the guard, and he kicks out the end at the point of attack. The wingback in motion will draw the cornerback out of the play. The full back leads off-tackle, which is what we call the "power hole" to get a body on one of the linebackers, which are likely to try and fill that hole.

Like most youth football teams, running your tailback off-tackle was the bread and butter play for our team. Nothing fancy about it, and certainly not unexpected.

It's all just a question of how you do it, and how well you execute it. If executed properly, it is a mathematical certainty that it will result in huge gains. But math never calculates intangibles. And there are many of them in youth football.

In youth football, another advantage of going to the unbalanced line for a play here and there, is that it's a great opportunity to put in one of your MP's. I mean, scrub players—like Andy Feingold. But those MP's are intangibles.

With both guards on the right side of the line of scrimmage, Feingold could be inserted at the weakside tackle position, with practically zero risk. Mathematically speaking.

Oh, he'd miss his block for sure, as he always did. But the play would be so far to the other side, that it would be out of the defender's reach. So, at whatever point that defender might come steaming past Feingold and into the backfield like a locomotive, which he inevitably would, it would not affect the play.

It therefore seemed like a good time to get Andy Feingold in for a couple of his six required snaps. I sent him into the game at weakside tackle. In doing so, I sent the play in with Feingold as well.

"Zoo, heavy right, 26 power," I said to Andy on the sideline. And off he went into the huddle.

Yet, unbeknownst to me, when Andy gave the play to Bobby Thompson in the huddle, Bobby took the liberty to change the play to a pass play. Bobby was smart enough to use the same formation, so that I wouldn't be on to what he had done, until after the ball was snapped. So, instead of the off-tackle run play, Bobby called "Zoo, heavy right, waggle pass left."

A waggle pass is a play-action pass, in which the QB fakes the 26 power off-tackle play to the right, but instead, the quarterback keeps and bootlegs the ball, hiding it on his hip, while he circles back around toward the left side. Meanwhile the left side tight end hits the defensive end for about a two-count, and then releases on a waggle route, usually a short, five-yard, out-route.

And if everyone is faked out, which they usually are, especially when you don't throw the football a lot, the waggle pass play can result in huge after-the-catch yardage. Even if your tight-end is as slow as molasses (like ours), it didn't matter, because everyone was usually so faked out that he'd get wide open anyway.

Although we rarely called pass plays, the waggle pass to our weak side tight end, Marty Levine, was one of the few rare pass plays that we occasionally did call. Marty was the son of Steve Levine, whose giant image was one of two that watched over us on the scoreboard.

Even though I did not call that play, actually, when Bobby decided to change the play, he chose a good one. In other words, it was not a bad play to call in that situation. Except for one thing—Feingold was in the game.

You see, when you move your left guard over to the right side in the unbalanced-line, heavy set; and when you go all out to sell play-action to the right and leave no running backs to block in the backfield; and when you send the weakside tight end out on a waggle route; the only blocker you have remaining on the left side of the line of scrimmage is the weakside tackle. Which in this case was Feingold.

The tight end, by chipping the defensive end for a two-count, will slow him down just long enough so the quarterback can get the pass off. But if the offensive tackle misses his block, which Feingold definitely would, then you've got trouble. Especially if the defensive tackle is Choo-choo Jackson. Which it was.

Choo-choo was one of the best and fastest players in the league. A running back on offense, he played tackle on defense. Some teams liked to play their best athletes on the defensive line of scrimmage, and this was one of those teams.

Such players often get through the line and disrupt plays in the backfield. If running toward his side, typically, we would get a double-team block on Choo-choo. But so long as we were running to our right, away from Choo-choo, we were reasonably safe.

The huddle broke, and as Bobby Thompson approached the line of scrimmage, I saw him give a thumbs up signal to our parents in the bleacher seats. I didn't know what this could've meant. But I now realize this was a sign to his dad that he had changed the play in the huddle. Bobby Thompson got exactly what his dad wanted—a pass play. But it was a serious mistake doing it the way it was done, by overriding me, the coach. Thompson had no idea what he was in for. But, as the expression says, God was in control.

The ball was snapped, and as the play developed, Thompson made a beautiful fake to the tailback. All the linebackers, the safety, and the backside cornerback, bought the fake and were out of position, leaving our tight end, Levine, completely wide open on the back side, with nothing but green grass between him and the end-zone.

Indeed, the play would've been a foot race to the end zone, and in spite of his slow-footedness, Levine was so wide open that he probably would have scored. The play was perfectly set up and would have worked flawlessly—but for one factor. Feingold, as usual, totally missed his block.

With a quick stutter step to the outside, Choo-choo Jackson darted from the defensive tackle position unscathed, and directly past Feingold. Then, like a locomotive, he came steaming into our backfield.

After Thompson made the play-action fake, he circled back around, dropping deep as he made his circle. And as he turned his body, Thompson was met, full-force, face to face, by the wrath of Choo-choo Jackson.

It was a clean hit. But Thompson never saw it coming. Choo-choo steamed into Bobby Thompson in full stride, and with great velocity and force. As Thompson turned blindly into the oncoming locomotion of Choo-choo, the hit snapped Thompson's head in whiplash effect, similar to what happens in auto accidents.

Hitting Thompson head on, Choo-choo executed a clean, picture-perfect tackle, driving through the man with the ball, and slamming him to the turf, flat on his back, with Choo-choo landing on top of him.

The ball went flying, and it was a mad scramble to get it. No one in the stands knew that Bobby Thompson had changed the play. But everyone knew Feingold had missed the block on Choo-choo Jackson.

Still, as much as Feingold might have been blamed for missing the block, he was to be forgiven. For, in another sense, Feingold may have been the one to keep us in the game. It was Feingold who dove on the fumbled ball.

Second and 20 on our own 25-yard line. But still our ball. Game delayed due to Thompson being down.

There is a fire station just a few blocks from the park, so the paramedics arrived about five minutes later. Thompson could not be moved until they arrived. And even then, it took another ten minutes to get him off the field on a back board.

During this fifteen-minute delay, Mr. and Mrs. Thompson knelt by their son, as the paramedics attended to him. I came out to offer my support, but Mr. Thompson shooed me away. He motioned for my assistant coach, assistant Pastor Billy Parker, to remain by their side as the paramedics attended to Bobby Thompson.

The Wildcat:

Meanwhile, Choo-choo Jackson's dad shouted high praise to his son for knocking Bobby Thompson on his butt.

"Choo-chooooooooooo!" He hollered, imitating the sound of a locomotive. "That's what I'm talkin' 'bout, Choo-choo. You do what you gotta do. You keep bringing it, son!"

The encouragement coming from Mr. Jackson seemed to garner the support of many of the fans on his side of the field, who were laughing it up, and high-fiving Mr. Jackson.

Finally, Malone got on the P.A. system and admonished the visitor's side to please pipe down while Bobby Thompson was being attended to. This announcement had no effect.

"Choo-chooooooooo!" continued Mr. Jackson, often with a chorus of a few other parents joining in.

Mr. Thompson did not appreciate the celebratory attitude from the opposing fans. At one point, Thompson left his son and his wife, and went over to the visitor's side to confront Mr. Jackson.

Malone saw this before it developed. He had already sent security to the visitors side to stop Mr. Thompson, who clearly would have otherwise got into a physical altercation with Choo-choo Jackson's dad. This surely would have resulted in a melee, that likely would have prematurely ended the game, which, per league rules, having completed one half, it would have gone down as a loss to us.

Thanks to Malone for diagnosing the situation, both Mr. Thompson and Mr. Jackson were escorted off the premises by security.

The Thompson boy was removed by the paramedics. Later on, we found out the diagnosis was severe concussion. Thankfully, the boy would be fine. He would play again next year. But, in spite of Mr. Thompson's plea to the Athletic Director, league rules prohibited Bobby from playing again until he could get doctor's clearance. No doctor in his right mind would do that. Bobby Thompson was done for this season. And we had a game to finish.

We did not exactly have a back-up quarterback. In the event of losing our quarterback, our backup plan, was to run a different offense, one in which the tailback takes a direct shotgun-type snap from the center. From this offense, called the "Single Wing," the tailback doubled as a running back and quarterback.

The Single Wing, also known as the "Wildcat" offense, has many advantages over the traditional QB under center type of offense. The main advantage is that you gain an extra blocker at the point of attack. This is because when the quarterback is under center as in the "Power I" set (our regular offense), he is practically never a running threat.

Except for the occasional scramble after dropping back to pass, the QB under center cannot ever be used to run at the line of scrimmage due to taking the ball from under center. This factor is compensated for when a team has a true passing attack. We didn't.

Moreover, when under center in the Power-I, after handing the ball off, the QB was not in position to make a block either. Simply put, unless he is a threat to pass, the QB in that offense is essentially a wasted position.

In the Single Wing, however, with the tailback getting the ball via direct-snap from center, at his position about four and ½ yards back he might run, pass, or hand-off. Which means he's a multiple threat. And if he runs, no hand-off needed, so we gain a blocker at the point of attack.

I had been studying the Single Wing offense since pre-season back in August. Unfortunately, I had allowed Thompson to talk me out of it. Simply put, his son didn't fit well into that offense, since he was not a good runner.

But since we had no backup quarterback, I had been rehearsing the Single Wing in practice, at least once per week, as our plan "B" just in case of the event that Thompson might go down. We only had a few basic plays out of that set, about six of them, but it was enough.

The tailback/quarterback position in the Single Wing did not require a player with great passing skills. It did require a player who was smart enough to know the plays, who had the speed to run the football, and could throw an occasional pass if necessary. The only player who met those qualifications, the only player who had the speed, the smarts, and at least the limited passing ability needed, was Skywalker.

During the interval, when the paramedics were tending to Thompson, I was caucusing with my offense, sketching out the six plays: Off-tackle, a dive, a sweep, a sweep pass, a counter, and the wedge play.

While I drew on the white board, Skywalker motioned to his mom to bring his puffer. She scurried over to us, and as she came within range of Skywalker, she tossed that puffer in his direction. It seemed surreal, almost as if in slow-motion, even though it wasn't. I reached out, and intercepted that puffer. In full possession of it, I turned toward Skywalker.

His eyes were wide, eyebrows raised, like a child who for the first time is watching his mom take away his blankie, and stash it somewhere out of reach. Such a child knows that he doesn't need a blankie anymore, but still can't fathom that he is actually giving it up.

"My puffer!" said Skywalker, with a deer-in-the-headlights expression, as I closed my fist around it.

Then, the words came out of my mouth, almost as if they were not my words. My voice spoke almost as if not my voice. Yet, as I looked into Skywalker's astonished face, from somewhere beyond myself, came forth these words: "God's grace will be sufficient for you."[96]

Something about children, they are much more teachable than adults. What might take me years to teach an adult, a child can learn in five seconds. I guess that's because they are a clean slate. Their level of preconceived ideas is far less than the adult. No wall has yet been erected. They are less developed, but more inclined to take things at face value.

Through some mystery of divine intervention, or whatever it was, Skywalker understood and responded to the words that came from me. He took it to heart. He trotted onto that field—puffer-less.

The first play out of the Single Wing was 18 sweep. The wingback blocks down on the end, we pull a guard around the end, along with two backs, leading Skywalker wide around the end, and up the sideline. Nobody even touched him. It was a 75-yard run. Touchdown!

Andy Feingold was standing next to me on the sideline. Andy gave me a big high-five as Skywalker ran into the end zone.

"New strategy," said Andy. "Get the ball to Skywalker."

Before the end of the game, our defense gave up another touchdown, but Skywalker scored three more touchdowns that day, and we ended up winning 28-21.

After the game, as we circled together, with parents, for the post-game speech, I said:

---

[96] 2 Cor. 12:9.

"Winning isn't everything. But it sure is a lot sweeter than losing."

This, naturally was followed by loud cheers, laughter, a round of high-fives, and applause.

As the cheering died down, Skywalker walked into the circle, in plain view of all. He extended his hand toward me, looked me in the eye, and said softly: "My puffer, please."

I reached into my pocket, retrieved the puffer, and, reluctantly, extended forward my hand toward Skywalker.

Skywalker then snatched that puffer from my hand, raised it up over his head for all to see, and let out a howl. He thrusted that puffer right down into the ground and proceeded to smash it into smitherines with his cleats.

This gesture was followed by much tribal rejoicing by parents and players alike. In fact, from that time forward, chest bumps, high fives, and celebratory howling became the norm for us.

That was the end of Skywalker's puffer. He never looked back. And neither did our team.

I was now, once again, officially loved. Our team rolled on to the playoffs, and all the way to the Superbowl.

Sticking with the Single Wing offense, and relying heavily upon Skywalker, we defeated a team that was 12-0, and we won the County championship.

There's no doubt about it. Winning is way sweeter than losing. And it's better to be loved than not loved.

But either way, whatever the circumstances, I know that people are fickle. They will fail us. The good news is that whatever else may happen, there is a love that never fades.

God IS love. And that love is right here in the midst of us. Always. And if we know this, then whatever else might be going on around us, well, all things tend to work together for good.

5

The Change

The Seed Has Sprouted:

When that football season was over, I realized that I had undergone a change. It was only the beginning, but the seed had sprouted, and new life was emerging.

One of the ways I would describe this change is to say that I was becoming a minister of the Spirit, instead of the letter.[97]

Let me qualify that by saying I think that everyone has the Spirit of God within them, as we humans are all created in the image of God. Whether we are in touch with the image or not is the question.

So when I say I was becoming a minister of the Spirit, as opposed to of the letter, this is not to say I was previously without the Spirit. To some extent Spirituality is always going to be a question of degree. The issue of "how much" is an issue applicable to everyone.

Being "born" of the Spirit as a theological concept is intended to mark a time when a transformation takes place. Even though the Spirit of God is the image in which all were created, there can be a moment where a reversal takes place, in which the government of a person's life is no longer their human self, but rather, selfhood of the Lord.

It is a transformation in which the image of God bursts forth, and takes over. Accordingly, the errant, flawed human, through extended periods of oneness with God, experiences that reversal. It's a coup d'état, really. The old

---

[97] 2 Cor. 3:5-7.

man is overthrown, and the Messiah becomes the reigning Prince of that person's life. Such a person becomes a new creation, part of a new humanity that is destined to live forever on planet earth.

When this coup takes place, we who experience it, become the righteousness of God thru abiding in Messiah.[98] Again, "righteousness," which is God's image and nature, as revealed via the instrumentality of human beings, is always going to be a question of degree.

No man should ever think himself to be a "tzadik" or "righteous man." No human can ever be. However, the image of God in every man and woman is perfect and wholly righteous. Therefore, our task is to join ourselves to the Tzadik within, the Righteous One, that we might be made the righteousness of God in him.[99] As I found, this happens not just by believing in him. But by establishing and maintaining actual, ongoing kesher or contact.

This reversal of government, this coup d'état of which I speak, comes about as a person partakes of the divine nature to such an extent that the image of God, which is the Spirit of the Lord, becomes the governing authority and the law of a person's life. By partaking of the divine nature, a moment comes when a shift occurs.[100] And when it happens, that is the moment a person becomes "messianic," which means "of the Messiah" or "Messiah-like."

So, this is the change that happened in me. Whereas, up till now, what I had to impart to the world was coming from the storehouse of my brain, now it was coming from a different storehouse. Not my mind, not my knowledge. But from God. I was becoming qualified and competent to convey unto the world the invisible, ineffable Truth of the Spirit, as opposed to the letter.[101]

The Law had come to be written on my heart. And not a law to regulate sin and death. But the Law of the Spirit. The

---

[98] *See*, 2 Cor. 5:21.
[99] Ibid.
[100] *See*, 2 Peter 1:4.
[101] 2 Cor. 3:5-7.

law which is in Messiah Yeshua.[102] I always knew, empirically, that the essence of the New Covenant is the law upon my heart. I could teach on that topic all day. But was it the reality of my life? What about you?

As for me, well, I would've said that the law was written upon my heart. And I would've said it without blinking. But it was only true in a small way. So, until this change happened, I could never have known that I was deluding myself with empirical knowledge and with ideals about the way things ought to be, as opposed to actual real-time experience.

You don't have to say you're faithful, when you are. When God is known, you don't have to convince anyone. You can be silent about that before God and before men. And in that case, nothing speaks like silence. Ideals have to be defended. Ideals can cause all kinds of violence. But when God is revealed, instead of ideals, you begin to impart Truth. When this happens in the world, it will be a very different world, no doubt. For the meantime, it is one here, one there. Are you one of them? Well, if you are reading this book, I am sure that God's grace is drawing you closer to the image in which you were created.

The religious world consists mainly of people reading books and repeating quotations. One book in particular. The bible. That's great in many ways. But there's much confusion over what it means. Conclusions are drawn. And they are sometimes correct conclusions, and sometimes incorrect. But conclusions don't add up to much. No one is set free from the ills and afflictions of this world by reading and formulating conclusions. There has to be something more. There has to be a spiritual awakening. Because only the divine nature made manifest in the world can ever bring healing to the world. And Messiah is doing that through raising up messianic ones. People who, through spiritual transformation, are molded in the Messianic image.

---

[102] Rom. 8:2.

However, it also seems clear to me that no one can effectively be a minister of the Spirit, without a thorough basis and foundation in the letter. Indeed, as it is written the letter kills, but the Spirit gives Life.[103] Nevertheless, the two go together.

We all need instruction in the letter, in order to grow and mature in the Spirit. To be an instrument of God to impart the Spirit, which is the essence of New Covenant, growing to maturity depends on both the letter of Truth and the Spirit of Truth together.

The problem is when the letter is all we have. Or when it is overemphasized to the point that the Spirit of God is pushed out of the picture as irrelevant. Or even dangerous. Taken by itself, when the letter is picked up with tweezers and placed into a petri dish to be dissected and examined and discussed, this is only going to lead to spiritual death. As it says, the letter kills.

Searching For More Information:

So, after that football season was over, I began a period of a few months in which I built up my foundation of knowledge through the letter of truth. By that, I mean reading materials, as well as audio and video files. I was aware that God was doing a new work in me. And I immediately began searching for more information so that I could better understand it. And grow in it.

I would've liked to see Marley again, but I didn't. After Marley talked to me on the sidelines that day, we played the playoffs, through the championship, at away stadiums, which had their own videographers. I stopped in at Starbucks a few times, but Marley was not to be found. And I couldn't take that scene anymore. So I stopped going.

Over the next several months, I holed up in the public library and began studying. I started with the bible. I poured over the scriptures. But not only the bible. I also reviewed my

---

[103] 2 Cor. 3;6.

own notes, my audio files, and whatever I could get my hands on that was related to what I was experiencing, so long as I felt that the material was biblical. I do not accept anything as reliable unless it can be scripturally validated.

I also took a lot of long walks and jogs. Many of them were on the beach. Florida is quite beautiful in the Winter, and the climate is perfect for being outdoors, right up until about April, when it gets blazing hot. And something about walking or jogging along the ocean is incredibly inspiring.

Anyway, on my walks and jogs, I always brought along my sport headphones. I listened to the audio files which I had from Marley, Capt. Rosenblatt, and Shlomo. I listened to them over and over. And I also found other audio files that related to the message about which I was searching.

When I began to search for more information, it was not difficult to find other materials related to this message of the iPath. By "related" I mean, as I said, scripturally validated. But I narrowed it down to a particular corridor. I was looking for materials which taught as Paul called it, the message of "*Messiah in you*."[104] That message which Paul said was a "*mystery that was hidden for ages and generations but now has been revealed*."[105]

It seemed most obvious to me that this "mystery" which had been revealed, was still nonetheless being missed by the religious world, including, but not limited to, that massive part of the religious world which had dubbed itself to be the "followers" of the Messiah. And I had been one of them all along. Now the change had come.

Immersion:

I realized what had happened to me during this sabbatical period was that I was becoming conscious of that mystery of which Shaul spoke, the mystery of "Messiah in me." I realized that was the change. And that was the thing

---

[104] Col. 1:27.
[105] Co. 1:28.

which was happening. The Spirit of the Lord began to open my mind and endow me with wisdom and discernment to see many wonderful things in the scriptures. These were things that were always there, but I simply wasn't seeing them. Things that made me go, "Ahhh!"

I saw Messiah in me. And I began to establish and maintain contact. Some might call that "tevila," which means, "the immersion" or "the baptism." Tevilat haRuakh or baptism in the Spirit was a key promise found in the scriptures. The scriptures say that John immersed in water, but Yeshua would immerse his followers in the Spirit of God.[106] This topic was nothing new to me. I had always thought of myself as one who had experienced it already. Now I began to question that. I began to wonder if maybe the immersion in the Spirit was not what I thought it was.

Something happened to Yeshua when he went into the river under his cousin, Yochanan (John), to be immersed.[107] His ministry officially began there. He was anointed with the Ruakh HaKodesh, and thereby, he went about the land preaching the Kingdom of God, healing the sick, and setting people free from demonic oppression, because God was with him.[108]

And you can see, after receiving the baptism of the Spirit, Yeshua grew in it. The miracles he did and signs he showed became greater and greater as time went by, until pretty soon he was raising the dead. And by the end, even a man who was dead four days was raised. And then he was ready to show to the world his divine sonship and infinite power as deliverer and savior of the human race. He showed it by laying down his own life, knowing that the same Spirit which raised Lazarus and was doing all these miracles, would raise him from the grave as well.

And so it happened, because Yeshua was fully conscious, he was one with the Father, in the same way that he was one

---

[106] Acts 1:5, Mat. 3:11.
[107] Mat. 3:13-17.
[108] Acts 10:37-38

before coming into the human scene. That is why he could say in truth, "I and my Father are one," as he often did. But humans are a fallen race, created in God's image, yet cut off like a branch that is withering and dying.

Hence, as a human walking on planet earth, the son of God's oneness with the Father was at all times in jeopardy. Being human, he was at all times tempted to fall into the same state of alienation as the rest of the human race. He suffered as a human, had his moments of temptation, but he never fell into the mesmeric grasp of the human scene. Even living at a time when the entire known world had come under the grasp of one empire—Rome.

Anyone who refused to submit to Roman rule would be put to death. Anyone, of course, could deny Rome's authority in their heart, as many Jews did exactly that. But Yeshua did not simply deny Roman rule in his heart. He also maintained connection and conscious contact with the Kingdom of God within his heart. The Kingdom which according to him is "not of this world."[109]

Even standing before the Roman Procurator Pilate, who didn't want to crucify Yeshua. And yet, knowing that if he simply said the right things, Pilate would set him free, he maintained "My Kingdom is not of this world." And Yeshua was not just saying it, or proclaiming it, but being conscious within himself of that eternal Kingdom, which was known to Yeshua, revealed to his followers, and will at the appointed time make its visible appearance on earth.

Now, with respect to the Kingdom that is not of this world, Yeshua bore witness to it. He intended to bring to the world even before the day it becomes visible to all. As those who see it beforehand, are the heirs of it. And now, I understood it. This revelation was beginning to unfold in me. As Isaiah said, *"The Spirit of the Lord God is upon me, because the Lord has anointed me to proclaim good news."*[110]

---

[109] John 18:36.
[110] Is. 61:1.

Not that I compare myself to Isaiah. Only that there is a paradigm set up here. Because we each have a unique purpose, individually, a raison d'être, a reason for being here.

I don't know how it all works. I just know that Yeshua is at the right hand of God in heaven.[111] Whatever that means exactly, is hard to describe. But I know this: That a time comes when a person who follows Yeshua is immersed in the Spirit of God for some purpose of God to be accomplished in that person's life. It isn't that person doing it—it is the Lord. And it's something that is happening quite mysteriously, because it is happening by divine grace. And when it happens, the person sees this great truth, that "It is no longer I who live, but Messiah lives in me."[112]

Even on the cross, dying, writhing in agony, Yeshua never lost his oneness with the Father because he was at all times conscious of the Spirit within him. From this anointing, he was able to stay true to his mission as Savior of the human race, and thereby found the strength to say, *"Father, forgive them, they do not know what they are doing."*[113]

I saw that the immersion in the Ruakh was the key to sealing his capacity not only to shine forth the Life of God into the world for the healing of the sick and hurting, but moreover, to keep himself in constant kesher with God, being fixed in the awareness that the Spirit of the Lord was with him. He otherwise could have fallen into the same state as the rest of humanity, but for our sake, he did not.

Something was happening to me. I didn't know what to call it. Nor did I care. I had no desire to tell anyone. Nor did I tell anyone. Whatever I might say wouldn't matter anyway. Either there was fruit to be born of it, or not. So, I kept quiet about it. I just wanted to grow in it. But I didn't know how. And I couldn't find Marley. Or anyone else.

---

[111] *See*, Acts 7:55, Heb.1;3, Rom. 8:34, Eph. 1:20.
[112] Gal. 2:20.
[113] Luke 23:34.

Building a Foundation:

So, I sought to build a stronger foundation of knowledge. And I buried myself in study and learning for those next few months. I was searching for the means to buttress what I had learned so far. I reiterate, I soughtto advance in the higher calling of dwelling in the Messiah. Which, as Shaul put it in the scritpures, *"Messiah lives in me."*[114]

This is what the iPath is all about, as I had learned thus far. It is walking in the nexus between two worlds. It is living in this perishable world, all the while retaining conscious connection to the infinite, imperishable Kingdom of God. This is the very paradigm set up by Yeshua, the immortal son of God, having appeared on earth to live the life of a mortal man. For the purpose to bring us, the human race, back into our original immortality.

There is so much information out there and available to us today, especially with the help of internet search engines, practically anything that has ever been written on any subject can be found if one looks. It's really just a matter of what we are looking for.

I found a wealth of material available. I found some materials as old as the hills. Others from the modern era. But whatever I found in my research, that was of interest to me, I was at all times careful to use the scriptures as my measuring rod. Everything I got my hands on, was carefully measured against the scriptures, to see if it measured up.

I do not intend to elaborate on the details of what materials I was studying. But I will say mention this. Other than the bible, which I poured over, there was one book that was the first material I got my hands on during this time that I call "building the foundation."

It was a book that had given to me ten years earlier by a friend. I hesitate to mention it, because I know very little about the author of this book, and moreover, that particular

---

[114] Gal. 2:20.

author has had only a small influence on me as a whole. There are others who I will not mention that have had a far more significant impact. But nothing out there had more of an impact than the bible. I simply was given a richer way to see it and understand its teachings. Especially the teaching of Yeshua HaMashiakh.

People give me books all the time. They say, "Rabbi, you've got to read this book!" I've got an entire garage full of those kind of books. CD's and DVD's too. I never read, listened or looked at most of them. Once in a blue moon, I might peruse through them and see if something perks my interest.

There it was, on a shelf in the garage, a little moldy, and the binding starting to disintegrate. This happens with old books in Florida, due to the humidity. But the pages were in pretty good shape nonetheless. There was an inscription from the friend, on the inside cover:

"Shalom, Gary, there's a _wealth_ in this book.

Blessings always in Yeshua, J—."

I note that the word "wealth" was underlined by the friend who gave me the book. To be honest, I still haven't read the entire book. And by no means did this book influence me to the extent that I became a disciple of this person or anything like that.

As I said, I don't really even know a great deal about the author, except I do know that he is thought of by many as the greatest healer of the modern era. The record speaks for itself in that regard. Whether it's true or not, I don't know. I am not an apologist for this author, nor am I of any mindset or position to defend, advocate, or promote, this particular author or his teachings. I hope I am clear on this point.

The Author's name is John G. Lake. I think he defies categorical placement, but if you had to, I guess you would call him a Christian, healing evangelist. He was, apparently, a former businessman, quite successful, who forsook everything to be a follower of Messiah.

And quite frankly, at the time I picked up that book which sat on a dusty shelf in my hot, humid garage, I had scarcely heard of Lake. And I knew practically nothing about him. Except that during the early 20th century, he became known as a great healer, and that most people today who follow that kind of thing are of the opinion that Lake was the greatest healer of the modern era.

I reiterate. I am not a disciple of John G. Lake. I have to say this because I know that as soon as you mention that you were influenced by a person, others seem to get the idea that you are a disciple of that person. And then everything you have to say about every topic might be thought of as if an extension of that person.

It would be like if Tom Petty says Bob Dylan was his greatest influence, then everyone will see Petty as if he's just doing Dylan. Well, in Petty's case it's true. But in mine, I think I am more influenced by Dylan, than I am anything like John G. Lake. But I am simply Rabbi Gary Goldman. Not Dylan, or Lake, or any of the wide array of teachers, poets, philosophers or kings, that I refuse to mention by name. Because I am not doing anyone else's shtick—except Yeshua HaMashiakh. I am definitely doing his shtick. Or at least trying.

And I suspect Lake was too. In his own way. And I am doing likewise. Therefore, simply put, the book which I found in my garage made an impact on me at that moment, propelling me forward in the direction I was going.

I repeat my disclaimer: Even now, I still don't know much about Lake. By no means is John G. Lake the biggest influence on my life. I have many other influences, actually some of them far more influential on my life than Lake.

However, what I found in Lake's writings made a deep impact upon me in that particular season, as I was building a foundation of understanding regarding the transformation that was happening to me. In fact, it catapulted me forward in the direction I was going.

I Opened the Book:

So, I opened the book. It was a collection of sermons by John G. Lake. I noted right way that it was published by Kenneth Copeland Publications.[115] Now the need for another disclaimer arises: I realize that Copeland is a famous personality in Christian Television. But I don't know much about Copeland. Don't know what he teaches, good or bad, right or wrong. I've never looked into Copeland. Maybe one day I will. But I never have. I didn't care who the publisher was. And I still don't.

So, I went to the table of contents and something caught my eye. Chapter 40 was entitled "Christian Consciousness." That grabbed my attention. Chapter 41 was entitled "Development of Christian Consciousness." That also grabbed my attention.

I took Lake's book with me to the public library and began to research it. In my little cubicle at the public library, where I had precious peace and quiet, and a good wifi connection, I read what Lake had to say.

Apparently, those two chapters, 40 and 41, were taken from a Sermon that Lake gave in Chicago, in 1920. He starts out with this statement, in which the publisher uses caps for certain words:

> *"There is a wonderful single word that expresses what God is trying to develop in us. The word is CONSCIOUSNESS. I love it. It is an amazing word. Consciousness means THAT WHICH THE SOUL KNOWS. Not that which you believe, or that which you have an existent faith for, or that which you hope, but that which the soul has proven which the soul knows, upon which the soul rests, the thing, bless God, which has become concrete in your life."[116]*

---

[115] John G. Lake. *His Life, His Sermons, His Boldness of Faith*. Kenneth Copeland Publications, 1994.

That one word—consciousness—seemed to reach out and grab me. Not that I had never heard that word before. Of course I had. But I had never heard it used by anyone in the mainstream Christian world. Because normally, the word "consciousness" was associated with Eastern philosophy. Why was Lake, the world's greatest healing evangelist of the modern era, using this word?

As I read on, Lake describes how his life and ministry career was impacted by a particular event that shook America and the world in 1893. It was the Chicago World's Fair. I read about that World's Fair, as described here in Lake's 1920 Chicago sermon; and also, simultaneously researched it on my laptop to find out more.

Apparently, among the features of that World's Fair in Chicago was something called the 1893 World Congress of Religion. Back then, nobody in America had ever heard much about the Eastern world of India and China, let alone whatever they believed or practiced in terms of their religion.

The age of the telegraph, which was the precursor to the internet, connected the world in a new way. The telegraph, together with the steamship, and particularly the British shipping industry, had brought on a great period of globalization during the latter half of the 19th century. By 1893, there was a tremendous exchange of information going on in the world. Peoples and nations were getting acquainted with one another for the first time ever. And there was some excitement about it in those days.

All of this bringing the world together as one was interrupted in the 20th century, thanks to a period of intense nationalism, which gave rise to two horrible world wars. But then the latter part of the 20th, on into the 21st century has been marked again as a period of advanced globalization and intense cultural exchange.

In 1893, at the World Congress of Religion, with this grandiose media spectacle going on in Chicago over the

---

[116] Ibid, p. 445..

World's Fair, and the whole world watching, that was the first time that the Eastern Religions had the opportunity to be introduced in America, and to the Western world, upon a far-reaching platform.

What happened was that Swami Vivekananda, who came from India, and reputedly had never spoken in public before, made such a splash with his presentation, that there was great excitement and enthusiasm over it. He became a celebrity and a hero in America and in the world as people were amazed with what he and his compadres had to say at the Fair about their philosophy of religion.

The Christian presentation, on the other hand, did not go over so well. As Lake describes it:

> *"The result of that Congress of Religions was that Christianity was so poorly presented that the Indian philosophers ran away with the whole thing, and in the minds of thousands who listened, it left a belief that their knowledge of God, and God's laws, and the laws of life, were greater than the Christian possessed. And fellow Christians, there began in my soul a prayer that Almighty God would reveal in my soul what the real secret of real Christianity is, in order that in this world Christians might become Kings and Priests and demonstrate the superiority of the religion of the Son of God beyond that of every other in the whole earth."*[117]

I think that what happened was that Lake saw two things at this event. First, that the "religion of the Son of God" was the one which was above any in the earth. But secondly, that Christianity, as it was understood and practiced in his time, was not the "religion of the Son of God" that it claimed to be.

This seemed to provoke Lake to a deeper and deeper immersion in the Spirit of God, so that at least in his own

---

[117] Ibid, p. 448.

life, he might be a follower of the Son, as well as a teacher and a worker in that religion of the Son of God.

This event at the Fair in 1893 catapulted Lake forward onto a new trajectory in which he sought after the prize of knowing the Son of God in a way that was true and real. After all, if Yeshua is King of Kings and Lord of Lords, then those who are witnesses for Yeshua ought to be the ones who make the big splash at the World's fair.

But as it was, what the Christians presented at the World's fair was something that made everyone go, "Ho hum." It was received like old news. Thus Christianity was embarrassed before the whole world, in the face of these visitors from the East, that came to Chicago for the 1893 World's Fair. And Lake was provoked to jealousy over it.

As I continued to read those two chapters, addressing the topic of what Lake called "Christian Consciousness," I saw that one of the keys to Lake's ministry was that he was open to learn about other religions. He wasn't open because he doubted his own faith. But he seemed to use what he learned from others in order to give himself a better understanding of his own faith in God.

Lake spent many years in South Africa, which was a unique place because it was inhabited not only by Western Europeans and by native Africans, but also, by millions of workers from India and China. Most of these came from the East to work in the diamond mines.

In this unique cultural mush-pot, Lake, in fact, made it a practice of studying and learning other religious scriptures, as well as attending interfaith meetings where he could hear from other leaders about their understanding of God. These "other" religions included Judaism, and also the various religions and philosophies of the East, which had been brought to South Africa by the workers and their spiritual leaders.

It is clear that the reason that Lake did this was not to affirm or validate these other religions. But, rather, to learn and grow in his own faith and understanding of God. Presumably, one undergoes similar experience in seminary or yeshiva, where courses in World Religions are commonplace. But that is happening in a sterile bubble of the classroom. This was real life. And it enriched his faith, learning from these Easterners.

Lake states:

> "*No other religion under the heavens has the same consciousness of God or the same means of producing a consciousness of God that Christianity possesses.*"[118]

In essence, what Lake did, was he took an eastern principle—consciousness—and applied it to the teaching and ministry of Yeshua. He says:

> "*I have studied the great Eastern philosophies. I have searched them from cover to cover. I have read them for years as diligently as I have read my bible. I have read them to see what their consciousness was. The secret of salvation is NOT in them. But in my Bible is seen that the Son of God saves men from their sins, and changes them by His power in their nature, so that they may become like him.*"[119]

It seemed clear to me that Lake, having studied Eastern thought, and having maintained dialogue with religious leaders from India and China during the many years he was in South Africa, had taken their core idea—consciousness—and came to the conclusion that there was no fulfillment of it, except through Messiah Yeshua.

They in the East were missing it. Because their revelations of God, whatever they may have been, were not on the level of the one which the Son of God, Yeshua, brought to the world.

---

[118] Ibid, p. 448.
[119] Ibid, p. 552.

But, Lake seemed to see also what I saw, that those in the West who may believe in the identity of the son of God as Yeshua (Jesus) the son of a Jewish carpenter from Nazareth, and may believe in all the facts pertaining to his miracles, his atoning death, and resurrection, etc., nevertheless, are still missing the very thing which the son of God brought to the world—consciousness. Lake says:

> *"Oh yes, bless, God, I am coming back to that word which I started. Do you know the secret of religion is in its consciousness? The secret of Christianity is in the consciousness it produces in your soul. And Christianity produces a higher consciousness than any other religion in the world...it comes breathing and throbbing and burning right out of the heart of the glorified Son of God. It comes breathing and beating and throbbing into your nature and mind, bless God."*[120]

Granted, I am uncomfortable with Lake's use of the term "Christianity" and his suggestions that it is a superior religion, and that sort of thing. I understand, though, the crowd which Lake was addressing was a Christian one.

The word "Christianity" is a word that has a thousand different meanings today, depending on whose saying it. And I'm sure it wasn't much different in Lake's time. So whatever "Christianity" may mean, John G. Lake obviously had a different idea of "Christianity" than say, Pastor Buddy and God's Awesome Ladies from the Sunny Lake Community megachurch.

And to Lake, to be a true follower of the "Christ" meant to walk in Christian consciousness, as the Christ did, not as one who only identifies Jesus as the Christ, but rather, one who shows forth the divine nature and the righteousness of God in oneself.

---

[120] Ibid, p. 452.

I saw plainly that this divine consciousness about which Lake spoke, at least from his point of view, was the key to his ministry. And that made sense to me.

The Age of the Jew-Bu:

As a Jew, I am well-aware of the fact that to my own people, unlike the Christian world, the word "consciousness" is quite commonly known. For one thing, historically, Jews are not a Western people, but Eastern.

The land of Israel, from which Jews originate, is not a Western land. It is located plainly in the East. The middle East, but still gravitating culturally more toward the East, being geographically located in the East. This fact should not be overlooked in interpreting the bible, and in particular the teachings of Yeshua.

But it has always been overlooked. Because even though Jews from Israel, an Eastern nation, brought the message of the gospel to the world, Christianity arose in Europe. And there it became institutionalized, and its interpretation and doctrinal foundation became Western in orientation. Which tends to skew the message, as it is misunderstood when taken out of its cultural context.

As part of the middle-east, Israel historically is the nexus point between the Eastern and Western world. Many of the key trade routes of antiquity went through Israel, and the ports of Israel connected Western Europe to the Eastern world of Persia, India and beyond. The Eastern presence in the land of Israel can be greatly seen and felt, not just historically, but today as well.

So, we should make no mistake about it, the King of the Jews, and all the Apostles and practically all of the early followers of Yeshua, were citizens of an Eastern country— Israel. Naturally, then, their religious ideas and practices, therefore, were more Eastern than Western.

This fact is vastly important in correctly understanding, rightly dividing and accurately discerning the bible. In particular, the New Testament, which has been popularized from a Western, European institutional point of view. But the reality of it is Jewish, and Eastern by nature.

As far as Judaism, the Jewish people today are for the most part disillusioned, disenchanted, and disengaged from traditional Judaism—much of which developed in Europe, not in Israel.

Today is the age of the Jew-Bu. That technically means "Jewish Buddhist," but it is a term often applied more generally to Jews in the West that have embraced some form of Eastern religious practice.

In fact, Eastern religion is as popular among Western Jews as traditional Judaism—if not more. The numbers of Jewish people in the West who have become acquainted with and/or oriented in Eastern religious philosophy and practices is quite staggering.

Now when you talk about these kinds of statistics, it's going to always involve some speculation and opinion. It's not easy to find out through surveys and polls how many Jews read the Bhagavad Gita or the Upanishads, for example. And even harder to determine what people might believe about such things. But anyone who's paying attention knows. Especially if you're Jewish.

When you are Jewish, it is common knowledge that Jews are heavily into Eastern spirituality. Jews were very much a part of the hippie movement in the sixties. And it was at that time that Jewish youth began to embrace, on a broad basis, things like meditation, yoga, and holistic practices. Not to mention mind-expansion through psychedelic and hallucinogenic drug use. (Note—this is not to in any way confirm or endorse such practices, it is only taking note of what is going on. I also note that it was out of this religious climate that the Jesus movement, and consequent messianic Jewish movement arose).

Mainline Judaism understands what is going on with Jews turning to Eastern thought. It is trying to adjust. It is commonplace today for mainstream synagogues (not messianic) to include yoga, meditation, and mysticism, not only as midweek classes, but actually incorporated into the weekly Shabbat services.

Today, not only with the baby-boomer generation, but also with the millennial generation, meditation and yoga is as common among Jews as matzo ball soup. Many of the yoga teachers in America are Jewish. And the synagogues in America are trying to meet the people where they are at.

Even among Jews who practice traditional Judaism, and might be considered observant or even Orthodox, many of them commonly supplement their religious life and beliefs with Eastern philosophy and practices.

For Jewish Americans, Eastern practices which are presumed to advance higher consciousness are more commonly adhered to than, say, the dietary laws of the Torah. Which, I note, most American Jews do not observe a kosher diet anymore. I do. But most do not.

Something Dawned on Me:

As I thought about all this, something dawned on me there in the library. But first, I decided to do some quick research on my laptop. Even though I know all this about my Jewish people's interest in Eastern philosophy, as I sat there in the public library, I was shocked to discover the number of Jew-Bu's. It is estimated that approximately 30% of all Western-born Buddhists are of Jewish heritage.[121]

I began to ponder some things. Obviously, as a messianic Rabbi, I am a talmid of Yeshua, called first to the Jewish people, but also to the Gentile.[122] But I think that whatever it is that the Jewish people are looking for spiritually, that is causing them to turn away from traditional Judaism toward the Eastern religions, is the same thing that many Gentiles are looking for, who are likewise put off with the church.

---

[121] Frankel, Ellen. "Ju-Bu's." *Author Ellen Frankel,* http://www.authorellenfrankel.com/ju-bus-4.html. Accessed March, 22nd, 2017.
[122] Rom. 1:16.

And as I thought about what I read in chapter 40 and 41 of John G. Lake's book of sermons, I began to see something that Lake articulated well in his sermon on Christian consciousness. I began to see that everything the Jewish people were looking for in Eastern thought could actually be found in fullness and perfection in Yeshua HaMashiakh. Because Yeshua was the fullness of divine consciousness in the flesh. So, I thought, why are my people not seeing this? Why are they turning to other religions instead?

And it dawned on me there, in the public library, as I read Lake's 1920 Chicago sermon on Christian consciousness. It's because they don't care if the divine consciousness is to be found in Yeshua. No more than they care if it is to be found in Moses or Elijah, or, for that matter, Gautama the Buddha. They don't care because they who look for it, are not seeking someone who walked in consciousness. Not even if that person walked in the perfection and fullness of consciousness (as Yeshua did). What they are seeking is to become conscious themselves.

Because it's not enough to know that consciousness was in someone else. From their point of view, what good does that do them? If they are interested at all to hear about a man who was divine consciousness in the flesh, the interest would not be so much in that person, but in how will this person help *me* become conscious? Can you blame them?

Yeshua is King of Kings, Lord of Lords. The son of God, he was perfect, sinless, and, as Lake suggested, he was divine consciousness in the flesh, and that's how he knew he could be crucified and go into the grave, and come up out of death's grasp three days later.[123] There is none like Yeshua, and never will be.

But, as a Jewish Rabbi, the message which Yeshua brought to the world was not just a message which said who he was. If it were like that, then we'd all be lost, until the day that he returns. But, rather, his core teaching, and the reason he suffered, and the whole purpose of his ministry, was to

---

[123] Lake, p. 452-53.

bring forth the divine Life in each of us. And I saw that day, that this idea of being a "partaker of the divine nature,"[124] as Peter put it, is the whole idea of the ministry of Messiah.

It is the essential truth, the abiding principle, and the overarching purpose, that we might be made the righteousness of God in him.[125]

So, it's not just divine consciousness in Yeshua. But also in us—that is, if we are truly his followers. Not that we will ever be him. There is only one perfect man who ever lived. But being the Son of God, as the pioneer of a new humanity, he has made many into children of God. And if we are truly "messianic" then we are born of Messiah. Then the same Messiah which Yeshua is, therefore, lives within us. If only we become *conscious* of the One who lives within us.

I saw that this is the gist of what Lake was saying to his people in giving that sermon in Chicago in 1920, which was 27 years after the Eastern world made its mark at the World's Fair in that same city. And in seeing this, it helped me hone in on what was happening to me.

Indeed, I was becoming conscious. And this wisdom that I received, most unexpectedly, from a Christian, healing evangelist—or whatever he was—that I knew very little about, catapulted me forward on the iPath. What I didn't know was how to grow in consciousness. To become more conscious. That would come later.

Scribbling and Assembling Notes:

So much new understanding was coming to me, that I needed to process it all. I found it necessary to scribble down notes and assemble them into some semblance of order.

So, during that Winter, I occupied myself not only with my research and my studies, but also with writing down my thoughts. In fact, day by day I was furiously writing down

---

[124] 2 Pet. 1:4.
[125] 2 Cor. 5:21.

notes in yellow legal pads. I went through quite a few of those yellow legal pads.

The notes I scribbled out on yellow paper, just seemed to flow right out of me. Fresh thoughts were swimming around in my mind.

It was stream-of-consciousness stuff, that came forth, without me thinking about it. Like a free-flowing river of thought, reduced to yellow paper. I basically just wanted to get down on paper, everything I could. And then I would read back over it, measuring it against the scriptures, to see if it measured up.

Most everything I wrote down on the yellow legal pads had to do with one of two things: 1) the nature of God, and 2) the nature of human error pertaining to God.

Later on, toward the end of my Sabbatical, I began to assemble these notes, and started drafting a book. The book that I couldn't write because I had nothing of value to say to the world.

Now I note that this book you are reading here, *The iPath*, is a prequel to that book. That first book, entitled *One God*, was actually sort of the "first fruits" of the experiences that I am describing herein.

In drafting and publishing *One God*, I did feel that I had something of value to impart to the world. But I did not feel a release about sharing with the world how the teaching in that book had come to me.

Therefore, not long after my Sabbatical was over, I published *One God* without explanation. After publishing *One God*, I held weekly video webinar teachings, live streamed on the internet through youtube and social media. As a result, the teaching in *One God* has touched tens of thousands of people all over North America. Quite a few, in Israel, and in Europe as well.

After nearly two years of teaching on the principles of *One God*, I felt it was time to share this personal story of how that particular teaching came to me, which is what I have documented here in *the iPath*.

None of this could have come about if a change hand not occurred in me. What changed was mainly in terms of the way that I *saw* things. Seeing things differently than I did before, changed everything.

I note that at the time it happened, I did not know what had happened. And even later, after I came to understand it better, I did not know how to explain it to anyone. Even to this day, I find it hard to explain to others what happened to me.

So when, for example, the Spirit of God said, "*You are me,*" on the sideline of the football game, something was happening. I didn't know what it was. But now that I've had some time to process it, I understand that what was happening to me, was that this inner voice, this internal power, was becoming the government of my life.

Not My Will:

It was not my will that brought about this change. No, I stress, it was not a conscious decision made by me. It was not something where I chose this instead of that. It was not a "choose this day whom you will serve" kind of a moment.

I had done that already. Twenty-five years earlier. When I became a "believer" in Yeshua. Now that is another story entirely, to be told some other time.

That, too, was a work of God's grace, but I didn't understand it that way. As I understood it, I had made a decision on that day to believe in the Messiah. Oh, I might have paid lip service to the idea that it was a work of God's grace, but I still saw it as a decision that I made.

From that day forward, I went on in the understanding that I had made a choice, and that it was the right choice. Which it would've been, if it was a choice.

Just look at Joshua, who put it to Israel, and told them to choose. And they did. He said, "*As for me and my house, I will serve the Lord,*" and the people Israel totally agreed with him.[126]

179

Well, it didn't work for them. Despite their "choice," even though it was indeed the right choice, nevertheless, they still went after other gods. Because it isn't about us making a decision. Our decisions don't add up to much.

I see so many examples of this in scripture. God chose his nation—Israel. Even when Israel repeatedly went after other gods, and did everything conceivable to blow it, God never will forsake the fact that Israel is the chosen nation. Not that Israel chose God, but God chose Israel. It's inexplicable. But it's irrevocable and irreversible.[127]

In the same manner Yeshua chose his followers from every nation tribe and tongue on the face of the earth, to participate in the covenant with Israel. Yeshua said to his followers, *"You did not choose me, but I chose you."*[128]

But I never really understood it that way. And when I did see it as a work of God's grace, and as something having to do with his choice, not mine, then the way was clear for me to be on the iPath. Because I got myself out of the way. The recognition of God's grace took the emphasis off of me. And it allowed God into the driver's seat. To do whatever work is to be done in me.

I have learned to maintain an attitude that says: "Not my will, but yours."[129] But even that can be willed. So it has to be a work of God's grace that causes a person to do that.

Otherwise, we are just like the people of Israel who chose God in Joshua's time, and vowed to serve no other. But then they still went after other gods.

Or like the masses, in Yeshua's time, who hailed him as Messiah when he entered Jerusalem, but then days later, they still chose Barabbas and were screaming for Yeshua to be crucified.

Or like the people Israel, when Moses came down the mountain and presented the law, and they said *"All the words which the Lord has spoken, we will do."*[130] Then just a

---

[126] Joshua 24:14-18.
[127] *See*, Rom. 11:28-29.
[128] John 15:16.
[129] Luke 22:42.

few weeks later they broke the first of ten commandments when they built a golden calf and said, *"This is your god, O Israel, who brought you up out of the land of Egypt."*[131]

I remember the day I chose the Lord. Twenty-five years earlier. It's darn near impossible for a Jewish person to believe that Yeshua is the Messiah. Everything is stacked against it. It doesn't make any sense to us, because the whole matter is so convoluted by history. Church history in particular. All the worst things done to us in Europe were done to us in the name of "Jesus Christ." And so we're supposed to believe he is the Savior? Please.

But it is possible for a Jew to see, what any Gentile also can see, if his or her mind is open to it—that the real "Jesus" is not the one that the world has been talking about for the last two thousand years. That one was invented by people with an agenda.

I chose the real one. Yeshua. Or Jesus. Or whatever language. It doesn't matter one iota how you say that name. What matters is what you know about him in your heart. Then there is at a bare minimum a root that can sprout.

I learned all the facts about who he was and why he died and rose from the dead. I became learned in the scriptures. I had the gift to communicate knowledge in creative ways. I learned how to teach the facts in ways to be applied to life.

But my knowledge of God was mostly from printed materials. Mainly the bible. Of which I had developed much expertise, as would be expected of a professional minister, like me. And I learned to run a congregation. To keep offices, administrate, manage, counsel, perform rabbinical services, etc., etc. And I was good at all these things. Well above par, if I may say so. But how well did I actually know God?

All I can say is ask yourself that same question. And if you are comfortable with the answer to that question, you'll never go much further than where you are when you ask it.

---

[130] Ex. 24:3.
[131] Ex. 32:8.

Well, I was comfortable too. But then, suddenly I wasn't. And so I started asking—*Who am I?*

I suppose the whole matter of how well a person knows God is always going to be a question of degree. But how well can you know anyone, let alone God, when the only fellowship you have with that person is through reading about them? What about real-time, panim el panim (face-to-face) communion? I didn't really know how to have that with him. Not in a consciously intentional way.

But during the year of my sabbatical, messianic consciousness dawned in me, and I came to see things that I had not seen previously.

When this happened to me, I stress, it was not a thing that I chose. It was not a decision that I made. It was something that crept into my life and revealed itself unto me. It walked in. Crept in. Slowly but surely. But most ardently and intentionally.

It didn't show up all at once. It came in stages. And not by my will. Nevertheless, with clear will and purpose. It was an inner revelation, but it became the guiding light and the operative principle of my outer experience.

It would take a while before I could grasp what was going on, and before the fruit would come of it. I would need further help. Who doesn't? But as time progressed, I learned to establish greater contact with what I came to know as my "new Self" or "true Self."

Of course, the idea of "new Self" comes from the scriptures. Naturally, I had read one thousand times before each and every one of the New Testament verses about the new self.[132]

I knew all about the doctrinal concepts of renewal, and spiritual rebirth, letting the "old self" die, and putting on what is called the "new Self," etc. Indeed, I often taught about these concepts at length in my sermons and bible study classes.

---

[132] See, e.g., Col. 3:10, Eph. 4:24, 2 Cor. 5:17, Rom. 6:6.

But my understanding of the new Self/true Self of scripture was somewhat limited.

The Opening of the Almond Blossom:

In Israel, one of the most beautiful sights of nature is the blooming branch of an almond tree. It is no wonder that the Menorah, in the Temple, which represents the Tree of Life, was made after the likeness of almond blossoms. Branches, buds, and flowering blossoms are fashioned right into it.

God commanded Israel to make the menorah that way.[133] The seven cups of the Menorah, which are fashioned in the image of the almond blossom, are opened up at the top of each branch, so that they might hold oil, and therefore be a vessel that shines the Light.

Likewise, something in us has to open up so that the Light might shine forth. There has to be an awakening. The Menorah as a vessel of light before the holy of holies in the Temple, bears witness that there must be an awakening.

When you awaken to consciousness, the Light has dawned. But if our consciousness remains closed, there is no vessel to shine forth the Light of Messiah. And darkness remains. Without the opening in us, as represented by the almond flower in the Temple Menorah, there is no means for us to be the vessel in which the Light of the world can shine.

Yeshua said, "I am the Light of the World," but he also said "You are the Light of the World."[134] This may seem contradictory, but it isn't. The simple fact is that the Light which is God is also within us. But there has to be an awakening, or an opening up, so that the cup which holds the oil might shine forth the Light.

What I have observed is that there is a transformative experience represented by the opening of the almond blossom, which Yeshua referred to as spiritual rebirth.[135]

---

[133] Ex. 25:31-40; Ex. 37;19,20.
[134] John 8:12, and Mat. 5:14.
[135] John 3:3.

When it happens a person begins to see themselves as an instrument of God. A transparency for shining the Light of the Lord in this perishing, dark world.

The biblical concept of "true Self" is the Light of God, individualized in us. The true Selfhood is something hidden. Like a seed planted below ground, maybe it has taken root. But for it to become the actual goverment of "me" or of "you," then it has to be brought forth above ground.

Otherwise, as individuals we remain in a somewhat embryonic stage of spiritual life. We go about our business thinking ourselves to be mature and developed, but who out there is going to tell us that it isn't so? It's rude to say things like that. And would you even listen if someone did tell you?

Marley was the first to confront me about this, and I was put off by it at first. But for some reason I took it to heart. That's how I got where I am now. Where is that? It's much further along than I was before. I can say that for sure.

I note that I always previously considered the true Self to be vastly important. Was I in touch with it? Far less than I thought. Hence, unknowingly, though I often spoke of the Kingdom of God, I was speaking of it not as one who lives in it, but as one planning a trip there. Or as a romantic dream.

And you see, the problem was that I didn't know I was out of touch. I thought I was in touch. Practically everyone thinks that about themselves. I was no different.

But then came into my path certain messengers of Truth, who bore witness to me. And I was willing to listen and learn. I can't fully explain why. I wish I could. But I just know that this is how the almond blossom opened up in me. And that's how it opens in anyone.

And I know that faith comes by hearing. That's how it came to me. Therefore, by telling my story, people who read it may get touched by the same grace of God that touched my life, and opened up the almond blossom in me.

Put on the New Self:

As my Sabbatical progressed, an inner revelation was unfolding in me. Now that the almond flower was opening up, I was seeing a new and true Self emerge.

I started to become aware of the plain truth that I had not yet experienced, in a significant way, the very transformation which I believed and preached was fundamentally necessary for a true Messiah-follower.

In fact, I did regularly preach and teach on the need to be reborn, transformed, become a new creation, or however you may want to put it. I made it a point to emphasize this in my teachings. That was not the problem.

The problem was that I thought I had already attained to the new Self. I was sure that I had. And for years I had been teaching others about this all-important concept, which is also called being "born again." Or "reborn" or "born anew" or "born from above," or "born of the Spirit." It's all the same concept. And the scriptures say we can't see the Kingdom of God without this occurrence of spiritual rebirth—or whatever you want to call it.[136]

Everybody who knows that the bible says we must be "born again," therefore, believes that they are "born-again" because they know you are supposed to be. Either that, or you have to ignore the matter altogether. Which lots of people do. But not people who value what the scriptures say.

Consequently, the world is populated by millions and millions of people who consider themselves "born again"—whatever that means.

Therefore, you have three options: Either 1) claim that you are born again just like everyone else who says they are; 2) ignore the matter altogether, or 3) realize that you are not born again in the true sense of it, and try to do something about it. After many years of being in group #1, I made a change. I guess I was converted. Because I selected group #3.

---

[136] John 3:3.

I guess to some extent the whole "born again" thing is a question of degree. Like how "born again" are you? I mean, is there a point where you can say "I have arrived?"

For me, walking with God is an on-again, off-again experience. The goal is to maximize the on-again time. The iPath is a road without beginning and without end. But there are times in life I feel that I am being pulled off of that road, overcome by the burden of living in this perishable world with all of its craziness and strife.

This is the whole challenge of living between two worlds—the Kingdom of God vs. the Kingdom of this world. There is a push and pull between them.

I know there is a point where the Reality becomes the law and the governing principle of a person's life. It takes control. You still waiver and vacillate between two worlds, but there is that pivot point, wherein a change happens. The change is that God is in charge. Instead of you. You are still around. For now. But not in charge anymore. Whereas, it used to be the reverse. God was around. But you were in charge.

That pivot point, I think, is spiritual rebirth. But the struggle isn't over. The world continues to try and pull you down. Oh sure, you'll never give up your faith. But can you live in abiding peace, joy, prosperity, health and happiness?

The world knocks you down. And you've got to get back up and get back on the iPath. Yeshua spoke of this saying, *"In the world you will have trouble, but take heart! I have overcome the world."*[137]

Our true nature, the true Self, is the image of God in which all human beings were fashioned. And only one man, Yeshua, ever walked the earth in the perfection and the fullness of that image.

Nobody else is ever that perfect, or ever that fully "born again." That's why he's the Messiah. And the rest of us, at best, are "messianic." Which means, "Messiah-like." Then it

---

[137] John 16:33.

becomes a question of degree. How much "Messiah-like" are you?

If you were to ask me, at what point has the image of God so fully emerged in us that we can accurately hang the label around our necks that says "born again"? I can't answer that, nor can anyone else. Because there is no litmus test for it. It can't be put into a petri dish and examined for authenticity.

I just know that there is a pivot point, where God is in control. Firmly. How do you know when it happens? When it happens in you, then you know. When it happens in someone else, God only knows. And the person in whom it happens. They know too.

And I know that my view on this might sound pessimistic or negative to some folks. So be it. But as a Jew, I always look to history. In particular, what happened to my people. Not to lament about it. But to learn from it.

Most of our suffering in Europe for nearly 2000 years was at the hands of "Christians." Most of whom, if asked, "Are you born-again" would have answered yes. So what have we learned from that? Many things. But at a minimum, we have learned that "born again" doesn't mean what people think it means.

Let me just add my feeling that it's better to err on the side of humility. It's better not to think oneself to have arrived, but rather, to go through life in Messiah with the attitude that Shaul had, believing that I have not attained the goal, but I am pressing on to the higher calling. As he stated:

> "If somehow I might arrive at the resurrection from among the dead. Not that I have already obtained this or been perfected, but I press on if only I might take hold of that for which Messiah Yeshua took hold of me. Brothers and sisters, I do not consider myself as having taken hold of this. But this one thing I do: forgetting what is behind and straining toward what is ahead, I press on toward the goal

for the reward of the upward calling of God in Messiah Yeshua."[138]

In this respect, on the all-important topic of spiritual rebirth, i.e. the emergence of the new Self, the most common mistake ever made among people who "believe" in Messiah is the idea that one has already arrived. Shaul didn't see it that way. Great as he was. Nor should we.

Instead, true Selfhood in the sense that Shaul saw it, is not something we became. Nor is it something we one day become. But rather it is something we are *becoming*. Always becoming.

The infinitive form says it all, because we are talking about the eternal soul from which God has created Man. Which happens to be infinite. Which we can't be busy "becoming" if we think we've already become.

In this sense, there is a way of working at becoming. Which I learned, thanks to those who showed me. And thanks to the grace of God which sent them my way. My only hope is to do the same for others—if they will listen to my story. Because faith comes by hearing.

In my story, like a breath of Life breathed into my nostrils, this realization of the new Self became the operative principle, the law of my life, and burst through an open almond blossom to emerge, carrying with it, the revelation of the Kingdom of God on a regular, ongoing, continuing basis. And my goal is to press on, to the high calling, as the power of an indestructible Life emerges as the Supreme authority which it is. Just as we are instructed:

"Be renewed in the spirit of your mind, and put on the new Self—created to be like God in true righteousness and holiness."[139]

---

[138] Phil. 3:11-14.
[139] Eph. 4:23,24.

Of course, I knew that scripture for a long, long time. But let me just say that knowing the concept of "put on the new Self," is not the same as actually doing it. And when I learned how to do it on a regular, routine, repeated basis, with conscious intent and purpose, then I became the new Self more and more...and am very much still engaged in becoming it.

Anyone can read a passage of scripture, and say "unless you are born-again, blah, blah, blah." Actually being "born-again" is quite another thing than just accepting the idea of it. And I think we all need a little help to push us forward in this regard.

Child of God:

"You are me," said the Spirit to me on the sideline of a youth football game. And it was life-changing. This simplistic little statement, is actually the deep Truth that most of us have been missing all along.

And no, it doesn't mean we are "little gods" or "little messiahs" or anything like that. Nothing about any human being can ever be divine. And anyone who goes around saying or even thinking, "I am God," is in a terrible state of sin.

What I am is a child of God.[140] Created in the image of God. Having been born of a fallen race, I am reborn of the Messiah who is God, living in me. He was always in the world, but the world knew him not. He came into the world and preached the Truth, but the world rejected him.

The Messiah told the world, I am the vine, you are the branches, so abide in me and I will abide in you.[141] And that's what I'm doing. He told me to be one with him, even as he is one with the Father.[142]

---

[140] *See*, e.g., John 1:12.13; Rom 8:16, Luke 20:36.
[141] John 15:4.
[142] John 14:20.

The human race is a branch, cut-off from God, that is withering and dying. The Son of God came to tell us "abide in me." But how?

This is the great paradox of what Yeshua told us to do. How can we abide in the son of God, being human? Humans are mortal. Not divine. Yet, we are told that the Son of God abides within us, and that we should abide in him. And in doing so we become heirs to eternal life and immortality.

The truth is that humans are human. But God lives in the midst of us. For me, when I could say, *"It is no longer I who lives, but Messiah lives in me,"*[143] that changed everything.

As many as receive him have the right to be called the sons and daughters of the Lord.[144] This is the hope of the world. But saying so doesn't make it true. Saying I am the son of God. Or daughter. That doesn't make it true. There has to be a change.

The entire basis of messianic life depends upon whether that change occurs—and continues to occur.

God is the center of our being. God is infinite. We are all created in that image, but we are not naturally aware of it.

That image is the true Self. Or call it the new Self. The human image is the old man. Or call it the old Self. What I'm saying is that there is no selfhood apart from God. And the more we know that, then the more we know what Yeshua meant when he said:

> *"In that day you will know, that I am in the Father, you are in me, and I am in you."*[145]

Messiah Lives in Me:

Truth is always there, right in the midst of us. But Truth means nothing to anyone unless we *know* it. The Truth will

---

[143] Gal. 2:20.
[144] John 1:12.
[145] John 14:20.

not set anyone free. It's only in *knowing* the Truth that we are set free.

When God imparted to me this simple little tidbit of information, "You are me," I suddenly came to know something that had always been true. But I wasn't seeing it before.

Oh, of course, I'd read Galatians 2:20 a million times: "*It is no longer I who live but **Messiah lives in me**,*" but it never really clicked until the Spirit of God said it to me: "*You are me.*"

Sure, I'd read Paul's statement in Col. 1:27 about the mystery of "*Messiah in you,*" and John 14:20 "*I am in the Father, you are in me, and I am in you,*" but I guess it just never had registered before.

God's Love is Spirit. It's invisible. And omnipresent. There is nowhere you can go from his Spirit.[146] But can you see love, hear love? Taste or smell love? No. We need a different kind of faculty to apprehend love. For God IS Love. God is invisible. Communion with God has to be an inner communion. Not outer. Not sensual. Spiritual.

Of course, it's cliché to say that God loves you. Or that God IS love. Or that to love God and love your neighbor are the two most important things. "Ho hum."

It's been said billions of times before, and everyone has heard it. All it does it make you go, "Ho hum."

But it's true! God is love. And to love God is the solution. So why isn't everyone doing it? Why isn't everyone living in God's love? And why doesn't everyone love God? And love each other? If it's all so simple, why isn't the world filled with love?! Therein lies the irony.

Because the message of love is cliché, and the world has heard it countless times, the world rejects it. It spews it right out. God is love. Ha! We know that already. Tell us something we don't know.

But, what I'm saying is that as many times as the world has heard—God is love—the world still does not know it.

---

[146] Ps. 139:7.

That's the thing. They've heard it. And they think they know it. But they don't know it, because they think they already do. So, the world goes right on like this, either rejecting it outright, or reinterpreting it. Which is the same as rejecting it.

Messiah is God. And God is love. The same yesterday, today, and forever. Messiah is with us always. But, as I discovered, it is true that Messiah "lives in me," only because, I, Gary Goldman, have become aware of this "I" which is the true Self, living in me.

And when that revelation came to me, this voice that said to me, "You are me," well, that is the revelation that comes on the iPath. But, I stress, it did not come of my choosing or by a decision I made. But by the grace of the One who is doing it and living it through me. Because the "me" is not the Gary Goldman me. The "me" is the Messiah who lives in Gary. That me is the me that I am. That me is the I am that I am.

The Word that Is Near To You:

Moses said to Israel, as recorded in the Torah, *"The word is near to you, it is in your mouth and in your heart."*[147] Shaul taught the same principle to the Gentiles.[148]

Nobody needs to go up to heaven to get it for us, nor go into the depths of the sea. Because the word is right here in the midst of us.

The bible itself testifies that the "Torah" or teaching of God, is upon your heart. That's just another way of saying God is upon your heart. Anybody may know that to be a fact or not. But either way, the value is not in knowing the fact that God is there. The value is in knowing the God who is there.

As a Rabbi by profession, I can testify to this: It is quite challenging as a Rabbi to tell people that the law is upon

---

[147] Deut. 30:14.
[148] Rom. 10:8.

their heart. Most want the Rabbi to teach them the law. "Teach us Torah," they say. "Tell us what it says. Show us how to apply it to our lives."

When God revealed Himself to Israel at Sinai, the people were so terrified, they told Moses, *"You speak to us and we will listen. But don't let God speak to us!"*[149]

So Moses gave them the written law, but the face-to-face communion with God, which Moses experienced daily, he could not give to Israel. It was as available to them as it was to Moses. He tried to tell them. The word is near to you, it's in your mouth and upon your heart...but they didn't want to hear that. Like a silly love song on the radio. Too simple. That's why they ended up instead with a complex law.

I can teach the law, and I can teach the New Testament, and I can show anyone how to apply it to life. But the value of it pales in comparison to the value of the revelation of Messiah. That is what it means to have the law within your heart. That is messianic consciousness. It is truly a transformation, and that is what Yeshua brought to the earth.

But the masses say, *"You speak to us and we will listen. But don't let God speak to us!"* They want to be told what God has said, and be instructed how to apply it to life. They don't want to be told that God is in their heart. And if someone rose from the dead to tell them that, then they still wouldn't be convinced.[150]

Messiah Yeshua, for example, rose from the dead. And the world has either rejected him outright, or reinterpreted him to fit their profile.

The Masses vs. The Narrow Gate:

In every generation, there is always a remnant, chosen by grace.[151] A remnant who aren't satisfied with a law written

---

[149] Ex. 20:19.
[150] Luke 16:31.
[151] Rom. 11:5.

on stone or parchment. They want more. They want to know this Spirit that lives in the "heart." And to walk with him. This walk is the iPath.

The scriptures are clear. The way is broad that leads to destruction and narrow that leads to life.[152] Yeshua told us to enter the narrow gate. So which one are you—the masses or the "narrow gate." The masses or the remnant?

If you are reading this book, I submit to you, that you are unlikely to be one among the masses. You probably are moved by God's grace, as I was, and are being drawn to the path that I am on. The iPath. And that's probably why you picked up this book. And why you read this far. Lots of people buy a book and never read past page three or four. You have. Why?

The people Israel, ended up with a complex law. One that they could not keep. And it made a big mess for them for generations to come. Because nobody could keep it.

Even though that very law testified to the simple truth that God is near to you, and dwells within your heart, that is not the message that the masses naturally want to hear.

Mankind searches the scriptures looking for the very Truth which is already written upon our hearts—but we just won't believe it. The scriptures themselves bear witness to this fact:

"You search the Scriptures because you suppose that in them you have eternal life. It is these that testify about Me. Yet you are unwilling to come to me that you may have life." [153]

Now I am not saying that one ought not to study the scriptures. God forbid! There is great value in learning the scriptures. I personally study them every day.

---

[152] *See*, Mat. 7:13.
[153] John 5:39-40.

Yet, we ought to know that people who become experts on the bible can still be, and often are, deluded. Just as the scripture says:

"Let no one deceive himself. If anyone thinks he is wise in this age, let him become a fool so he may become wise."[154]

My point is simply that bible knowledge and belief in that knowledge, in and of itself, does not bring someone to know God. Moreover, neither rites, rituals, sacraments, nor theological doctrines could ever transform a human being into a child of God.

So, when we read and study the scriptures, as I believe all people should, we ought to know first and foremost why we are doing it. For the Kingdom of heaven, which indeed one day will be established in the earth for the whole world to see plainly with open eyes, is at the very same time already right here in the midst of us. So, we ought to read scripture not for the acquisition of knowledge. But with the goal of entering into fellowship and communion with the Spirit of God.

For the very Kingdom which we seek in the scriptures is within us. And the scriptures tell us that. So we need to know not just what is written in the bible. Not just that Yeshua said, as he did: *"The Kingdom of God is within you,"*[155] but we need to actually know that Kingdom which is within us— for real. Not just know the fact that it is there. But know *it*.

But who wants to hear that the Kingdom of God is here, in the midst of us? If you do, it's only because the grace of God has put that on your heart. And if so, then it's only a matter of time. If you don't already, then soon you will know the Truth and that Truth will make you free.

Meanwhile, "Show us the Kingdom," that is what the masses are saying. It's akin to saying "Show us that you are

---

[154] 1 Cor. 3:19.
[155] Luke 17:21.

the Messiah. If you're the Messiah save yourself." Well, he did exactly that. But not on their terms. He rose from the dead. He did save himself, in a manner of speaking. And he did show that he is the Son of God. But that was only part of the message.

The world refuses to see the Rabbi's message in full. Not just that he is the Son of God. But that the Son of God is in each and every one of us. It's not just about *his* identity. It's about *our* identity. To wit, our identity in him. The image in which we were created.

It's easy to see that he's the Son of God. Can you also see that the same Spirit which raised him from the dead, lives in you? That same Spirit is crying, *"Abba, Father? For the Spirit himself bears witness with our Spirit that we are the children of God."*

The True Hope:

I am a Rabbi, so I know what kind of things people consider to be worth learning from me. And the one thing people want to know more than anything else is the most bizarre thing that they ever could want to know. But so it is. Above all other things, they want to know when this world will come to an end.

Therefore, they want the Rabbi to tell them the signs of the time. They want me to explain if the collapse of the stock market last month is a sign that the end is at hand. They want the Rabbi to explain the meaning of the mark of the beast in the book of Revelation. They want to know if there is going to be another war in Israel, and if this time Russia will get involved. Is this the fated battle of Gog and Magog?[156] Etc, etc.

Oh, how the people desire to hear their spiritual leader tell them that the end is at hand. Well, the coming of the Messiah and the Kingdom of God is indeed a certainty—one

---

[156] Ezekiel 38 and 39.

day. And I do think it is near. And I find it important to speak about it sometimes. But not much.

When it will happen, nobody knows for sure. Is it soon? I think so. Israel's rebirth is a sign to the world that the day is near. That's what I think anyway. But generally, I don't like to talk about it.

The reason I don't like to talk about the end of the world, and the return of the Messiah, is because it won't help anyone with real life issues today.

When, God forbid, you've lost your job, or been diagnosed with a fatal illness, or your marriage is broken, or you can't pay your rent or buy shoes for your children, or you're depressed, drug-addicted, or stuck in some cycle of some horrible sin, it won't do you any good to know that there are signs in the world saying that the end time is near.

It may be near. But how near? It may not happen in your lifetime. But even if it does, that is not the hope that the Messiah has given to the world. When things aren't going well in life, it's easy to put your hope in the end of this world, and the return of the Messiah. But that is not the hope of the good news of Messiah.

The hope which Messiah gave to the world is Himself. The hope is expressed most profoundly in these words: "*I am with you always, even to the end of the age.*"[157]

When you realize that the "I" of you is the "I" which Yeshua said is "with you always," then you are on the iPath. Then, you have your hope realized in the Messianic Kingdom which is right here in the midst of us. Not a tomorrow thing. But a thing that is without beginning or end. Which makes it a today thing. A now thing.

That does not deny that Yeshua is coming back. He is coming back for sure. And the whole world will see. And every knee will bow, and every tongue confess that He is the Lord.[158]

---

[157] Mat. 28:20.
[158] Phil. 2:10.

But what good does that do you today? If Messiah is already living in you then look to him and find him now. Don't look to a future date when he comes down from the sky with a legion of angels, riding in chariots. You and me may not be around to see it. And that is not our hope. Our hope is "Imanu-el" (God with us). Not God is coming. But God is here.

When Messiah is living in you already, then His return is kind of a moot point. Because Messiah's return is not your hope. Messiah in you is your hope.

Then, whether He returns today or tomorrow or a hundred years from now, you won't care. God will handle that. And you will be perfectly happy about it. You will then be a transparency for God, to help others live the life of "Messiah in them" even as you are already living the life of "Messiah in me."

But I know for a fact that the masses generally don't want to hear this. People want answers. They go to their Rabbi or Pastor or Priest for answers. They insist. They demand answers. They may have all faith and commitment to serve God, but the moment you tell them *"the Kingdom of God is within you,"* or any of that kind of stuff, you've lost them—unless the grace of God opens their spiritual ears to hear. As Yeshua said, *"My sheep hear my voice."*[159]

When Yeshua was faced with this same situation, he "compensated" for it by healing the sick and delivering people from oppression of every kind. In other words, because they could not embrace the message he brought, he imparted unto them the blessing which they would otherwise have if they were able to appropriate the gospel message for themselves.

If the world could grasp Messiah Yeshua's message of oneness with the Father through the Son, then there would be nothing left in the world to heal. His closest followers did, and they went forth doing the works he did, healing the sick, raising the dead.

---

[159] John 10:27.

Rest assured there is indeed a second coming of Messiah, a resurrection of the dead, and a final judgment. Don't believe anyone who says there isn't. There is. But we may not be the generation to see it. Or we may. Either way, how much does it matter right now?

When Yeshua returns, the whole earth will be filled with the knowledge of God. With messianic consciousness. There won't be any sickness, lack, sorrow, or even death. For the meantime we must understand that the afflictions and the sorrow of this world is due to our human ignorance of God. And you can't study and learn your way out of this problem.

Spiritual consciousness is the cure for mankind's ills, and this is what the Savior brought and brings. The higher we rise in consciousness, putting on the "mind of Messiah,"[160] bringing forth the true Self in whose image we were made, then the more we have fulfilment of the life Yeshua brought to the world.

Until that day when the perfect Son of God, Yeshua, returns to planet earth, filling the whole world with messianic consciousness, that is, the knowledge of the Lord, as the waters cover the sea.[161] So the earth once was in the day mankind was first created.

We have to understand that the steady path of God is a work of grace, and it has nothing to do with ceremonies, rites, or rituals. Although these things may have meaning and purpose in your community, as they do in mine. They are merely for corporate teaching and testimony.

What human beings need is not religious rites nor theological doctrines, but a restoration of consciousness. It is a restoration of what we once knew in Gan Eden. There we were busy eating the food of Life, before we started to partake of the consciousness of good and evil.

The way back to the tree of Life is already made available by Yeshua's sacrificial payment. The penalty of our peace was placed upon him. By his wounds we were healed.[162]

---

[160] 1 Cor. 2:16.
[161] Hab. 2:14, Is. 11:9.

199

Look to the fruit of that Tree which is eternal life. Yeshua made it clear he was going away, and would one day return. But he did not teach that his return was the hope of the world in the meantime. God is in the midst of us. A vine of Life, running through the garden. And our task is to abide in the vine today.

The Secret:

Yeshua came preaching the gospel of the Kingdom of God. And that message is a message of freedom. By now, billions of people have heard that message. But even though Yeshua has been hailed as Messiah by 2.2 billion today alone, his message to the world has largely been rejected. The fact remains, as he taught, that no one will come to their true Self, unless the Father draws them.[163]

In the year of my sabbatical, the Father was drawing me. Something was indeed happening. But I did not know what it was. A great mystery was being revealed to me. It is only now that I am beginning to try to share my story. Because it's hard to do. I'm still figuring it out.

I do know this: The secret which had remained hidden from the world since the most ancient days, and the mystery which Yeshua himself came to reveal to a remnant of his followers was being revealed to me. What secret?

There are clichés such as: Born of the Spirit. Filled with the Spirit. Baptized in the Spirit. Walking with God. Living for God. Saved. On Fire for God. I have used all of these expressions, too. I'm not saying they are wrong, or that we should stop using them necessarily.

I am saying, when certain language referencing the spiritual birth in Messiah becomes so cliché due to overuse, the meaning is lost. Much of the time I don't even know what the heck does any of this mean?

---

[162] Is. 53:5.
[163] John 6:44.

We are still feeling the effects of the tower of Babel. Unable to communicate clearly about matters of the Spirit, we resort to language coming out of the corporate world. It's all we have. But it's babel. It makes no sense. However, there is an ancient secret, revealed by the hand of the Lord to those that are drawn to him by grace.

To be clear, the secret is *not* God. The world knows now, and has known, in large part, that there is a God. It knows and believes that there is a Creator, of some kind, who reigns over all.

To know that God exists is not to know a mystery. It's plain and obvious. Of course, atheists don't believe it, but about 85-90% of the world believes there is a God of some kind or another. And they are right. But they don't know the secret.

The "secret" of which I speak is not that there is a God. The "secret" is *God in you.* As Shaul said, "*Messiah in you.*" Shaul said it was "the mystery" which he as a Jew, was sent unto the Gentiles to reveal.

> "*The mystery that was hidden for ages and generations, but now has been revealed to His kedoshim. God chose to make known to them this glorious mystery regarding the Gentiles—which is **Messiah in you**, the hope of glory!*"[164]

Now that secret is coming back to the ones who brought it to the Gentiles. Back to the Jews. So, I guess I was born for such a time as this. For I no more did anything to discover this secret than Shaul did, when he was on the road to Damascus. Not that I am comparing myself to him. Only making the comparison in the sense that this is a work of God. Not of man.

I did not know the secret until the secret was imparted unto me. The secret which Shaul called "*Messiah in you.*" The secret which I call "Messiah in me."

---

[164] Col. 1:26,27.

The result of Messiah in me, or Messiah in you, is messianic consciousness. Also known as "Christ consciousness." But there again, the world has been invaded by many clichés.

Although I am a perfectly normal and ordinary person, something extraordinary happened to me. And I guarantee you it can happen to you. I have been personally transformed. And you will be too. If it happens to you.

On the iPath, we are all walking together. And God is the one doing it. God in me. And God in you. If, indeed, you are being drawn. I suggest, maybe that's why you are reading this book. And nobody comes to the iPath unless the Father draws them.

So, I've now shared with you how, with the help of others, I came to the iPath to begin with. After the football season, after the Spirit said, *"You are me,"* and through that Winter, I was writing down my thoughts. I knew I was on the iPath. And that a change had occurred in me. But there was much more to come forth in Springtime. That is when this transformation, like everything else in Springtime, truly blossomed.

6

Sacred Ground

The Certified Letter:

One early March morning, as the sun came up, it must've been 6:30 a.m., I looked out my window, and there was Mother Theresa on the sidewalk by the side of my house. She was taking pictures of my lawn with her cell phone.

Within a week, I received a certified letter. I note, I have never received a certified letter bearing good news. People who send letters like that, always seem to be trying to strike fear in you.

This certified letter was from the Homeowner's Association, replete with photos attached. The letter stated that the condition of my lawn violated Rule 24, section 2, subparagraph b of the Homeowner's Code. The text of that particular rule was gratuitously included in bold print.

At first, I figured, it was no problem. Not for me anyway. As a renter, lawn maintenance is not my responsibility, but is taken care of by Tiffany Feingold-Spiegelman, as the landlord and house owner.

I did not anticipate a problem. I'd lived there for over ten years at this point. Everyone knows that a lawn must be re-sodded every once in a while. So, no big deal. I simply called Tiffany Feingold-Spiegelman, who had been copied on the letter from the Association, and she told me that her lawn man would take care of it.

So, Tiffany sent her lawn man, a guy named Jed, from her church—Sunny Lake Community megachurch—who also does the landscaping for them. He'd been cutting my yard for years. I did not know him, and rarely paid much attention to him.

Tiffany's lawn man, Jed, completely re-sodded my yard. However, by mid-May, it had been two months since fresh sod was laid. Yet, it was still totally brown, and showing zero signs of life.

It had not rained hardly at all during the last two months. We were officially in a drought. And due to the ·drought there were restrictions placed on watering one's lawn.

Nevertheless, the local water restrictions allowed anyone with fresh sod to water twice a day every day for the first thirty days. Which I did. But it didn't work. After that, watering was only permissible twice per week. Which I was doing. But at this point, it seemed obvious that it was not working. It was not going to bring this lawn back to life.

He Didn't Dig It Right:

"He didn't dig it right," said Larson, my next door neighbor. Practically every day for the last month, I heard this from Larson. And he typically added, "Would've been glad to show you how to do it. All you gotta do is ask."

Larson was a retired Midwesterner. One of the hoarde of folks who flock from the Great Lakes region down to the Gulf Coast of Florida. Most of the time, Larson reeked of marijuana.

Larson was neighborly, but in a proud way. He often boasted that he worked as a teenager in the very first Target store back in the 1960's. He then spent his days as an exec, working in the corporate offices in Minneapolis, before retiring to Florida.

Larson had long, blonde hair and a sweat band around his head. He spent his days working in the yard. I suppose that up in the frozen tundra of Minnesota they didn't have much opportunity for yard work. He certainly made up for it.

Whether tending to his vast array of shrubbery, or working on his near-perfect lawn, Larson seemed to always be out doing yard work. He obviously took great pride in his yard. Some people enjoy that kind of thing. I guess when you're retired, and stoned all the time, you've got to find something amusing to do.

But yardwork is not my thing. In any case, my lawn was already under contract by the owner, who had a service that took care of my lawn on a weekly basis. It wasn't my responsibility. But Larson didn't seem to accept this.

"You should've asked," he would say to me over and over again. "I gladly would have helped, but you didn't ask."

While plodding around in the yard, there was always music pouring out of Larson's garage. Always show tunes. Larson was awfully fond of show tunes. As a blonde, fair-skinned Swede, Larson clearly could have passed as a member of the Swedish pop band "Abba." And the soundtrack from *Mama Mia!* was one of Larson's favorites.

But Larson also seemed to like the old classics. On any given day, as Larson worked in his yard, many of the greatest hits of Broadway and the sounds of the Golden Age of Hollywood musicals could be heard blaring at high volume from a boom box located somewhere within his garage. It was like living next door to Ethel Merman.

So, with the sound of "There's No Business Like Show Business", or "Send in the Clowns," or "Oh, What a Beautiful Morning!" blasting at top volume from his garage, Larson made it a point each day to come over and tell me how the sod wasn't laid right. And that it wasn't going to grow. And he could've done the lawn for me, if only I'd asked. Etc, etc.

Then he'd go back to his yard work. And every once in a while, if you watched him, you might catch him acting out Judy Garland's part as "The Trolley Song," trumpeted from his garage. Or doing a disco number to "Dancing Queen." Or something like that.

In some ways, Larson was an annoyance. But I know he was a well-meaning neighbor. And I always heard him out, and treated him kindly.

The fact of the matter is, I tolerated Larson because, frankly, I felt pity for him. I knew that the hair on his head was a wig. Larson was a cancer patient. He was undergoing chemo. Which is probably the reason he was smoking weed all the time.

He told me that the doctor had only given him a year, maybe two. But he had already made it through two full years. I assume that he was in some pain, but so long as he could work in his lawn, he was going to keep doing it. And I admired that about Larson. He was a fighter.

Standing My Ground:

Tiffany's lawn man, Jed, who provided lawn care for her church, called his landscaping company "Confederate Lawns." The company slogan, painted boldly in italics on Jed's pick-up truck: *"Because your lawn is sacred ground."*

Jed referred to himself as "Tennessee Jed." I don't know why. I assume he may have been originally from Tennessee. I never asked. Jed was not the type of man that you would want to ask such questions. And I didn't much care to know anyway.

I just called him Jed. And though he reminded me a couple of times that folks called him "Tennessee Jed," I just wasn't gonna go there. And he seemed okay about it. In that regard, I think we had an understanding.

Apparently, when it comes to laying sod, Confederate Lawns offers a 10% discount to anyone who will agree to stick a miniature confederate flag into their front lawn, right next to the mailbox. Sort of a promotional scheme for the company. I actually had seen a few of those little flags in various re-sodded lawns throughout our neighborhood.

However, up until the time that my lawn needed to be re-sodded, I did not know that the flags were connected to Confederate Lawns. I just assumed these homeowners were proud southerners. Not unusual in our neighborhood. I didn't know about the connection to Confederate Lawns until the time came for my lawn to be re-sodded, and I was personally offered one of these flags by Tennessee Jed.

Now, I should say, as a Jewish-American, I am also a Southerner at heart, in the sense that I have lived my entire life residing upon Southern soil, in the deep South. This fact notwithstanding, I politely declined the flag when it was offered to me.

"You can't get the discount without the flag," said Jed.

"That's okay. I'm good," I replied.

"Ms. Feingold-Spiegelman told me I could give you one," he said, planting the little flag next to my mailbox. "That was part of our arrangement."

"Thank you," I said, pulling it out and handing it back to him. I was standing my ground on this. "I'm not interested."

"Yessir." Jed took the flag back. "No flag, no discount. Fine with me."

"You'll have to take that up with Ms. Feingold-Spiegelman," I said.

"I surely will," he said, spitting a long, brown, chewing-tobacco-induced spit onto the pavement of the sidewalk.

In all the previous years that Confederate Lawns had been moving my lawn, I had never before had any problem with Jed. I had always accepted the honor of having my lawn mowed by "The Robert E. Lee," a riding mower which bore the Stars and Bars painted nicely onto its hood. But putting a confederate flag into my lawn was simply going too far.

Would I have hired Confederate Lawns to begin with? Probably not. But, as the tenant, with lawn care not being my responsibility, per the lease it was not my choice. And, frankly, I really didn't care who cut my lawn. As long as they did the job, and left me alone.

Hence, I was perfectly content to have my lawn manicured and cared for by a self-described secessionist. Because as long as he was mowing my lawn, it didn't matter to me what his views were on State's Rights, the Tenth Amendment, or the downside of belonging to the Union. And in any case, the opportunity to converse was rarely present. And I preferred to keep it that way.

The iPath

Over the years, once in a while, if pressed into a conversation with Jed, I would have to oblige. I wouldn't want to be rude. But I otherwise generally kept my distance.

Because, for one thing, Jed liked to bend a person's ear if given the chance. He was a talker, but not a listener. Conversations with Jed were mainly monologues, a one-way street, with him doing all the talking. And usually something having to do with politics.

Furthermore, Jed talked real slow. And he didn't ask questions. He simply talked. Like he knew something the rest of the world did not yet know, but needed to know.

Jed never looked at you when he talked. Other than a quick, periodic glance back at you, Jed always spoke as if he was talking to someone else. Someone out there in the trees, up in the sky, or across the street perhaps. But not you. Even though, it clearly was you that he was talking to.

I greatly preferred not to be drawn into these one-way diatribes with Jed. In fact, before this whole matter arose with my lawn needing to be re-sodded, I could count on one hand the number of times I had conversed with Jed. Otherwise, as long as I kept my distance, Jed did his work. And I ignored him. In this manner, things were fine.

But when this need arose for my lawn to be re-sodded, Jed was working in my yard for several days. During this time, I decided to stay home and work from there. Call me paranoid, or whatever, I simply was not comfortable with Jed being around while my wife or kids were at home. She is home on the weekends, and also in the afternoons when the kids are out of school. I did not want Jed engaging Laura or my kids in any of his political monologues.

Accordingly, I gave Laura specific instructions to stay inside and keep to herself. I even made sure that her car was parked in the garage, so that whenever she got in the car or returned home, she would not be out in the driveway, exposed to a possible conversation, or monologue, from Tennessee Jed. Laura felt I was overreacting. But I don't think so.

At this time, I worked in the house and stayed busy going through my notes, and drafting on my laptop. However, with Jed in my yard each day for about a week, my ability to keep him at a distance and avoid conversation with him was greatly challenged.

The situation was particularly complicated by the fact that I made the mistake of offering, without considering the potential consequences, to bring Jed a cold bottle of water several times during the course of the day.

I definitely found it strange that Jed did not bring his own water. It can be quite hot working in the sun in Florida, even in March. However, having noticed that he had no water, I offered to bring him a cold bottle of water, as needed.

I made this gesture for several reasons. One, in order to be kind. Jed was clearly bothered by the fact that I refused to plant the miniature confederate flag in my yard by the mailbox. I felt that some cold water might help smooth things over with him.

But to be honest, a secondary concern, or maybe actually my primary concern, was I did not want to leave open the possibility that Jed might come knocking on my door for water. In fact, call me paranoid, but I even suspected that might be the very reason that Jed did not bring his own water.

I had no inclination to have Tennessee Jed come inside my home, wherein, once he started talking I would surely be challenged to get him back out the door. I therefore came up with the idea of offering to bring him a cold bottle of water, as needed. This was offered as sort of the lesser of two evils.

A World Gone to Hell:

Consequently, on day one, as Jed was busy at work, I brought Jed that first cold bottle of water. I had hoped to hand him the bottle and walk off. But to no avail. When he saw me coming, he turned off the rototiller machine that he was using to dig up the soil. He accepted the water, and then started talking.

Without provocation, and without any concern about relevance, Jed particularly liked to talk about what he felt were the "real" issues that led to the civil war. In that regard, he started in on one of his rants.

"Industrialism, banks, railroads. That was always the issue," said Jed. "Just look at the world today. It's a world gone to hell."

Tennessee Jed spat on the ground a big brownish stream of spit, coming from the giant wad of chewing tobacco in his cheek. I wondered if or how he was going to drink the water with that wad in his mouth. But the chew was no obstacle for him. He took a big gulp of water, then wiped his lips with the palm of his bare right hand. Then he went right on:

"It's the land that's sacred, my friend. The soil. The very stuff upon which our feet stand. That's what we were fighting for."

I nodded. Cleared my throat. Jed continued:

"That's why they want to take away our muskets," said Jed. He stared me down, right into the eyes, as if gauging what, if any, response I might have.

"Muskets?" I responded.

Jed spit, and then wiped spit from his chin on the back of his right hand. He shook his head in the negative.

"You ever heard of something called the right to bear arms?"

"I've got a firearm in the house," I said. "Several of them. Shotguns, handguns, rifles."

"Dang," he said. "I didn't figure you for a gun owner."

I smiled proudly. Of course, I was greatly exaggerating. I only had one firearm. A Beretta, nine millimeter. But I felt it wise to let Jed think there was an entire armory in my home.

With a flip of his right index finger, Jed expelled the wad of chew from his cheek. And I thought to myself, I'd have to remember not to shake that hand. Ever.

"You ever killed a man?" asked Jed.

"Uh, no. Can't say that I have."

"Yeah," he said. He pulled a stray piece of chewing tobacco out of his mouth and took another chug of water. "That's about what I figured."

"Hey," I said, "I got work to do, so—"

"The problem," Jed continued, "is that we don't know who we are anymore. You see what I'm saying?"

"Yeah. I think I know what you mean."

"We're disconnected from the land. Disembodied. Dis—, uh, dis—?"

"Dismembered?" I said. I wish I hadn't. But somehow I did.

Jed's eyes got real bright.

"Listen to you." With a thud, he spat another stray piece of chew out of his mouth. "Dis-friggin-membered." He slapped me on the shoulder. "I like you." He laughed. "Hell yeah, I do."

"Alright," I said, taking a couple of steps toward the house. "I gotta get back to work in there,"

"A man's gotta work," he said, with a disappointed look. "Thanks for the water, good buddy."

I gave Jed the thumbs up. But somehow I felt he wasn't finished with his speech. Unfortunately, I was correct.

"This country is totally lost. Out of touch with our God. And don't know who we are or what we are no more. Or why God made us a nation to begin with."

"I hear ya," I said, turning toward my front door, and hoping he'd get back to work. But even as I walked away, and with my back to him, Jed continued.

"It's the land, my friend. The land! That's what America is." Out of courtesy, I stopped and looked back toward him. Jed reached down and picked up a handful of dirt.

"The land!" he shouted. "God gave this land to our fathers. And the friggin' People's Republic of California, and the dadgum liberal Northeast establishment, well, they ain't never gonna understand that." He tossed the dirt back on the ground.

"I'm gonna be inside for a while, so I'll see ya tomorrow, I guess." I said, walking toward the door. But Jed wasn't finished.

"They think they're running this country. But I tell you what. They don't know nothing. They can take their factories, and their cannons, and go straight to hell. Cause one thing's for damn sure. Ain't nobody, and I mean, nobody, ever gonna take me at the point of no bayonet. As God is my witness. Nobody. Or, they gonna die trying. I tell you that much."

On that note, Jed pulled the starter cord on the rototiller and got back to his duties of turning the soil. Thank God. So, I went back inside.

A Quick Rant About Politics:

I try not to judge people based on their political views, and I don't want anyone to judge me either. I think every person has to have some idea of whatever they believe would make the world a better place. And how the world ought to govern itself. I try to respect that. Because it's only human to have opinions about such things.

As much as we may focus on the Kingdom of God, unseen with human eyes, we are all nevertheless touched by what happens in this world. Everyone therefore has to have political opinions, one way or another. I have mine, too. So I feel I should put this out there, not because I am trying to sway anyone on political issues, but simply because it's part of my story.

Politically, I definitely see myself as a conservative. But I also feel that conservatism is not always what other so-called conservatives think it is. Nor what non-conservatives may think. I think there's a lot of confusion over these labels.

So, first and foremost, let me just say I believe in individual freedom, above all. Therefore, politically, I want to see limited government, and individual freedom emphasized. Why people wouldn't want freedom, and would prefer more government, I don't know. To me, individual freedom is the main thing. And government is a necessary evil. The reason people created government in the first place is to uphold individual freedom.

To me, ideally, politics should be about liberty. I always think of the scripture which says, *"Where the Spirit of the Lord is, there is Liberty."*[165] Government should never be a means to impose the values of one group of people upon others. But it should be about ensuring that all people have the means to live freely.

Secondly, I want to live in a country that supports Israel. Yes, I think the scripture is plain—the nation that blesses Israel will be blessed.

But whatever I believe, politically, I am committed to extend the courtesy of respect toward other human beings, who may see things differently. That commitment, however, is particularly difficult to maintain toward people who refuse to extend the same courtesy of respect toward me.

<u>A Question of Law</u>:

We are all originally made in the image of God. I try to recognize this in all human beings. But I found that to be a challenge in the case of Jed.

Although he didn't seem to understand that military technology had long since moved beyond cannons and muskets fixed with bayonets, that was not the problem I had with Jed.

I was willing to grant that, perhaps, Jed referred to such military relics for some symbolic purpose. Or maybe he really just remained oblivious. Frankly, I'm not sure which. In any case, I had no issue with Jed about that.

Accordingly, there was something about Jed which caused me to feel that he just might do something totally out-of-the-box one day in furtherance of his belief that his political principles were God-ordained.

---

[165] 2 Cor. 3:17

Indeed, I worried that one day Jed's frustration with the liberal Northeast establishment might just take precedence over sanity and civility. And that he might very well decide that his purpose in life, his raison d'être, was to personally rectify all that which, in his view, has gone wrong in America.

I think that people who mix fanatic religious beliefs with extremist politics, are dangerous to civilization. Whether we're talking about Islamic terror, or angry, fanatical white people in America. Jews, historically, have been hated by both types. From our point of view the ideology may be entirely different. But there is always a danger with fanatics. Because fanatics operate under a presumption of self-righteousness. Fanatics lack respect.

Jed struck me as a fanatic. In any case, for the time being, so long as Tennessee Jed focused on fixing my dead lawn, I was content to give him that occasional bottle of cold water. But always with the hope that I would not have to listen to him speak his peace about what had gone wrong in America.

Yet, I found that Jed was not easily quieted. As much as I tried to avoid it, through my body language and/or excuses about being too busy to chat, every bottle of water resulted in another political monologue from Jed.

At first I refrained from vocalizing my disapproval. Was it my compassion for what seemed to be a twisted and confused soul? Or was it my concern that this twisted and confused soul might not respond in a proper, civilized manner to my disapproval? Probably the latter.

It took Jed about a week to finish the job of re-sodding my lawn. The problem was, two months later, the fresh sod was all brown.

As a result, I received a letter from the homeowner's association, warning that if I did not get my yard fixed within thirty days, I would be subject to legal action by the association. Immediately, I contacted Tiffany Feingold-Spiegelman, and she said she'd come by to take a look and to talk about it.

I peeked out of the front window, and saw a Mercedes sport utility in front of my house. Tiffany was standing on the sidewalk, speaking on her cell phone. I proceeded out the front door. Catching a glimpse of me, she took the call off speaker and held it up to her ear.

"Ok, I'll tell him," she said into the cell phone. "No I won't. I said, I wouldn't and I won't. Okay? I said, I will tell him. Gotta go. Love ya."

She ended the call.

"That was Murray," said Tiffany. "My husband is a lawyer, as you know."

"Right."

Her insanely high heels clicked as she took a few paces along the sidewalk, perusing the yard. She then proceeded to take a few photos of my brown lawn with her phone.

At that moment, I glanced into the car. The window was down. I noticed that Andy Feingold was sitting in the passenger seat. He nodded, and gave me a salute.

"Hey Coach," said Andy.

Tiffany stopped and turned back toward me. At that point, there was a long pause, as we both looked out at the horrible condition of the lawn. Tiffany took a few more clicks along the sidewalk.

"Can you believe this?" I said.

With hands on her hips, she shook her head negatively. Her tone and her countenance had now clearly indicated that she was not taking my side on this.

"Okay. Here's the deal," she said. "You didn't water it properly."

"Not true," I responded. "I watered it as often as the local ordinance allows."

"You got any proof?" she asked.

"What kind of proof?"

"Pictures? Videos?" she retorted, smacking on a wad of bubble gum.

"Who takes pictures of their automatic sprinkler system watering their lawn at 4 am?" I said.

A bubble popped.

"People who don't want to get sued when their grass dies. That's who."

Tiffany was now pacing up and down the sidewalk, hands on hips.

I said, "That confederate lawn man, Tennessee Jed, didn't prep the lawn properly before laying the sod."

"You got any proof?" retorted Tiffany.

"You can tell by looking at it. It sits too high. And he left too much grass and weeds underneath the sod."

"Oh yeah. Says who?"

"Just ask Larson, my neighbor." I pointed over to Larson, who was out in his lawn, trimming his shrubbery to the sound of Liza Minelli singing "Caberet."

"That guy? I don't think so."

"Yeah. Larson knows a thing or two."

"Hey, listen, I already paid Jed. And I'm not paying him again to fix this problem. My husband won't let me. He says it's a matter of principle."

"But it's not my responsibility."

"My husband says it is."

"He's wrong."

"Look, I don't know all the legalities on these things. But if Murray says you gotta fix this lawn, then you gotta fix the lawn."

"I can't afford it," I said.

"I'm sorry," said Tiffany. "The homeowner's association is threatening to sue me, and Murray says, if they do, then I am going to have to sue you as a third party."

"Can't you just talk to Theresa? She's the one who made the complaint."

"Theresa is my prayer partner. So please don't trash-talk Theresa."

"I'm not trash-talking her. I'm just saying she's the one who complained. She's constantly on my case with her petty little complaints to the homeowner's association."

"You've got a completely brown lawn here, bud. This is not petty. And it's not Theresa's fault your lawn is brown."

216

"No, it's the fault of that wacko lawn man that you sent over here." I said. Then I let out a deep sigh.

"Jed attends my church. He's been doing our church landscaping for years. No one's ever complained about him."

"I guess that makes me the first, then," I said.

"Look, I don't want to stand here and listen to negative talk about other people," she said. "You've been a good tenant. You pay the rent on time. You're a decent guy. You won the championship in football. And my kid really likes you. But the Homeowner's Association is not backing off. My husband says you're the one in breach. He tells me I'm not to pay for new sod. And believe me, you don't want Murray to file suit against you. But he'll do it if we have to. He wants me to sell this house anyway. So, if you don't want your family evicted, you need to take care of this."

"You would evict me over a brown lawn?"

"Just get it fixed. If you do that, everything's cool. Like it never happened. Otherwise, you leave me no choice."

With that she clicked her way back to her Mercedes sport utility. As she did, Andy leaned out the passenger side.

"Hey, Coach," said Andy.

"Yeah," I said, as I walked right up to the passenger side window.

"Let me give you a name."

"Okay," I said.

"The lawn doctor."

"The lawn doctor?" I asked, as Tiffany started the vehicle. Tiffany heard me.

"You think Jed is a wacko," she said. "Hah. Wait'll you meet the lawn doctor."

"Just google search it," said Andy.

The Mercedes pulled away. And I began to weigh it all out in my head. What to do? All the varying possibilities began racing through my mind. It's a question of law. But not God's law. Man's law. And while God's law is always right, with man's law, it's not so easy to put your finger on what is going to happen.

The iPath

On the one hand, I could hire an attorney and duke it out. I strongly believed that I would win in court. I am quite certain that whatever the true cause of the brown grass, the condition of the lawn was ultimately the landlord's responsibility, not mine.

Could they really prove that I didn't water it properly? Not a chance. Did it even matter? I doubt it very much. I went back and read the lease, and it states clearly that the condition of the lawn is the responsibility of the landlord. Not the tenant.

However, even when the law is on your side, you still have to go to court in order to get justice. And that can be a long and winding road. And an expensive one. Especially when dealing with people who don't mind litigating because their husband happens to be a lawyer.

I felt confident that the terms of the lease would exonerate me from responsibility for the brown lawn. But if not, I could still prove that the browning of the grass was not my fault. I am sure that Jed did not lay the sod correctly, and I am sure that I could prove it if I had to. Maybe put an expert on the stand. Of course, I'd have to find a lawn expert, and pay him to testify. And that would be expensive too.

I figured a total re-sod would cost me about $5,000.00. Money I really did not have. However, even though I felt my case was strong, it would cost more than five grand to hire a lawyer, an expert witness, and litigate in court. Not to mention the time involved. And no guarantee winning. I did not want to risk a face-off with Murray Spiegelman in court.

My biggest concern was that if I went to court over this, Tiffany would resent me about it. If I somehow kicked her husband's butt in court, I'd have a new lawn at her expense. But she most certainly would not renew the lease with me again at the end of the year. In that sense, even a win would be a loss.

After going through all the possibilities in my mind, I came to the conclusion that litigation was not an option. There was but one thing to do—talk to Tennessee Jed. He

218

was the real culprit here. Tennessee Jed needed to have a "come to Jesus" moment.

I knew in my heart that Larson was right, Jed did not lay the sod properly. The grass was dead because of Jed's laziness and sloppiness in failing to prepare the surface. Maybe if he'd pay more attention to laying sod instead of the causes of the civil war. Anyway, I decided to confront him about it, in love, of course.

Dug In:

I contacted Jed by phone and invited him to come and look at the condition of the lawn, and give me a quote on how much it would cost to fix it. Of course, I had no intention of paying him to fix it, but I felt like if I could confront Jed in person, I might be able to persuade him to see that the condition of the lawn was attributable to his own incompetent work.

So, Jed came right over and as expected, he said that a total re-sod was needed.

"It's totally dead," said Tennessee Jed. "No chance of saving this lawn. I'll do a total re-sod for $5,000.00. That's with no discount. $4,500.00, if you take the flag."

I then went on to try and explain, in all kindness and reasonableness, that the brown lawn was Jed's fault. And that, therefore, Confederate Lawns needed to fix it at their own expense. Not surprisingly, Jed did not take it well.

"You didn't water it correctly," said Jed in his defense.

"Yes, I did."

"If you watered it right, it wouldn't be dead," insisted Jed.

"It was sloppy work, Jed. Legally, you've got to re-do this lawn, and I am not paying a dime for it."

"You're dreaming, buddy. And I ain't taking no orders from no greedy, Jewish, Yankee-sympathizer," he responded.

I do try not be offended by ignorant people. But I was really bothered by this statement. Not just because I am Jewish, and the statement was anti-semitic. I've been hearing anti-semitic remarks all my life. You learn not to let it bother you. But I am not a Yankee-sympathizer. My family moved to the South when I was three years old. I grew up in the South. So, if we did live in a universe where it even mattered, how does being Jewish automatically make me a Yankee-sympathizer?

This had nothing to do with politics. Nor with nationality. Nor was it about the Yankees vs. the Rebels. It was simply about a brown lawn. My lawn. I needed my lawn to be green. But it wasn't. It was brown. And it was Jed's fault.

I love the South. I really do. But, as I saw it, whether one believes that the South might rise again, or not, it still would not change the color of my lawn. My lawn was brown and nearly dead. I wanted my brown lawn to be green and full of life. Like Larson's. And not at my expense.

But Tennessee Jed was dug in tighter than tick on a hound dog. He would not be moved. After all, he was not in a contractual relationship with me. He was hired by Tiffany, and as far as she was concerned, his job was done. The fact that I felt differently about it didn't mean anything to him, since he wasn't really working for me. And I didn't care whether she was getting a discount or not—I wasn't putting one of those flags in my lawn.

Anyway, what are the legal rules on sod failure? Does anyone really know? Does a man purchase sod at his own risk? Or does the sod-layer bear the risk? Whose responsibility is it when the sod does not work, when the grass does not turn green and stay green? Is brown sod an inherent risk? Or is it Confederate Lawns' duty to provide a healthy, green lawn?

These are the kind of pressing questions in life for which no one really has hard answers. Which is the reason why the world so often turns to lawyers to solve its problems. Which, of course, is really no solution at all.

"So, what would you have me do?" I asked.

"The way I figure it, well, it's kinda like what you get when an elephant mates with a rhinocerous."

"What?"

"Ele-fino," he said with a shrug. "Heh, heh, heh..."

Can't believe I fell for that one. I heard that stupid joke when I was ten years old. And now I was getting upset.

"You need to make this right," I said.

"My work is done, son. We don't guarantee our grass against death. It ain't life insurance, ya know," responded Jed.

That's when Larson came over.

"You didn't dig it properly," said Larson.

"Whose this guy? A gay Bjorn Borg?"

Admittedly, Larson, with his head band and long hair in the back, actually did look a bit like Bjorn Borg.

"I watched you do it," said Larson. "Shoddy workmanship. Just look at it. It sits too high. You must first remove the old grass completely. Otherwise, the roots can't sink into the soil."

At that point, Jed got into the driver seat of his truck. But just before he drove off into the sunset, he rolled down his window.

"Why don't you just get one of your lawyer friends to sue me. Ain't that what y'all people do?" He spat out the window and nearly hit me.

Going to court over dead grass didn't seem like the smart thing nor the right thing. Yet, surely if I didn't get that grass green again, it would be me getting served with a lawsuit by the homeowner's association. I had a real mess on my hands...so that's when I remembered what Andy had said to me from the car.

So, as Andy had suggested, I went inside my house, and google searched "The lawn doctor." I got the number, and made the call. He arrived the next morning, first thing.

7

The Sound of Life

The Lawn Doctor:

The monogram embroidered onto a patch on the right side of his shirt said "Carlos." He looked to be early 50's in age. Dark hair, tan, and he wore a mustache that was thicker than the average man could grow.

Carlos was my new lawn man. He did not like to be called a lawn man.

"Lawn *doctor*," he said, correcting me when I mistakenly told him how pleased I was to have him as my new lawn man. He pointed me to the title embroidered onto the patch on the left side of his shirt, which stated "The Lawn Doctor."

Seemed odd. But our last lawn man was neither a lawn doctor nor much of a lawn man either. I had an urgent situation on my hands. And I needed someone good. So I was open to find out if the lawn doctor could live up to the name.

"Mucho gusto, Carlos," I said, showing off my skill with the Spanish tongue.

He looked at me, puzzled.

"What do ya think, every lawn man speaks Spanish?"

Surprised, and a little bit embarrassed, I said, "Uh, no, but with a name like Carlos, I just figured—"

"It's Feldman. Carlos Feldman."

"Feldman? Jewish, huh?"

"Yep," he said.

"That actually makes two of us," I said, extending a hand. "I'm Goldman. Gary Goldman. He shook my hand.

"L'khayim," he said. "Actually, just kidding ya. I do speak Spanish. Ladino really."

"You're Sephardic?"

"My mother. She was born in Portugal. My father was born in the States."

"Where are you from?"

"I'm from forever," he said. "When you come from forever, you can be everywhere."

"I've heard that before. C'mon, seriously."

"Well, I'm mainly from Israel. My parents were both olim[166], met in Israel. I'm a sabra, born in the land. Raised there. But I've traveled the whole world. And not too long ago, I came here. And for right now, I am the lawn doctor."

"I guess your mother must be proud. I mean you being a doctor and all. I know how Jewish mothers are," I said.

His blank expression indicated that he did not seem to find humor in my remark.

"My mother's dead," said the lawn doctor.

The Diagnosis:

"Okay, Mr., or I guess I should say, *Dr.* Feldman," I guess we may as well get on with the diagnosis, huh?"

"Good idea, Goldman," he said sternly.

"So, anyway, as you can see, I've got this brown sod here. And I'm quite sure it's dead."

"It wasn't dug properly," said Dr. Feldman, most confidently.

"Yeah. Well, I've heard that," I said.

Carlos got down on his hands and knees, and started pulling at it. He tore a piece of brown grass, looked at it, and tossed it up into the breeze.

I had no idea what this ritual was all about. But then he put his ear to the ground. A smile came to the corner of his mouth. Very slight, but I distinctly noticed it. He nodded in the affirmative.

---

[166] Jews who immigrate to Israel from other nations.

"Not dead," said Carlos. "Only sleeping." He brushed off his hands. Smiled. "You're gonna be okay, my friend."

I would've liked to believe the lawn doctor's diagnosis. I would have been overjoyed to know that somewhere, somehow, the mystery of life still lay quietly hidden beneath my lawn. But the lawn was brown and brittle as toothpicks. I was not buying it.

"Hard to believe," I said.

"Believe it," said the doc.

"All appearance is to the contrary."

He scoffed at my remark.

"Hah. Did you see that!" he pointed excitedly to a tree a few yards away, where a squirrel seemed to run head first into the tree.

"The squirrel?"

"Of course the squirrel," he said. "He ran right into that tree."

"Why does it matter?" I said.

"Look closer," said the lawn doctor. Do you see something in that squirrel's hand?"

I looked closer, and yeah, I did see something.

"He's got an acorn," I said.

"Well, there's your answer, Goldman."

I looked around. Larson was out there, trimming the hedges to the voice of Judy Garland singing, "Meet Me in St. Louis" at top volume.

I thought to myself that the lawn doctor must have some point. But it was a mystery to me.

"I'm not following you," I said.

"He's blind!" laughed, the Jewish lawn man.

"Blind? How can you tell?"

"He ran head first into that tree."

Okay, I thought to myself. So the squirrel is blind. What this might have to do with my lawn being dead or sleeping or whatever, was still escaping me.

Dr. Feldman continued, "How do ya think he got that nut?"

"Beats me," I said.

He looked deep into my eyes. "Listen to me," he said.

I waited. He didn't say anything.

"Okay," I said.

"You aren't listening."

"Yes, I am." He seemed to stare a little deeper at this point. "I am listening," I insisted.

"I want to tell you something really amazing," said the lawn doctor.

"Okay. Lay it on me." I said, his eyes still fixated within mine.

"Even a blind squirrel finds a nut once in a while." He paused for a moment. Then he broke out in hysterical laughing.

"Uh-huh," I sighed in frustration. I don't know if he was serious or joking. But I saw neither wisdom nor humor in this.

I had a dead lawn. I have lots of squirrels in my lawn. Was this one really blind? If I could have given that squirrel a vision test, I might have done it. Of course, Feldman was trying to make a point. And I sensed that he was trying to impart some wisdom to me. But I wasn't interested in the kind of wisdom that involves silly clichés about blind rodents.

I needed by lawn healed! But typically, for situations to be healed, someone needs to get to the root of the problem. And the root of the problem is something the lawn doctor understood much better than me.

Asking the Right Question:

Now, as he continued laughing, presumably about the blind squirrel, I folded my arms across my chest and watched Dr. Feldman rifle through his tool box in his van.

"You're mocking me, aren't you? " I said.

"No, no," Feldman responded, "Don't take it personal, Goldman. I don't mean it that way."

"I see."

"Because you say, 'I see,' you are blind. And you don't know who I am."

I was stunned by that. Not just because it seemed to come totally out of left field. But, moreover, I wasn't expecting Feldman to be the kind of guy to quote a bible scripture. Especially not New Testament. Jewish followers of Yeshua are growing in number, and they seem to spring up in the strangest of places.

"I don't know who you are?" I said.

"No. You don't know who I am?" responded Feldman.

"Ok. Who are you, then?" I said.

"Wrong question," said Feldman. "The question should not be who are *you*? The question should be who am *I*?"

"Isn't that what I asked?"

"That's what you think you asked."

"Well, then, you're right. I don't see," I said.

"That's what I said, isn't it?" said Feldman.

I uncrossed my arms and let out a big sigh. I re-crossed them. Then stood there, paused, quietly staring at Dr. Feldman. He was smiling, like he knew he'd made his point.

"I don't know what you're talking about," I said.

"You don't see, because you don't know. And you don't know because you don't believe who *I* am. If you believed in my words, then you would know who *I* am."

"Why don't you just tell me plainly who you are?"

"If I tell you earthly things, and you don't believe, how will you believe if I tell you universal things?"[167] said Feldman.

Exasperated, I said. "Okay, I get it. I'm the blind squirrel, right?"

"You are from below. I am from above. You belong to this world. I do not.[168]"

At this point, the lawn doctor located and selected his tool. A metal rod, about four feet in length, with a cross bar at the top that formed two handles. Like a golfer deciding

---

[167] John 3:12.
[168] John 8:23.

upon just the right club, the lawn doctor took the rod in hand with confidence.

He turned to me and said, "Listen, my friend, that squirrel found a nut and he can't see a thing. How did he do it?"

"I don't know. Luck, I guess."

"You believe in luck?"

I had to think for a moment.

"Not really," I said.

"Good. Because there's no such thing," said the Doc.

"Well, he must have like a sixth sense or something."

Dr. Feldman put his hand on my shoulder.

"You mean he can see without using his eyes?"

"I guess so." I shrugged.

"How 'bout that?"

I didn't like this illustration. I was starting to see that, in it, I was the blind squirrel. I didn't like being the blind squirrel. But Feldman had a point. This idea of seeing without using the eyes, seemed important to me. In fact, it connected with me.

"So what is the blind squirrel supposed to do when he finds the nut?" I blurted out.

Feldman found that question quite amusing. He laughed so loud it even caught Larson's attention. He must've heard it, even over the blaring sound of "Singing in the Rain," as he stopped trimming for a moment and looked over toward us.

"He's supposed to eat it," said Feldman. "What else can you do with a nut?"

At this point, Feldman took his rod and inserted it into the ground, about a foot deep. He put each of his hands on the handles, and started twisting and turning the rod.

On the end of the rod, just above the handles, the rod was open. After he twisted and turned several times, he put his ear up to the opening. Then he motioned to me.

"Put your ear right there."

I politely declined. But he insisted.

"What are you chicken or something?" he said. "C'mon, put your ear right up there like this."

"Ok." So as not to be rude, I went along with it.

"You hear that?" said Feldman.

I shook my head in the negative. I didn't hear anything. Maybe I was too distracted by Larson's dancing. But not just his dancing. I was concerned that Larson might be watching this charade. Which I likely would have to address with him at a later date, when the inevitable, neighborly discussion about my lawn would ensue.

Do You Hear What I Hear?:

"Try again," said Feldman.

I looked over at Larson, who I now knew for sure had definitely taken an interest in what was going on.

"Don't worry about that guy," said the lawn doctor.

So, with "Singing in the Rain," playing in the background, and the lawn doctor urging me to listen to my lawn, I agreed to give it another try.

"Listen a little closer this time," said Feldman.

This time, I did hear something. As I put my ear up to that little opening in Doc Feldman's divining rod—or whatever it was—I heard a sound that I can only describe as something like a stream or a brook running down the side of a mountain. I was familiar with that sound. It was like the sound of a mountain stream.

I often go hiking in the Appalachian mountains, in Virginia. I very much enjoy sitting by the bank of a mountain stream, listening to that beautiful sound of water trickling down the mountain, over the rocks. The sound I heard through Feldman's rod reminded me of that.

"You hear it, don't you?" he said.

"Yeah. I do."

"What do you hear?"

"It sounds like running water. Like a stream or something."

He slapped his thigh.

"Exactly. Now do you see?"

"See what? All I see is dead grass."

"No. Listen again, Goldman."

I listened again.

"Same sound," I said.

"It's the sound of life!" He grasped me by the shoulders. "You got life down there!"

I stepped back, out of the lawn doctor's grasp. I still wasn't buying it.

No doubt, by now, I knew that Carlos Feldman, the Israeli-born Jewish lawn man, was, shall we say, not normal? Of course, I suspected it right away. There was something extraordinary about Doctor Feldman.

But that didn't change everything. You see, my overriding concern was with the condition of my lawn. Not whether or not my lawn man—excuse me, lawn *doctor*— might hold the key to all the secrets of the universe.

Bear in mind, I was still nursing battle wounds from my experience with Confederate Lawns. And I was super aggravated because Mother Theresa had turned me in to the Homeowner's Association for the crime of having a brown lawn. And I was concerned about being sued by Murray Spiegelman on behalf of Tiffany Feingold-Spiegelman.

My worries and concerns over lawsuits and the possibility of losing our home overrode whatever enthusiasm I might otherwise have had about Feldman's good news. The thing is, I simply was not open to the idea that the sound of life could be ascertained audibly through a metal rod inserted into my yard.

Hence, even though I had clearly heard the sound of running water hidden beneath my lawn, I didn't accept it. Because, at that moment, I remained focused on my problem, and thus resorted to skepticism. Wouldn't you?

"Maybe it's the underground plumbing," I said to Feldman. "There's pipes running all underneath this lawn, ya know?"

Feldman walked away from me, toward his van, and mumbled: "Underground plumbing, he says."

It was clear to me that Feldman was packing up his van as if preparing to leave.

"You're not leaving, are you?" I said.

"Yeah."

"What about my lawn?"

"What about it?"

"You said there was life down there, didn't you?" I argued.

"There's life everywhere, my friend," said the doctor.

"Can you fix my lawn or not?"

"No," said Feldman.

I shook my head in frustration, and put my hands over my face in consternation.

"There's nothing you can do?"

"Nope," said Feldman. "I can't do anything. But you can."

"Tell me," I said.

"Are you willing to listen?"

"I'm pretty desperate actually, so yeah."

"You got a place we can talk. A back porch or something?"

"C'mon. I'll show you." Feldman followed me around back of the house.

My Back Porch:

Practically every home in Florida has what's called a "lanai," which is a screened-in area behind the house, sometimes with a pool, or as in my case, just a back porch area. It's a place where you can have backyard BBQ's, or just sit and watch the sunset. And thanks to the screen, the bugs cannot get to you.

I opened the screen door connecting to the back porch, and let the lawn doctor in first. I heard the screen door slam behind me.

"Perfect," said Feldman. He seemed impressed. I had no idea why. But I felt relieved.

"We're good then?" I queried.

"We'll have life back in your lawn in no time."

"Great!" I said. I clasped my hands together in enthusiasm.

Doc Feldman said, "Let's sit and talk. Ok, Goldman?"

I offered the lawn doctor a chair. And we both sat down. Now, maybe you're wondering why I was willing to invite the lawn doctor onto my back porch. Why was I willing to listen to him? Simply put—desperate people do desperate things. So, that morning, there I sat with the lawn doctor, and listened to what he had to say.

"This world, as it appears, is not the Reality," began Dr. Feldman.

"Huh?" I said.

"What we behold as Reality, is not Reality, but it is an appearance. It is an illusion of the human mind. The true creation, the divine Kingdom is unseen by the natural eyes."

"Okay," I said.

"For ages, ministers of the divine Kingdom have been visiting the earth. Angels. They come as emissaries, to represent the interests of the King, and of the divine Kingdom. They come to help bring about God's will on earth, as it is in heaven. They are still coming. Secretly."

"Alright," I said.

"Furthermore, at various times, God has raised up prophets for the same purpose. But two thousand years ago, God sent not an angel, not a prophet, but a Son. God spoke to the world through a Son, through whom the universe was created, who is the very imprint of his being, and who has been appointed heir of all things."[169]

"Okay," I said.

"You don't disagree?"

"No," I said.

"I'm going to talk to you about Yeshua, then. Is that alright?" said Feldman.

"I'm a messianic Jew, so we're of the same mind on that one."

"Oh," said Feldman. "We'll see about that."

---

[169] Heb. 1:2,3.

He stretched out. Cracked his knuckles. Then continued.

"The Son of God came with the specific mission to set mankind free, by preaching the Truth. He went about teaching the Truth and demonstrating the Truth. And his words remain until this day. Actually, he was in the world since before the world began. Invisibly. But the world, for the most part rejected him. The word became flesh and dwelt among men, but he told his disciples that he would be rejected by the religious establishment."[170]

"Which he was rejected," I said.

"Yes. And in this there is a paradigm. The very people who teach that the Messiah is coming, and that he will save the world from evil; the very people who claim to have authority concerning the identity of Messiah and concerning his teaching; the very people who have positioned themselves as God's representatives on earth; are oftentimes the ones keeping the earth from ever knowing God. And it's still going on today. And the reason for this is because they haven't known God themselves. They are guardians of the gates, but they can't go in. And therefore, they won't let anyone else in either.[171] This is the whole problem with religion, and always has been. Religion has its place. But if the Son sets you free, then you will be free indeed."[172]

"Sure. I totally get that," I said.

"Fine. Now, after the Rabbi endured being crucified, he was literally dead for three days. His body was laid to rest in a sealed tomb, and he appeared in every way to be lifeless. To remove any doubt he was pierced through the side. But he proved that death as a power over man was not the Reality. It was only the appearance. The Reality of who the Messiah is revealed itself when he arose from the dead. Eternal life is indestructible. By rising from the dead this testifies to the Reality, and to the non-reality of the power of this world. Which is death. It is not a power. It is nothing. And the

---

[170] Mark 8:31.
[171] Mat. 23:13.
[172] John 8:36.

232

Rabbi not only taught this. He not only said, 'Anokhi ha-T'khiya' (I am the Resurrection), but he demonstrated it by his own resurrection.

"The coming of Messiah Yeshua was perfectly, flawlessly the Reality of the Divine Kingdom made manifest in this imperfect, flawed world. The imperishable revealed in the perishable. The Truth is not what passes away, but rather, it abides forever, unchanged. The indestructible Life of the Rabbi is in the world always and never passes away. It was the Life of him, and it raised him from the dead.

"God is one and God is the Reality of the universe. There are not two but one Reality. But the human race is under a delusion of two powers—good versus evil. This is our natural state. But Yeshua taught that we can see the Kingdom of God by spiritual rebirth. Because Yeshua was God acting in the form of a man, as a human life, Yeshua could act on behalf of the entire human race.

"The Rabbi overcame the delusion of two powers—life versus death—the duality which is brought on the human race by a false belief in two powers—one good and one evil. The Rabbi destroyed the duality on behalf of all humankind. That we who are his followers might be children of God.

"He voluntarily laid down his life. Suffered and paid for our debts at the tree of sacrifice. He arose from a sealed grave after being three days gone. He arose in the same body which previously was dead. All of this was so that we might know the Truth."

"What Truth?"

"The Truth IS the Reality, Goldman."

I threw up my hands. I sighed a deep sigh, but then regathered myself.

"Okay, what Reality?"

The Life:

"I am speaking of the Reality that the Rabbi wanted us to know," said Feldman, "even suffering a gruesome death, paying for the debt of mankind, so that we might come to know it."

"What is it?" I said.

"You tell me," said Feldman. "What is the reason that the Rabbi came, and why did he do what he did?"

"So that we would not perish. But have everlasting life."

"You're close," said Feldman.

I rubbed my chin, pondering it for a moment.

"Well, it says *'I have come that they might have life and have it abundantly.'*[173] So, I guess the Rabbi came to give us eternal life."

"Very close. But not quite. As long as you approach it that way, there is always going to be a separation between you and God."

"What do you mean a separation?"

"A chasm. Like the Grand Canyon."

"I know what a chasm is. I just don't know what you're saying here."

"I'm saying God doesn't give life. God IS life."

"You're splitting hairs," I said.

"No," he said, "there's a world of difference."

I paused for a moment. Took it in. And Feldman continued:

"When you recognize eternal Life not as something I give, but something I AM," he said, "it changes your approach. God isn't just something to believe in. And God is not something to be given to you because you believed. God is something which IS. It is "I AM the Life." Not the "I give you Life.""

"I see the difference, but not sure what you mean by 'approach' it differently."

"Be patient, Goldman. I'm just getting started here," he said.

"I'm all ears," I said.

"Eternal Life is Reality. But Reality cannot be part of anyone's experience so long as there is a separation between you and it. It will remain a far-off, distant dream. Something

---

[173] John 10:10.

perhaps for a future time, when you're not around anymore. But eternal Life is the abiding, ever-present Reality of now, and it is the same yesterday, today and forever.

"The Rabbi's mission to planet earth, as Messiah, was for the purpose that we might have Life in us, even the same Life which he is. He doesn't give eternal Life. He IS eternal life. And that eternal Life which he IS, is the very seed of his image, planted in us. But we can't see this. He came to bear witness to it, to remove the blindness, to open our eyes to the Truth."

"Ahhhh. Now, I see."

"Do you?" said Feldman.

"I don't?" I asked.

"Look, me telling you the Truth is not the same as you knowing it. If Truth was a wad of spaghetti thrown at the wall, how much of it would stick to the wall?"

"Are we talking cooked spaghetti?" I inquired.

"Yes, of course" said Feldman, a bit frustrated. "You know what. Let's just forget the spaghetti."

"Okay. No spaghetti at all then?"

"None. Let's move on. Just know that he IS Life. Are you following me?"

"Yeah, I think so."

The Resurrection:

"The resurrection proved who the Rabbi is. It proved what he said, "Anokhi haKhayim—"

"I am the Life," I said.

"Yes. The Rabbi IS Khayei Olam (Eternal Life). And Khayei Olam is the Reality. Not life and death. Because in that version of reality, even what is thought of as "Life" is not really what Life is. That kinda life is not Khayei Olam. That kinda life is here today gone tomorrow. But the Rabbi showed this to be an illusion."

"I see what you mean. The Life never ends," I said.

"It never begins either," said the doc.

"It just IS," I said.

"Now you are starting to get to the heart of it."

"Thank you."

"Don't get cocky, Goldman," he said.

"Alright, go on," I said.

"Khayei Olam IS. And that is the Reality. But, you see, Khayei Olam (Eternal Life), is not just the Reality of him, but the Reality of you as well. There are not many Life's. The universe is one Life. And all that is living is living through the Life. Even as there is one God, because God IS the Life."

"In him is the Life, and the Life is the Light of mankind,"[174] I said.

"There you go quoting scripture," he said.

"That's not good?"

"I didn't say that," Feldman. "But you've got to move beyond what you know intellectually. You know the Life is the Light of mankind. Good. But do you know that Life?"

"Do I?" I said.

"That is the number one question," said Doctor Feldman. "It is a question of consciousness. Reality is not automatically Reality in your experience. Reality doesn't need you to be Reality. But it becomes Reality to you when you become conscious of it. This is how and why people can believe in God, but then, in the experience of their life, God is not who God is supposed to be. Because they lack consciousness. God is perfect Love. But where God isn't realized to be who he is, therefore, the experience is not in accord with God's perfect law of Love. Instead of Reality, it's a dream. Oftentimes, a bad one.

"As the scripture says, *'Where the Spirit of the Lord is, there is liberty.'*[175] Well, the Spirit is omnipresent. But as long as someone remains ignorant of the Spirit's presence, then the Spirit's omnipresence does not result in liberty. The Truth only sets a person free when they know the Truth. God is consciousness, and without consciousness, it is as if God is not even there. Even though God is always there."

---

[174] John 1:4
[175] 2 Cor. 3:17

Illusion and Reality:

"Wow. I think I'm starting to understand. Please continue," I said.

"The Reality is the Truth. And the Truth is the Reality. Whether we know it or not. It never changes. It was, it is, it always will be the same yesterday, today and forever. But when you know the Truth, it sets you free, because then it becomes the operative, governing principle of your life.

"Instead of illusion?" I said.

"Exactly. The resurrection showed that neither the grave nor death were anything but illusion. When you look at the created world, the nature of it is mayim. Water. Water can take on whatever form in which it is contained, and then it takes on another form in another vessel. Mayim is the time-space continuum. It is an ocean of constant change. Mayim is not substance. It is form. The substance of mayim, the creative principle behind it, substance without form, the omnipresence, by which and through which all things were made, is without beginning without end. That, my friend, is Khayei Olam. Eternal Life. Beyond the time-space continuum. The Creator of it, and of all that is within it."

"Alright. You're beginning to lose me again."

"Sorry," said Doc Feldman.

"No, that's okay. Keeping going."

"You must put on the mind of Messiah, then you see things as God sees them. Instead of looking to a God who gives you this or that, or does this or that for you, look to God for God. For no reason or motive other than to know God. By saying 'to know' God, I mean to commune. In communion there is realization of Reality. Reality non-realized does no one any good. But when you connect yourself to the Reality of the universe, you see things as they are. Not through a distorted lens of good versus evil. But through the lens of Truth."

"Is this what the Rabbi meant when he said, *"I am the way, the Truth, and the Life?"*[176]

"Alright, let's consider that saying of the Rabbi. In saying, '*I am the Way, the Truth, and the Life,*' he doesn't mean to say he will *give* anyone the Way, the Truth or the Life. He is saying that he IS those things. So when you come to him, you have it. But so long as there is this chasm, then you don't. Do you see the difference?"

"Sort of. I'm not sure how you are supposed to get across the chasm, ya know," I admitted.

"You don't get across it. You get rid of it altogether," he said.

"Hmm. Okay, so, how do you do that?" I asked.

"You do that when you see that the chasm is an illusion, not the Reality," said the wise doctor.

The Same Spirit that Raised Messiah:

"I know that the chasm is an illusion. But it doesn't seem that way." I said.

"That is the delusion of this world, and the pull is strong. But you have to remember, and dwell upon this Truth, that the word is near. You don't have to ascend to the heights of heaven or go down into the depths of the sea, but the word of Truth is in your heart and upon your lips. Eternity is set within your heart, and the Kingdom of God is right here and right now, forever in the midst of us."

"I know, I know," I said. "The kingdom, and the word, and the Son of God, it's all here and now. I just find myself asking, sometimes, how do I get to it?"

"No doubt, you have heard it said that there is a path that leads to God. But I say unto you, there are no paths to God. God IS the path."

"The iPath," I said.

"Correct, my friend. I see you have had training."

"Thanks," I said. "but, I admit, it doesn't always seem that I am on that path. I am on it for a while, and then I get diverted. How does one stay firmly planted on the iPath?"

---

[176] John 14:6.

Feldman continued, "The key to the iPath is knowing the answer to the question—*who am I?* Have you asked yourself this question?

"I have," I said.

"You are not far from the Kingdom of God, Goldman," said Doctor Feldman.

"I guess that's good news," I said.

"The same Spirit that raised the Rabbi from the dead, lives in you, quickening your mortal self,[177] to see and know what the Rabbi wanted you to know—infinite Life. Not only to know that he is infinite Life. Which he is. But that he is the infinite Life *in you.* That is what makes the difference. When you realize that, and do not waver, and cannot be moved, then you are in a place of maturity on the iPath.

"Make no mistake, Yeshua as the perfect Son of God, was wholly conscious, without flaw, without imperfection. Completely and totally the Son. Human beings are born of that same Spirit but are a fallen race, having accepted a belief in two powers. There is one God, and human beings have not known this. But the Messiah-born remnant, though not perfect by nature, have awakened to the Truth and have inherited, by God's grace, the right to be called "sons of God and daughters of God through Messiah.

"No one becomes one of God's children by saying so. No one is one of God's children by endorsing a set of beliefs. Humanity was created as God's children, but are only restored to that status when that same word which became flesh and dwelt among the earth in the form of the Rabbi, is realized in the heart of an individual. This is what it means to be born of the Spirit. This is what it means to be a child of God. It means '*Messiah in you.*'[178] Not knowing the phrase. But knowing the Messiah. Who is the Reality of you.

---

[177] Rom. 8:11.
[178] Col. 1:27.

Vanity of Vanities:

"Yeshua said, "*My Kingdom is not of this world,*"[179] because that world from which he came is Reality, and this world is something other than that. This world is a world of appearances. Mayim. It is based on deception and the deceiver is the father of lies.[180] It is a world held together by mortal concepts. Such a world cannot remain, because mortal concepts will pass away, just as every thought does.

"That's why the Rabbi said, '*My kingdom is not of this world.*' This world is illusion of illusions. King Solomon saw deeply into this. This world according to Solomon is 'vanity of vanities'[181] and 'chasing after wind.'[182] God has set eternity in our hearts, but since the fall of the human race, it is in such a way that we cannot naturally see the Kingdom of the Lord at all times.[183] Even though eternity is there, planted in our hearts, we have to be born of a new nature to see it. And the Son of God came so that we could do exactly that.

"To try and take hold of mayim's illusion, is only chasing after wind. Because the sun will rise, and then set again. Everything changes, and there is nothing new under the sun.[184] It is a world of futility, built upon futility, and made for a purpose that is futile to begin with. But you have begun to recognize this. And I'm telling you when you can see illusion for illusion, then it becomes possible to rejoice in the beauty of God's creation. This joy is the gift of God. And it glorifies God when man rejoices and is happy in his creation.

"There is one God, and God is one. The whole of material creation is mayim. Illusion. But to the extent we remain under a belief in two powers, we see the created world of mayim without knowing that it is mayim. Based on this error, when we believe the illusion to be the Reality, and then

---

[179] John 18:36.
[180] John 8:44.
[181] Eccl. 1:2.
[182] Eccl. 1:14.
[183] Eccl. 3:11.
[184] Eccl. 1:5 and 9.

chase after it, this is the fallen state. This is "avodah" (slavery). It is the state of captivity into which mankind has fallen. The human race has fallen into it. But it is based entirely on deception. If only we know the Truth, even as a thief on a the cross, the realization of the Truth would lift us up out of the darkness of avodah, and set us free by the consciousness of the Light of Messiah.

"Mayim is the tool by which the thoughts of God are, as a divine revelation, painted onto the canvas of creation. From the eyes of the Creator, Mayim is beautiful and glorifies the Creator, because the Creator and all God's children are conscious of the fact that mayim is mayim. Illusion is not illusion so long as you know it is illusion. It only becomes illusion when you don't recognize it as illusion. Otherwise, mayim is what it is intended to be, merely an effect that glorifies the Creator and increases the joy that is in him, by causing creation to rejoice over the glorious works of the Lord.

"To behold creation as illusory effect, in consciousness, without delusion, is the function of an intelligent being such as man. By this, the Creator is glorified, through a being that God loves, and because of his love, he has created man with Creator-consciousness. And even though that being has fallen, he loved us so much, that he sent his Son to redeem us, even thru suffering and tribulation, setting us free to be what God created us to be. The full realization of this will one day fill the whole earth with joy. As the Rabbi taught, it is the intent of God to place the infinite joy of God in the hearts of his children.[185] For now it brings joy to each individual along the iPath.

"The human race is deceived. It has rejected one God. It has accepted two powers. It cannot of its own mind recognize one God, as it sees through the lens of good and evil. Reality cannot be seen through that lens. The goodness of God and His Kingdom is pure and absolute. It knows no opposite.

---

[185] John 15:11 – "These things I have spoken to you so that My joy may be in you, and your joy may be full."

"Therefore, the natural human sees duality. What humanity believes to be "good," it seeks after and what it considers "evil," it avoids. But it is a quest doomed from the outset, because it is based on a delusion of two-ness, and neither good nor evil on the human scene is truly the work of God. It is illusion. And the Truth of what Yeshua called "my kingdom" remains hidden.

"Mankind therefore has become enslaved unto the waters of illusion, having fallen into avodah. Instead of beholding mayim's beauty and celebrating it, the human mind is held captive by mayim's charm because it is stuck in delusion, not recognizing mayim as illusion, but believing mayim to be the Reality. And therefore desirng it, because he believes it to be necessary for his own 'good.' But this desire is the delusion of good and evil. It is avodah. Slavery."

The Government is Upon His Shoulders:

"That's a lot to digest," I said. I cleared my throat.

"It will grow on you. As you walk on the iPath, you will become one with the Teacher."

"What Teacher?" I asked.

"Who was the Rabbi's teacher?" said Feldman.

"The Rabbi IS the teacher," I said.

"Precisely," Feldman continued. "He was in the world before it was formed, and he is with you always. Right?"

"Definitely. So if this is going to grow on me, then what do I do in the meantime?"

"Let God govern his universe. The government is upon his shoulders. He is the omniscient one. Not you. When messianic consciousness becomes the government of your life, then you are abiding in the true vine. In oneness with the Rabbi, there is oneness with the Father. And fruit will come forth as a natural result. As the Rabbi used to say, "I am in the father, you are in me, and I am in you.[186]

"That's the way the universe is constructed, my friend.

---

[186] John 14;20.

But until the Truth dawns in consciousness in you, it is not the law of your experience. You have to know the Truth, or it means nothing to you. When you come to know the Truth, the Truth will set you free."

I said, "Yeah, I've heard that so many times."

"I know you've heard it. So have millions and billions of others. But hearing it is not worth much. Hearing Truth is not knowing Truth. Reading about Reality is not seeing Reality. That's why the Rabbi said a person must be reborn, or they cannot see the Kingdom of God.[187]

"It is only in *knowing* Truth that there is freedom. Not hearing it. Not reading about it. And not just believing it either. Truth must be *realized*. It's already there. But you have no natural sense of it. You have to get contact with it. When Truth is realized, then it becomes the operative principle of your experience.

"The government is upon the Rabbi's shoulders. But until that government is realized by someone, as the living Truth abiding in the depths of their being, then that eternal and perfect law of his Kingdom, his government, cannot become the operative principle of that person's life. Instead, until it happens, you are ruled by avodah. The power that holds mankind in avodah is death. It's not the Reality, but it seems to be in every way. Mankind became enslaved in it the first day that it accepted a belief in good and evil. Just exactly as God said, "In the day that you eat thereof, you will surely die."[188] Death is the illusion, but it came upon our consciousness in such a way that it seems real. It is swallowed up in the victory of the resurrection. But even knowing that, the delusion of mortality still seems to be the operative principle at work. Which places mankind in a state of avodah. Servitude. So, freedom was declared. The Rabbi came that we might have Life, and have it abundantly. That the Resurrection which he is, would not be just a promise of tomorrow, but the government of our life today."

---

[187] John 3:3.
[188] Gen. 2:17.

"Because he IS the Life," I stood up and stretched a little. "I'm getting it. But I have to say, this is a lot to swallow."

"It will grow on you. In a little while you will not see me. Then the words I have spoken to you will come back into your memory. Let the words I have spoken to you be planted and take root in your mind. Keep this teaching. Guard my words. Abide in it. And, as it says, *I* will abide in you."

So What About My Lawn?:

"Okay." I was quiet for a moment. Then I said, "So, what about my lawn?"

"Sit back down and I'll tell you," said Doc Feldman.

"Go ahead, I said, as I obliged and sat down.

"You must realize that your external experiences are simply the formations emanating out of your own internal dialogue. Your thoughts become your experiences. And whatever it is you are thinking, you are going to continue to experience. Start paying closer attention to your internal dialogue. And then you will realize that your thoughts are just as brown and dead as your lawn."

"Whoa, whoa. So, what you're saying," I reasoned, "is that I am what I think I am."

"Not exactly. You are who you are. There exists, independent of your idea of yourself, an objective reality of you. An absolute you. The absolute bears witness within you, declaring, 'I am *that* I am.' But you are out of contact with *that* I am which you are. It is a human condition. All are born into this delusion, believing themselves to be something other than they are, which is based in a belief that there is a selfhood apart from the one, eternal, God."

"So, basically, what you're saying is to stay positive. Like if I think positive, things will be positive in my life."

"No, absolutely not. The Rabbi's teaching was centered on revealing true selfhood. Not positive thinking. Positive thinking is based on human selfhood. It uses human effort to try and became all that a human can be. Positive thinking is no part of the Rabbi's message. It's premise is human will,

244

and therefore the key problem with positive thinking is that it is based in the delusion of two powers. It seeks to use a positive attitude to overcome negative situations."

"Are you saying that doesn't work?" I said.

"I'm saying it's not what the Rabbi taught. It's better to stay positive than negative, but the real victory is in a state of consciousness that is above the duality altogether. Because the duality is an illusion. This world is based on a delusion of two powers. A power of good and a power of evil. Positive thinking accepts two powers, and that is why it is not a good approach to life. It's better to dwell on the positive than on the negative. But it doesn't set anyone free. Because it doesn't get to the root of the problem."

"Which is?" I said.

"Duality. The root of the problem is the acceptance of two powers. God is one. If the world knew God as the one God then the human race would be living again as in the garden of Eden. Instead of trying to overcome evil by thinking good thoughts, we must abide in God, and thereby, rise above the delusion of two powers. Because the Truth is one God. Not two.

"God is omnipotent and unopposed. There is no power to contend with God because God is all-power. The only "power" contending with God is that of deception. The Son of God has been in the world from the beginning and all things were made through him. But the deception causes men to believe that God is not the only power. As many as receive the Son, and abide in him, they are the children of God. They walk in the consciousness of Reality. In that state of consciousness no weapon formed against us will prosper. This is the inheritance of God's children. To them, the Kingdom of God is the Truth, an unmovable rock. The key is in their hand, and the gates of hell will not prevail against it.[189]"

"What then? A child of God should never have any problems anymore?" I said.

"Not so. So long as you live in this world, there is trouble.

---

[189] Mat. 16:18.

But the good news is, *"Take heart, I have overcome the world."* [190]

"Okay, so when problems come, then shouldn't I at least try to stay positive?"

"It's better than becoming negative. But if you retreat into the Spirit of Messiah, making God your fortress and refuge, allowing yourself to be immersed in the consciousness of God's Kingdom, then, as King David said, because you have made the Lord your dwelling place, *'no evil will befall you, nor any plague come near your tent. For he will give his angels charge over you, to guard you in all your ways.'* "[191]

"The victory lies within. And when you commune with God's Presence, undoubtedly, you will come forth with a positive attitude. At times you may lose that composure, but it doesn't matter because composure and attitude is not where the victory lies. You can always go back to where the victory is—with God.

"A 'fear not,' positive attitude will come from abiding in the peace of God. But spiritual life is not mood-making. The peace of God can't be conjured up on human strength. And in any case, the victory is not in that positive attitude, the victory is in the source. Not because anything is to be done to the evil of this world. 'Vengeance is mine,'[192] says the Lord. But because by dwelling in the Lord, you become conscious, through the Spirit of God. The Spirit of the Lord is consciousness, and consciousness is freedom—for where the Spirit of God is, there is freedom.[193] Because to know the Truth, sets a person free.[194]

"The mental efforts of the human mind, on the other hand, will always fall short. Because it recognizes a separation. Evil never destroys good. But good never destroys evil either. They always come face to face again on

---

[190] John 16:33.
[191] Psalm 91:9-11.
[192] Deut. 32:35.
[193] 2 Cor. 3:17.
[194] John 8:32.

another day. But God is in control. Because God IS. And in that Kingdom there is no duality of good and evil.

"God is good, pure and absolute. But not 'good' as human beings suppose it to be, which is 'good' as part of a duality. Simply put, this world is based on illusion. But God IS. Belief in God is not setting anyone free from the ills and afflictions of this world. We are made in God's image, therefore, the task should be to seek reunion with the one God, in whose image we are made. Restoration to the God who IS. This overcomes the delusion of good and evil. The whole matter is a delusion. But God is the Reality. And God is one. And God is Shalom. Eternal and everlasting. That Shalom is within every one of us, but we must turn within to connect and commune with it.

"To insist on being positive is to accept that negative is power. Then you have two powers not one. And let's face it, no one can stay positive all the time. Some folks are better at it than others, but it cannot be maintained."

"True," I said.

The Self You Are Not:

"You see, the human condition is marred by a state of delusion in which the deluded self believes it is the power in charge. This is the human self. The old self. The self you are not. Separated from God. Separated from the true Self. Consequently, to the extent that the old self reigns, that life is based on illusion. Instead of the *I* that you truly are, you go through life as if you are the I that you think you are. Until true messianic selfhood emerges, thru messianic consciousness, you continue to be ruled by your old self. When it does emerge, that is the iPath. Not a path to God. But the path that IS God.

"The old self must pass away, in order for the true self, the new self, the eternal I am, to emerge in place of the old, dead human consciousness. This is what it means to be on the iPath. The new self becomes the "I" that I am. It always was the I that I am, but until the true selfhood emerges in consciousness, it means nothing. God loves everyone, and the Messiah lives in the heart of every person. But until a person recognizes it, and dwells therein, then it is as if it was not even there.

Messiah is infinite and eternal, and is always on the iPath. Not only on the iPath, but Messiah IS the iPath. Never veering. Never stopping to get off. The child of God walks in fellowship with Messiah. This fellowship is messianic consciousness. In that state of consciousness God is the law, and the government is upon his shoulders.[195] It is the law of Life in the Spirit of Messiah, which sets you free from the law of this perishing world, which is a law of sin and death.[196] God is the I am. But so long as the human self remains the governing authority of your life, then the I am is not in charge. Consequently, your experience of life remains based on a false concept of who you are, and is ruled by that same law that governs falsehood. Instead of the law of Life, it is ruled by the law of this passing world. The law of sin and death.[197]"

"The law of brown grass?"

"Exactly," laughed Dr. Feldman.

I rubbed my chin. I do that when I am thinking about deep things. Not sure why. I knew that Dr. Feldman was speaking some wisdom here. I could not, however, comprehend what it might have to do with my immediate situation—a brown lawn.

"I know you're not getting all this," he said. "Be patient. It will take shape soon, as the days go by."

"Okay," I said. "Let me just ask you one thing. What am I supposed to do with all this information?"

"Just know the Truth and the Truth will set you free."

"Yeah, yeah. Been there done that."

"Don't be so sure," said the lawn doctor.

"Fine. Let's just say, I accept what you suggest. That I

---

[195] Isaiah 9:6.
[196] Rom. 8:2.
[197] Romans 8:2.

248

don't know the Truth, but in time I will know the Truth and it will set me free. The question remains, what am I supposed to do in the meantime?"

Feldman smiled. He didn't respond, except with a Mona Lisa smile. The same smile I remember from Shlomo and from Marley. The smile that says he knew something.

The Love Song of Nature:

Right then, I noticed the buzzing sound of a prop jet flying over my house, barely audible though, due to the sound of crickets. Those crickets were getting into a rhythm.

I should say that crickets in Florida are not necessarily crickets. Usually they are cicadas. It seems to me that whether speaking of cicadas or crickets, most folks just lump all of them into the one category of crickets. I do too. But I realize there definitely is a difference.

Now, I am not an insectologist, so I don't presume to know all the differences between cicadas and crickets. But I am a Floridian. And everybody in Florida knows a thing or two about that sound we hear all day and all night, especially in Summer. Which, in Florida starts about late April and doesn't end till early November. There's no avoiding that sound.

You see, crickets go "chirp, chirp." It is sort of like the sound of a high-pitched "beep-beep." Like pushing a button on one's cell phone. We hear the crickets mainly at night in Florida. They are very beautiful when there are lots of them chirping together, especially when near a lake or pond. The sound resonates off the water. We have lots of lakes and ponds in Florida. My neighborhood has dozens of small lakes and ponds.

But Cicadas are different than crickets. Cicadas do not chirp. They do not go beep-beep either. Cicadas roar. They sound more like a lawn mower or a jet propeller whizzing at high speed. Moreover, they are not only heard at night. They go on all day. And night. And they get extremely intense in the summer months.

249

The iPath

Cicadas are like a chorus of insects beating on a drum. Literally. It's hard to believe they are insects at all. They make their sound by beating on a part of their abdomens called a "tymbal."

Crickets, by comparison, make their chirp sound by "stridulation" which is basically rubbing their forewings together. Cicadas are not rubbing things together. They are beating on things.

I guess it's like the difference between rubbing your finger on a glass to make that high-pitched noise vs. clanking your spoon on the glass. If you wanted to get everyone's attention at a dinner party, which would you do? Yeah.

In my back yard, cicadas are hidden away somewhere in the live oaks. Nobody ever sees them. But we sure hear them. In fact, I've never seen one. I wonder if anyone has. I wouldn't have a clue what they look like. They are definitely there, making their presence well-known. But quite hidden from sight. And if not for their tribal drumming, no one would know it. They are as good as invisible.

Typically, the cicadas start in little by little. As if one group of cicadas is reaching out to others, inviting them to join in.

I reiterate, I am not an insectologist. But, I have learned that the males make their drumming sound in order to attract females. And, apparently, once the females draw near, the males become quiet. Until that happens, the noise gets louder and louder. Like the sound of conga drums.

The sound of cicadas is quite mesmerizing. If you live in Florida in the summer, the sound stays with you. It's in your sleep. It's in your day dreams. It's in your night dreams. You hear it through the sliding glass door to your bedroom. It pours through the bay windows by your kitchen or sunroom. The rhythmic cicada trance of summer. That inescapable, intoxicating sound. It ebbs and flows, but it never stops. It's always there. In the background. And it's in your head, day in and day out.

It calls you forth. It lulls you into some weird kind of tribal communion with nature—without you even knowing it.

250

There's no avoiding the sound. It's a sound you know has been around since the most ancient of days. You couldn't get away from that sound. Even if you wanted to. Not in Florida anyway. Even in the modern, technological, air-conditioned, man-made world of today's Florida. You can't take your mind off of that sound. The cicadas simply won't have it.

Now, you have to understand that the whole time that Doc Feldman had been speaking on my back porch, that sound—the cicada sound—was there. It was strong. Real strong. It comes in waves. Then dissipates. Then another wave. And right now it was getting stronger.

That sound never seems to go away. But sometimes, suddenly, inexplicably, it gets louder and louder. As often happens, now the birds were getting into it also.

Sometimes, it seems the birds are harmonizing with the cicadas, even as vocalists harmonize with the drums in a band. I guess they act on instinct in doing this. I assume that they are not aware that they are doing it. They just do it. In any case, I am aware of it. And I can testify—it is beautiful.

There are several live oaks in my backyard, and thousands of them throughout the neighborhood. I am convinced that there are no more amazing trees anywhere on earth than the southern live oak. They are ubiquitous in Florida. The moss which hangs from the southern live oak gives it a deeply mysterious quality.

During the entire time on my back porch, Feldman and I both were looking out at the live oaks. As the cicadas drummed their song, and the birds joined in, it grew louder and louder. I had been listening to Dr. Feldman, but the whole time I think that neither one of us ever once made eye contact. It's as if he was speaking, but not necessarily to me. We both looked out on the live oak trees.

Therefore, as I noticed the prop jet flying overhead, which I could barely hear, due to the cicadas, it cleared out, and then suddenly the song of the cicadas became faint. Nature said, "Selah." Except for a few, that were already at work trying to renew the chorus of nature, otherwise, for that moment, nature was almost quiet.

What am I Supposed to Do?:

And at this "selah" moment, Feldman, too, was quiet. He sat there, smiling, looking into my eyes. He just stared.

So I said it again, "What am I supposed to do in the meantime?"

"Get free of the problem."

I took a deep breath, then exhaled a big sigh. "Free from what problem?" I asked.

"That is the problem."

"What is?"

"You don't know what the problem is."

"Exactly. How am I supposed to solve the problem, when I don't know what the problem is to begin with?"

"That's the problem."

I sighed again. Even bigger this time.

"But there is good news," said Feldman.

"Tell me!" I exclaimed.

"Even a blind squirrel finds a nut every once in a while."

"Oh, great. That's a big help."

"You worry too much."

"I can't help it. I feel like if I don't worry, then nothing good is gonna happen."

"Let me put it to you another way: '*My grace is sufficient for you. My power is made perfect in your weakness.*'"

"Second Corinthians 12:9," I said.

"You know the verse. But you don't know how to implement it in real life."

"Tell me, then."

"Grace is when the Spirit of God becomes the operative government of your life. Is it dumb luck that brought the blind squirrel to find the nut. Or God's grace?" said Feldman.

"Hey, can we just forget about the blind squirrel?" I said.

"That's up to you. But, let me ask you something, what do you think I am doing here?"

"You?" I asked.

"That's right."

"I google-searched your company, and I contacted you."

"Oh really," said Feldman. "Is that how it happened?"

"Well, yeah," I said.

"Didn't that boy give you my company name?"

"How do you know that?" I said.

"And how did he come to know me? And how did you come to know him? And what brought him to that moment of crisis where you needed a new lawn man?'

"Lawn doctor," I said.

"You're learning," said the lawn doctor.

We both had a laugh.

"The grace of God, I guess, I said. "Unless this turns out to be a total waste of time."

"You'll see. But just remember something. You did not choose me. I chose you."[198]

Just then, the cicadas started in again. Calling out to their mates. The birds joined them. It grew louder. And louder. And I was ready to know more.

Feldman sat back, and as we both looked out on the live oaks, the magnificent chorus of nature reached its crescendo. And Feldman continued:

"All things as they appear within the time-space ocean are illusion. Not knowing this, causes a sense of isolation, as if you lack something. And that gives rise to desire. That is why you worry. But it's not real. In Reality, you lack nothing.

"You have the answer already to your brown grass problem. There is life within that lawn. Just as there is life within you. But you don't know it. That state of not-knowing the Truth is what causes you to feel like you have a problem. But you don't have a problem. The problem is the illusion. The Reality is not what it appears to be."

"Okay, wait a minute. So, that brown grass right there," I said, pointing to my lawn, "which I am looking at right now, is nothing more than an illusion?"

"No. That's not what I'm saying."

"But you did say that?"

---

[198] John 15:16

"I said it is not what it appears to be. What it appears to be is not the Reality. It only seems to be the Reality because you have accepted it as Reality. But it isn't."

"Well, fine then. I accept it no more."

"Not true. You still accept it."

"I do?"

"I think so," said Feldman.

"Fine. Then how do I stop accepting it?"

"Illusion is nothing, because it isn't real. But you can't overcome the illusion by declaring it to be nothing. Declarations and affirmations are nothing more than positive thinking. It's based on duality. The problem is that you have inherited a belief in two powers."

"Fine. How do I get disinherited of that?"

"You are human. You can't help it. It's a universal human problem."

"What do I do then?"

"You shall know the Truth and the Truth will make you free."

"Urggh!" I said in frustration. "Give me something concrete."

"Concretizations are part of the delusion of two powers. Good is concrete and evil is concrete. You want the good, of course, but so long as you see two powers, instead of one, then it escapes you because good is not good in the spectrum of two powers. It is merely a diametric opposite. It is part of the dualism of the deluded mind.

"So where is Truth then?"

Dr. Feldman now looked at me square in the eyes. He pointed hard at my chest.

"Look within your heart," he said.

I shook my head in exasperation.

"Don't get frustrated," said Feldman. "The Truth is Spirit and Life. You've got to rise above this deluded vision of the world as seen through the lens of good and evil."

"Rise above it?" I said.

"That's the only way. Then you will know the Truth—"

"And the truth will make me free. I know, I know."

"You're getting the idea," he laughed until he coughed. "You got any water?"

I zipped inside, got two cold bottles of water from the fridge, and planted myself back in my chair on the porch. I handed Dr. Feldman a bottle of water. He chugged the whole bottle down, then wiped his face with his bare wrist.

"Thanks," he said. "Mayim is the water of illusion. But it's not necessarily a bad thing. Mayim is part of creation. All things were made by and through God. Apart from Him nothing was made that has come into being.[199] But God couldn't have everything looking exactly the same. Mayim is the secret of the diversity of creation. And in that diversity is the beauty of it. The key is that you know the difference between what is Reality and what is illusion. So long as you abide in the Truth, ask whatever you wish and it shall be done for you.[200] Because when you recognize God as God, and mayim as mayim, you can have all that the Father has given to his children. The earth is the Lord's, and all the fullness thereof.[201] And everything that the Father has belongs to the children. This is what the Rabbi said, isn't it?

"*All that the Father has is mine.*"[202] I responded.

"Exactly. Because I am in the Father, you are in me, and I am in you.[203] This is the oneness principle. The heart of the Rabbi's teaching, which he gave to his followers in order that the Life which he is, might also become the Life living in them.

A verse came to mind, and I pulled it up on my cell phone.

I said, " *'That they all may be one. Just as You, Father, are in Me and I am in You, so also may they be one in Us, so the world may believe that you sent me.'*"[204]

"Exactly," said Doc Feldman, interlocking his fingers.

---

[199] John 1:3.
[200] John 15:7.
[201] Ps. 24:1
[202] John 16:15
[203] John 14:20.
[204] John 17:21.

"Oneness."

"Although, I must say, it doesn't seem like oneness."

"That's what I'm saying. But when you find your true spiritual identity in the Rabbi, it changes the picture. It starts coming in clear as crystal. Not as an alternate reality. It is the one and only Reality," said Feldman.

"The Reality channel!" I said.

"Something like that," said Feldman, laughing. "Through oneness with the Son, there is oneness in the Father. This is why the Rabbi used to say, 'I and the Father are one.' Not just that he is one. But that we are also one, in him. Then whatsoever you ask can be given to you, but it's not really given. And it's not really asked either. It's all already there. In oneness, the asking and answering is really just a way of discovering."

"Discovering what?"

"Discovering the Truth."

"You mean discovering that the grass is green?" I said.

"Maybe. But Truth isn't always what we want it to be. It is what it is. The important thing is to know it. Because it's the end of the problem."

"I see."

"As the scripture says, '*Son, you are always with me and everything that I have is yours.*' "[205] What you seek in this world, is already yours, when you are on the iPath. Walking with God. Not *to* God. On the iPath, you know who I am. You know who you are and what you are, and the borders of the falsehood are no longer borders at all, when you know your true spiritual identity and in whose image you were created.

"The Rabbi taught to his followers that his identity was to be their identity. They are one. And this oneness comes in knowing your identity. That is messianic consciousness. That is knowing the Truth. When you know it, then you are on the iPath. Not a path to God. God IS the path. The path is individualized in you. That's why it appears as varied and diverse. But the diversity is mayim. The substance of it is the

---

[205] Luke 15:31.

same. One path. One God. One infinite Reality. One everlasting Life. There are infinite faces, infinite views along the path. But the path itself is the same. It is one path. The iPath. The path of I. God's path and that path is the path of the family of God. If indeed you are a child of God, then you are on that path. And bear in you the image of Messiah."

"I think I'm starting to get it," I said.

"Alright, then. Just remember my kingdom is not of this world. So, all that you behold with the senses is mayim. When you see this, you will recognize the source, and will be able to live life to the fullest, without being deceived by mayim's charm. As the Rabbi made clear, it is for this reason that I came into the world—to bear witness to the Truth.[206] The Truth is the Spirit of God. And, you see, just as Yeshua testifies of the Spirit of Truth, and sends the Spirit of Truth to his followers; so too, the same Spirit of Truth testifies of Yeshua.[207] Yeshua bears witness concerning the Spirit, and the Spirit bears witness concerning Yeshua. All so, that we might be one, as he is, in the one God. This is the magnificent wisdom of the one God who created all, and sustains all."

"Does this mean there is hope for my lawn?"

We both had a good laugh about that. Feldman then regained his composure and continued.

Omniscience:

"To be on the iPath, it is necessary to be transformed by the renewing of your mind.[208] Now, God is omniscient. A mind that knows all, sees all, and which created all by perfect wisdom. That is the source. The omniscient messianic mind is embedded in the fabric of the universe. But the human being, which was created in God's image, is now of a mind that is far, far away from the source."

---

[206] John 18:37.
[207] John 15:26.
[208] Rom. 12:2

"Thus, the need for transformation," I said.

"Precisely. As scripture teaches, that is why you need to be transformed by the renewal of your mind. That the mind of the Messiah might be the operative principle of your life. Do you see?"

"Clear as crystal," I said, giving Feldman the thumbs up.

"The mind of Messiah is clean and clear, unconditioned, unfiltered. It is Truth raw and pure. The one who puts on the messianic mind, as it is written, out of that person's innermost being will flow forth a river of living water. The tree of life grows on the banks of it, bringing forth the fruit of eternal life."

I popped up a scripture verse, and interjected: "It also is written, '*the mindset of the flesh is death, the mindset of the Spirit is life and peace,*' Romans 8:6."

Feldman continued: "The principles are known to you. But the next step is beyond knowing principles. It is the living and dwelling in the Ruakh. '*For those who live according to the flesh have set their minds on things of the flesh-*'"

"*But those who live according the Spirit,*" I interrupted, "*have set their minds on the things of the Spirit.* Romans 8:5."

"Took the words right out of my mouth," said Doc Feldman. We had a quick laugh. And then he continued:

"There are two minds out there. The eternal. And the finite. The human mind is a stream of thought producing the experience of mortality and isolation through self-dependence and self-reliance. And self-love. It is a mind that does not know God. It thinks for itself. Provides for itself. Or, at least, tries to."

"Well, I admit. I am a human. So what am I supposed to do about that?"

"So was the Rabbi. He was the son of God. But he also was human. Fully God, yet fully man."

"But he was perfect."

"True. And you never will be. That is why he is Lord of Lords, and is set apart from all. But the image in which you were created is perfect. And Yeshua came to reveal this to mankind. So that the human race might be capable of being restored to gan Eden."

"So what did the Rabbi mean when he said, 'your righteousness must exceed that of the Pharisees?' "[209] I asked.

"It isn't easy to master the things written in the law, but there are those who have. Yet, still, there is a veil that blinds every human being born into this world. It is a universal condition, and it is causing Mankind to continue in the knowledge of good and evil as its daily bread. That kind of bread is a food that kills. Man looks to the scriptures, and in them there is Life. Well and good. But even so, the veil keeps a person in blindness and unable to come to the Truth. The scriptures can be mastered, but to follow the Master is another thing entirely. Because only the Master can remove that veil. And until the veil is lifted, one continues to behold illusion instead of the Truth. By virtue of being born human. It is only by dwelling in the Messiah that the veil is lifted.[210] Not by religious belief, but by abiding in the Spirit of Truth that is hidden from sight, but is the Life right in the midst of us all. The abiding in it gives rise to messianic consciousness. Because the Spirit of Truth and Messiah are one and the same. The Son knows the Truth. And the Truth sets free. Not through belief, but through actual dwelling in the divine Presence.

"Now, the Rabbi was tamim.[211] He walked in perfection. But this state of tamim was not limited to the moral sense. The religious world has missed this. They have made it about morality. It was that, too, but morality is a by-product of messianic consciousness. The Rabbi's mission was not moral perfectionism. He was tamim in that he was one with God.

---

[209] Mat. 5:20. "*For I tell you unless your righteousness exceeds that of the Pharisees and Torah scholars, you shall never enter the kingdom of heaven.*"

[210] 2 Cor. 3:13,14.

[211] "Tamim" means perfect or unblemished. E.g. the Passover Lamb. See, Ex. 12:5 – "*Your lamb is to be "tamim" (without blemish), a year old.*"

He was tamim in the fullness of consciousness. No one ordinary man can be in that state of perfection. But at the same time, the Rabbi said to us, '*Be perfect, just as your Father in heaven is perfect.*'[212]

"How can we who are imperfect, be perfect? This is the very paradox from which the Rabbi came to deliver us and heal us. The answer is through consciousness. And consciousness is found in him, who is with us always, and is the very center of our being, and government of our lives. That is why, regarding the Pharisees, and religious leaders, Yeshua said to do as they say, but don't be like them.[213]

"The messianic life goes beyond the 'righteousness' of the ultra-religious, super-knowledgeable and legally observant. When the mind that was in Yeshua takes charge of your life, and becomes the operative authority in you, the veil has been lifted, and this is a state of consciousness coming from Messiah himself. It is not a point-of-view, it is a spiritual awakening. It is a new birth. To the one who awakens in Messiah, the moral high ground comes naturally as well. But it is the consciousness of the Rabbi, that he spoke of, which exceeds the righteousness of the Pharisees and the Scribes.

"So no one is perfect," continued Feldman, "except the perfect one. And, therefore, even though due to your humanity you may at times err, and sow seeds of the flesh, nevertheless, the Rabbi has dealt with that at the tree of sacrifice."

"Yes!" I said.

"As it says, '*The one who knew no sin became a sin offering on our behalf, that we might become the righteousness of God in him.*'[214] Again, Yeshua taught his followers that your righteousness must exceed that of the super-observant, religious establishment. How can this be? That can only happen when righteousness is not being

---

[212] Mat. 5:48.
[213] Mat. 23:3
[214] 2 Cor. 5:21.

sought by human will, or by observances, but it is the righteousness of God's own nature. As the prophet Jeremiah said, in reference to the Messiah, that his name shall be called, "Adonai Tzedikeinu," (the Lord is our righteousness).[215] If we are trying to create our own through rites and observances, it falls flat. Even good deeds, and scriptural knowledge is not the way."

"Because God is the way," I said.

"Exactly," said the wise doctor.

"You were talking about atonement?" I said.

"Yes,"

"I'd like to hear what you have to say about that," I said.

"Do you believe the Rabbi is the Lamb, slain for the sins of the world?" asked Feldman.

"I do. Of course."

"That he paid your debts, and the penalty of your peace was place upon him, and that the Father laid upon him the iniquity of all?" asked Feldman.

"Isaiah 53," I said. "His shed blood removes the stain of my sin."

"Well, ok then. Tell me something. Where is the blood?"

"What do you mean 'where'?"

"Have you seen it?" said Feldman.

"No."

"Has it been sprinkled upon you?"

"No."

Debt Paid:

"So, you know your debts are paid. Not only your wrong deeds, but your wrong thoughts as well, from which all wrong deeds originally flow. It is not your positive thinking that sets you free, but the atoning work of the Messiah, suffering and dying upon the tree."

---

[215] Jer. 23:6 and 33:16 – "Adonai Tzedikeinu" (the Lord is our Righteousness).

"Agreed," I said.

"The atonement is there. It's done. God's gift to the world. Blood upon the altar, to make atonement for your soul.[216] But, the problem is that it's invisible, just like everything else having to do with God's kingdom. So, you see, the crux of the whole issue of atonement is this—where do you go to get it? Because if you don't know, then it doesn't do you any good. So tell me, where do you go?"

"To God," I said.

"Exactly," said Doctor Feldman. "So that's the problem."

"How's that?" I said.

"Because if you have to go to God, then where is God?"

"Somewhere, in the heavens, I suppose," I said.

"Actually, God is omnipresent. The problem is that the human race is out of contact with God. Therefore, if we know that the atonement is with God, but we are alienated from God—which the human race is—and we don't know how to have kesher (contact) with God, or are unwilling, or both, then the atonement doesn't do us any good like that. Does it?"

"I guess you're right," I said.

"Because the benefit to mankind is not just in the fact that the atonement is there. It only becomes a benefit to the world if the world has a means to be there—wherever it is—that's what matters. But human beings do not naturally have contact with the invisible Kingdom of God. What the human race has, instead, is belief. Lots of belief. And from belief comes doctrines. Which are essentially a way of rationalizing the problem. It's like saying, we know there is a fountain of Life, but we don't drink from it because we don't know where it is. So what good is it?"

"Okay, I follow you. So, you're saying the problem is not having kesher?" I interjected.

"That's right," said Feldman.

"Okay. And the solution is?" I asked.

"What would the Rabbi say?" said Feldman.

---

[216] Lev. 17:11.

"He'd probably say, 'I AM the solution.' "

"Exactly what he would say. Because he's already said it in so many ways. One of the best is: *I am the Light of the world. And all who follow me will not walk in darkness, but have the Light of Life.*' "[217]

"So you're saying that God is the Light of the world, and the atonement of the Lamb's blood is in the Light?"

"I'm not the one who said it. The scripture says: *'Walk in the Light as he himself is in the light, and then you will have fellowship with him, and then the blood—*"

" *'Then the blood of his Son Yeshua will purify us from all sin!*[218]' I said, finishing the verse for Feldman.

"Yes," said Feldman. "You see, the power of the blood of the Messiah is not in religious belief. Because belief is mental. It's a human thing. The power of the blood of Messiah is in spiritual communion. The communion with the Messiah is not rites and rituals or opinions. Not symbolic. But Reality. As the Rabbi said, *'eat my flesh and drink my blood, then you will have Life eternal.*'[219] Right? The world has presented atonement as something gained through belief, and then added to that religious rites to symbolize it. Rites and practices are well and good for symbolism and as a teaching. But they have the mesmeric effect of convincing the human mind that they are the substance and reality, when in fact that is the illusion. The Reality is neither mental nor symbolic. The world offers the best the world can offer. But the true teaching came from the one who is the author of it, "by whose stripes we are healed."[220] And he presented the atonement, not as religious belief, but as spiritual communion."

"True. Yeshua did teach it that way," I said, and pondered it a moment. "So you're saying that the atonement is not just through believing in Messiah, but through abiding in the Messiah, as he taught us to abide in him?"

---

[217] John 8:12.
[218] 1 John 1:7.
[219] John 6:54.
[220] Is. 53:5.

"I am saying what Yeshua said, '*He who eats my flesh and drinks my blood abides in me and I in him.*' "[221]

"Wow. I never thought of it that way," I remarked.

"Spiritual communion, Goldman, that is where the freedom lies. Not in scriptural knowledge nor in religious belief. And definitely not in positive thinking. It's in kesher. Contact. The invisible Kingdom is in our midst. And that is where the spiritual food is, the bread which gives life to its inhabitants. On the iPath, your task is to be in communion. Communion—spiritual communion—is to take your dose of 'daily bread,' your messianic meal.

"A meal with God," I said.

"No. Not a meal *with* God. A meal *of* God."

It's All in the Communion:

"Okay, I totally get it. It's all in the communion. But then, the issue becomes, how do we commune with the Lord," I said.

"From the earliest day of mankind, even from the time of Seth, the son of Adam, '*then men began to call upon the name of the Lord,*' "[222] said Doc Feldman.

"What were they doing?" I asked.

"They were praying. But if only it was understood how they prayed, then the whole subject of prayer would be approached differently."

"How so?" I said.

"Prayer, as intended, is a spiritual activity. That is what human beings need in order to commune with God," said Feldman.

"Sounds like some kind of a ritual," I said.

"No. God is a Spirit. So, real-time communion with God cannot be about religious rites. Religious rites having to do with communion—whether a Passover Seder, or monthly sacraments of wafers and wine—are completely symbolic.

---

[221] John 6:56.
[222] Gen. 4:26.

Such things serve an important and good purpose for people who practice them. A symbol teaches. It testifies. It points the way. But it is not the way itself. God is a Spirit. Nobody comes into contact with the Spirit of God by eating matzo or sacramental crackers or drinking ceremonial wine," said Feldman.

"I understand that," I said. "But how then, do we come into contact with the Spirit."

"Prayer. Prayer is man's way of communicating with God. But there are many kinds of prayer," he said.

"What kind is the good kind?" I asked.

"Well first, there is always going to be a difference between what is done in public versus in private," said Feldman.

"Obviously, because public is corporate," I said.

"Right, so in public people must pray out loud, because they are communicating not only with God, but with each other."

"I understand that," I said. "Let's talk about private prayer."

"Fine," he said, "What you do privately, in prayer, is literally the difference between life and death of the individual. Spiritual rebirth happens through an inner communion. It cannot be handed to you by someone else. Organizations are vital, and have a key purpose in messianic life on earth. But no one is born anew by joining an organization of people. Nor can you read your way or think your way into the Kingdom. Nor arrive by joining a group."

"I get all that. Tell me more about personal prayer," I said.

"First, let me be clear. All prayer is good prayer. But not all prayer is effective. When a person turns to God sincerely in prayer, there is always some contact," said Feldman. "The idea of prayer is that there is a turning away from this perishing world, to the imperishable within."

"Agreed," I said.

"The key to effective prayer is keeping your eyes on the goal of it. By 'goal' I mean the reason why you are doing it to begin with. The motive behind prayer is going to dictate whether or not it is effective."

"Okay, so, what is the goal?"

"The goal of effective prayer is not content, but contact."

"Not content, but contact," I repeated softly, as I cogitated what he was saying.

"You see, it isn't the content of the prayer, but rather, the activity of prayer that makes the difference. So the more that prayer becomes a part of one's life, the better. Yet, to pray with much verbal content, is not very effective. Because you are putting yourself in God's place when you do that. You are telling God what needs to be done. And that in essence, is a denial of God's omniscience and omnipotence. Look, there is only so much time in the day. People who pray ought to use that time to connect with God. Make kesher. That solves the problem. Because the problem—whatever its nature—is caused by separation. So, in pure prayer, the axe is laid at the root. Go to God for communion with God. And let that spiritual food be sufficient. Because it is."

"So, the less words the better," I said.

Feldman nodded in the affirmative.

"Can't you be a little more specific than that?" I asked.

"If you'd like," he said.

Igud:

"God is an invisible Presence. Communion with the invisible Presence of the Lord is through some kind of spiritual activity. "Igud" is an activity that promotes union with God," said Feldman.

This word, "igud" (pronounced "ee-gud"), in spite of my familiarity with Hebrew, was unfamiliar to me.

"Igud?" I queried.

"Yes. It is Hebrew for 'union.' Igud is the practice of union with God. Igud can involve any spiritual activity which enables a person to practice the Presence of God. In this sense, igud seeks to bring a person into fellowship with God."

"Give me some examples," I said.

266

"It can be as simple as a quiet walk in the neighborhood, a bike ride, a hiking trip, walk on the beach, or a certain type of exercise. Igud can be any activity that relaxes the mind and helps direct our attention to God. Because the point is God-contact. Kesher. But igud in the purest, most effective sense has to involve prayer. There is no purer way to commune with God than through prayer."

"What kind of prayer?" I said.

"All prayer is good. But not all prayer is effective,"

"Alright, you said that already," I said.

"I may say it again, just to warn you," he laughed.

"Thanks for the heads up," I said.

"There is a science to prayer. Just like anything else. If you want to be effective, you've got to learn to do it the best way, and do it well," he said.

"What about praying the scriptures?" I said.

"It's important to be well-versed in the letter of Truth. I don't suggest you can be effective without a sound understanding of scriptural Truth," he said. "But the art of effective prayer is not about what you say, it's about what enables you to touch the Spirit. Scripture helps. But I can tell you this, God already knows the scriptures. And he knows all our needs. So, as long as someone is yakking away, they have erected a wall between God and them. The most effective prayer is the kind of prayer which cultivates and establishes kesher with God. So to begin with some scriptural Truth in mind, is good. But the Spirit of the Lord moves freely in us when we are still and silent."

"Alright," I said. "Tell me more."

"Well, the problem is that the whole issue of prayer is often shrouded with superstition. To talk to God without knowledge of God's nature, or how to enter into fellowship with God, is not very effective," Feldman said.

"So, what is the best way to have fellowship with God?" I said.

"Through prayer. But, first, the goal of prayer must be clear. The most effective prayer is when the goal is God. Not to get God to do something. But just God. The whole point of

The iPath

igud, in any form, is to be in contact with God. God is the hidden Reality of the universe. Igud is the practice of union with the invisible God. Practicing the Presence should not be something that a person believes, but something that really truly happens. And not randomly in a hit or miss fashion. But purposefully, consciously, intentionally, and by proven method.

"Igud as prayer is a means of taking the authoritative, written letter of Truth, applied in such a way to lift up the human being to consciousness of the revealed Spirit of Truth. It puts the visible, study-able, learn-able written word of God, taken together with the invisible, unseen, mystery of the infinite word of the Spirit of God.

"Mankind cannot connect to the invisible God without prayer. But there is a science to it. A practice of the Presence. The human race is cut off. Like a branch from a tree, broken off, it withers and dies. No fruit born on it. We must have communion or we have no means to communicate with invisible vine, which is God. This is why Yeshua taught an 'abide in me' kind of a message. His teaching was about communion. Not relationship, and not religious belief. He taught oneness. Do you see that?" said Feldman.

"Yes, I do." I said. "But isn't it important to seek to have a better relationship with God?" I said.

"Yeshua didn't teach relationship. He didn't say 'relate to me, and I will relate to you.' Did he?" said Feldman.

"No, he taught, 'abide in me,' of course," I said.

"Take, for example, a marriage. Yeah, there is a marital covenant. But marriage is not based on that. It might be held together that way, but the mystery of the man and woman in marriage is oneness. The joy of the marital union comes through the experience of oneness. No marriage is truly a 'success' until there is oneness."

"The two shall be one flesh,"[223] I said.

"Right. Messianic life follows the same principle. It is not a relationship with Messiah. It is oneness in Messiah.

---

[223] Gen. 2:24.

268

New Covenant, born anew, law upon my heart, or whatever you want to call the messianic life, is based on the transformational work of Messiah in you. That's not a relationship with God. It's communion with God. New Covenant is oneness. Old covenant is relationship. It is based on two-ness. And is held together, therefore, by the law. By vows, commitments, promises, etc. But this doesn't work. Because it's based upon a non-reality. A legal fiction. The spiritually reborn, messianic life happens when we have dissolved the separation outright. Not trying to cope with separation. But by doing away with the separation, in favor of oneness. I in you, and you in me. That is the Rabbi's way. That is the iPath."

"Yeah, I see what you mean," I said.

"In relationships, there is a wall between you, and you are trying to relate through the wall. Whether a good relationship or a bad one, the wall remains. Relationships necessarily depend upon mental effort. The wall needs to come down entirely. Then there is no relationship. There is oneness. No mental effort. It is Spirit and infinite Life flowing freely. When the Rabbi said *'abide in me and I will abide in you,'* he wasn't talking about relating to God. He was talking about abiding in your true spiritual identity. There is a world of a difference there. Abiding in the Lord, literally dwelling in Messiah, is impossible in the flesh. Flesh and blood have no part in spiritual things. This is why we need a spiritual practice. This is the point of igud.

"Communion and communication are mutually dependent. You can't have communion without communication. And vice versa. But to approach communication with God without true communion, always misses the mark. The Rabbi made it clear in his teaching that we must enter into communion with him by consuming the Spirit of God as if it were our daily bread. 'Eat my flesh and drink my blood and then you will have eternal Life,' he said."

"Yeah," I interjected. "And they turned that into a religious rite."

"True. But there's nothing wrong with these kinds of

269

rites and ceremonies. They are symbols. Teachings. They have purpose within certain communities. These things have meaning and purpose. But no one can be set free from the ills and afflictions of this perishing world through religious rites. There must be an inner communion. It has always been so, going back to Adam. God is Spirit and Life, not wafers, wine, or water. Not days of the week, nor seasons, nor holy garments. The Kingdom of God is not food and drink, nor flesh and blood, but God is the spiritual Reality, hidden from our sight. Without religious symbolism, the world might very well forget that there is a God. But when the Truth is replaced by religious symbolism, then the wall of separation is set up, and it's hard to bring it down."

"I see what you mean."

Messianic Meditation:

"Now, I reiterate, all prayer is good. But not all prayer is effective," said Feldman.

"Okay, okay. I follow you," I said. "But I am still waiting to hear about the most effective way to pray."

"The most effective kind of prayer is meditation. Messianic meditation," he said.

"You lost me on that one," I said.

"The Rabbi explained it best. So let's start there. Pull up Matthew 6, and read verses 6 through 8," said Feldman.

I did as he suggested and I read out loud:

> *"But you, when you pray, go into your inner room; and when you have shut your door, pray to your Father who is in secret. And your Father, who sees in secret, shall reward you. [7] And when you are praying, do not babble on and on like the pagans; for they think they will be heard because of their many words. [8] Do not be like them, for your Father knows what you need before you ask Him."*[224]

---

[224] Mat. 6:6-8.

"That's messianic meditation. It is done "secretly," as the Rabbi said. Because it is an inner work. No one can see it. Although they will see the fruit of it, and the fruit is what glorifies God. If the goal of prayer is communion with the Messiah, then messianic meditation is the purest and the most effective way to have it," said Doc Feldman.

"Sorry, but I'm still not understanding this," I said.

"The 'inner room,' that the Rabbi refers to," said Feldman, "is what King David called the 'Seter Elyon.' "

"The secret place of the most high," I said.

"That's right. From Psalm 91, as you know."

I typed in the search window and pulled up that Psalm on my phone.

"It says, '*He who dwells in the secret place of the most high shall abide under the shadow of the Almighty.*'[225] So, what about it?"

"B'seter," said Dr. Feldman. "In the secret place. That's where you are transformed. Or not."

"I still don't get it."

"God is a Spirit."

"Yeah."

"Can you see God?"

"No."

"Of course not. That's because God is invisible. That's why you need an activity, or a practice, in order to enter into communion with the invisible God. Some might call that quiet time, or devotional time. But it doesn't matter what you call it. The question is what you do during that time. Because that is the whole secret of messianic life. It is not what to eat, wear, or days to observe. Freedom from the ills of this perishing world comes secretly and sacredly through inner communion.

"Inner communion," I said softly, as I digested that phrase. "Yeah."

Inside-out:

---

[225] Ps. 91:1.

"However, that is not to say that the iPath is simply an inward journey. It is both inward and outward. Living consistently on the iPath is living both inside and outside. It is turning your life inside-out. Because messianic life starts within, but from that inner reservoir, you draw forth in order to carry the goods of the Kingdom with you into the outer world.

"The iPath is the way in which the children of the Creator are playing happily in Creation. This is the purpose of God, and the glory of his creation, that his own children, created in his own image, are living joyfully in the world that God created. So, to be on the iPath requires that you maintain constant contact with the Creator, which is inward. But also live the life appointed, which is outward. It's the inward, lived in the outward.

"So, regarding the whole subject of prayer, remember that you cannot live on the iPath entirely through inward dwelling. However, kesher or connection with God starts there. It's a state of within-ness, lived in the without. There is no way to have contact with an invisible Presence absent an inward connection to that invisible place of within. So what you do in your private devotional time, to journey to the world within, makes all the difference. If you don't have an inner witness, then you'll never have an outward one either," concluded Feldman.

"Sounds pretty complicated," I said.

"In practice it's extremely simple. It's only complicated to talk about. That's because you have to first unlearn what you think prayer is. In messianic meditation, as King David reveals in the Psalms, the realm of God is brought forth into this realm of delusion. The thoughts of Messiah are spontaneously livestreamed into your consciousness today, so that the seed of the messianic Kingdom becomes planted in your garden and watered by the water of life."

"Sounds like a good remedy for dead grass," I joked.

"Even more than that," said Feldman. "Instead of God's Kingdom being a dead, romantic dream and a distant hope of the future, the realm of the messianic Kingdom becomes the Reality of your life. Put another way, it is to see things on earth as it is in heaven," said Feldman. "It's the inside, shining forth outwardly."

"Cool," I said.

"Messianic meditation is the practice of abiding in the Messiah. It is spiritual communion. Not something of the human imagination. Not visualization. Not mood-making. It's transformational consciousness. It's putting on the Mind of Messiah, which is to say, the Spirit of God in you."

Be Still and Know that I am God:

"But how is it done?" I said.

"It all starts in the place which King David called 'Seter Elyon.' That can be anywhere private. But you know something, this back porch right here would be a good spot."

"What am I supposed to do here?" I said.

"Here it is: *Be still and know that I am God*.[226]"

"Um. Okay. Is that it?"

"Yeah. That's pretty much it," said Dr. Feldman.

"C'mon. Give me some more info here." I said.

"Pull up Psalm 27:4," Feldman said. "Read what King David said there. Read it out loud."

"Ok, fine," I said. I pulled up that verse on my cell phone, and read as follows:

> *"One thing have I asked of Adonai, that will I seek: to dwell in the House of Adonai all the days of my life, to behold the beauty of Adonai, and to meditate in His Temple."*[227]

"Do you see that?" said Doc Feldman.

"What?" I said.

"There was just 'one thing' David wanted above all else?"

---

[226] Ps. 46:10.
[227] Ps. 27:4.

"True," I said.

"Well, what was the 'one thing' that he wanted?" asked Doc Feldman.

"I guess, to be in God's presence," I said.

"Exactly. David was a man who practiced the Presence. He dwelt in God's presence, through meditation. The Psalms he wrote bear witness to this. He spoke often of his meditation. This is how he communed with the Lord. Especially in the early mornings and at night. And David knew that there is nothing greater than to meditate in the Presence of the Lord. This is the one thing he desired above all else, because he knew that it was amazing. And you will know what David knew if you pray the way that he prayed."

"Which was how?" I said.

"It was like this—*Be still and know that I am God.*[228]

"I don't see your point," I said.

"The point is to '*know that I am God.*' That is pure prayer. When you do that, you've reached the goal of prayer. That is the whole point of messianic meditation. To meditate is to abide in God. To join yourself unto God. God is the Reality. God is the "*akhat sha-alti.*" [229] The "one thing I have desired." When contact is made. Not a concept of God. Not a human idea of God. The real-time, actual Presence. But you have to 'be still,' because if when you are 'still,' then you put your human self to the side. There's a still, small voice, that comes to you. It speaks to you. Whether through a vision, a voice, a tender touch, what happens is that instead of your thoughts, it is the thoughts of the Lord."

"I am familiar with the Presence of the Lord," I said.

"Yes," said Doc Feldman. "No doubt you are familiar with the Presence of the Lord. But I am not talking about taking shots in the dark. This is a way to practice the Presence intentionally and effectively. Not as a blind squirrel that on occasion happens to find a nut. But with conscious intent, and with a clear goal in mind."

---

[228] Ps. 46:10.
[229] Ps. 27:4.

"So just be still, then?" I said.

"That's right," said Doc Feldman. In messianic meditation, you simply sit quietly and intentionally in the presence of the Lord. Take a written verse or two of scripture with you if you want. Or bring to mind some written scripture that you've memorized. Bring it into your thoughts, by reading it, or thinking about it, or maybe saying it softly aloud. Contemplate the scripture. We're not making declarations or affirmations here. Contemplation is internalizing the verses. Sort of like speaking it to yourself.

"By this, you are filling your human mind with the thoughts of God, recorded in the scriptures. This is sort of a wake-up call, a clap or a snapping of the fingers, which in a manner of speaking, frees the mind out of the delusive spell of this world, out of the belief in two powers, and into the glorious freedom of the Reality of one God and the everlasting Kingdom.

"So, you see, the written word is only to set the stage for the activity of meditative prayer. It is not the meditation itself. And once the stage is set by reading or bringing written Truth into mind, then contemplate it. "

"Contemplate?"

"Yes. 'Con,' which means 'with.' And 'temple,' which is the house of God. Go into the *temple* to be with *God*."

"Hmm. And do what?"

"Sit. And be quiet. And wait upon the Lord."

"That's it?"

"Yes. As you sit quietly in your secret place, in silence, contemplating, what happens is your mortal self gives way, and is subsumed by the immortal Life that is the Spirit of God."

"What do I do when that happens?"

"Simply, be still and wait on the Lord. Don't pray. Let God pray in you. Whether through visions, a gentle touch, or a still, small voice that gives you direction, instruction, confirmation, wisdom or whatever, you will know that a connection with God has been made. And God is taking care of his son or daughter. Contact made. Mission accomplished."

"That's it?"

"Yeah. Pretty much."

"Shouldn't I be saying something?"

"Only at first. But when the Spirit comes, be still and quiet. Let God be God," said Dr. Feldman.

"Through silence?"

"By you being silent, God speaks. If you want to do all the talking, that tends to leave God out of it. Let kesher be the goal, and be content to have kesher. Then, when it happens, let the Spirit move through you, and God will take care of his business. Don't feel the need to tell God what needs to be done. Let God's omniscience go before you, and his grace is sufficient. Let God govern his universe. Instead of you praying to God, let God pray in you."

"So I don't need to ask for anything."

"Being in the Presence is the answer. You will come away from each meditation with renewed vision, wisdom, clarity of purpose, authority, and everything needed to walk victoriously in this perishing world. Because you will have drawn forth from the reservoir. The reservoir is the storehouse of God's infinite good. In so doing, then you can go into the world and impart unto others."

"I think I follow you," I said.

"Just remember the goal of prayer is contact with God. You have to put aside your human self to make contact with the invisible Spirit of Messiah in you. The perishable cannot bring forth the imperishable. Only the imperishable can transform the perishable. As the scripture says,

For this perishable must put on the imperishable, and this mortal must put on immortality. But when this perishable will have put on the imperishable, and this mortal will have put on immortality, then will come to pass the saying that is written . . ."

At that moment, I interrupted, finishing Feldman's sentence: "... *death is swallowed up in victory.*"[230]

"That's right," Feldman said. "And, put another way, illusion is swallowed up in reality. You will see."

Green Pastures:

Doctor Feldman arose from his chair and extended a hand to me. We shook hands.

"I appreciate you sharing all this with me," I said. "I do have one last question."

"Something to do with your lawn, I suppose?"

"Well. Yeah, actually. Aren't you going to do anything to the lawn? Sprinkle some fertilizer maybe?"

He shook his head in the negative.

"Alright, but I gotta tell you, I'm a little uncomfortable paying your bill for this—"

"No problem," said Feldman. "I tell you what. If your grass comes back, you pay me whatever you think is a fair price."

"And if the lawn stays dead?" I asked.

"It's not dead," said Feldman.

"Only sleeping, right?" I said jokingly.

"If it doesn't wake up, then don't pay me anything. Fair enough?"

"Deal," I said extending a hand. We shook on it.

"Any last words for me?" I asked.

"This is your secret place," said Feldman. Just like King David had his, this will be yours. You must get into your secret place, and there you will find the good Shepherd, and he will give rest to your soul. Beside streams of living water, and in green pastures."

"Green pastures, huh?"

"Green pastures, my friend."

"Sounds promising."

"I assure you it is."

As it happened, I took to heart the instruction of the lawn doctor. After he left, that same day, I did as instructed.

At first, I really didn't know what I was doing. I began to

[230] *NAS*, 1 Cor. 15;54, Isaiah 25:8.

sit quietly on my back porch, waiting on the Lord. I took a scripture verse with me. "*I am the first and last. Beside me there is no God.*"[231] I spoke it. Softly. Then contemplated it.

It is difficult to describe contemplation. It's difficult because it's something going on privately, internally in the mind. But I'll try.

By contemplation of a verse, what I mean is, I thought about it. I didn't declare it nor affirm it, as if trying to make it true by saying so. Declarations are outward. But Contemplating a scripture is internal. It's more like digesting it.

I also thought about God. I thought about God's nature. Inwardly. But how do you think about infinity? You can't. It's like trying to put infinity in a bottle. No can do.

So contemplation has its limits. If God is a consuming fire, then contemplation is a fire starter. Not the fire itself, but the thing that starts the fire in a particular place. That's one way of describing it.

In contemplating the statement: "*I am the first and the last,*" I might just bring it to mind from memory. Or I might start by reading it, whether from Isaiah 44:6 or Rev. 22:13, for example. But then I put the book down and think about it. Inwardly.

I would think about the fact that there is something infinite out there. Something which always was, and therefore is here right now. Then I think about the word "I". Who is this "I" which is first and last? Is "I" doing the contemplation or is "I" someone else?

Then I might think who am I? Who is Gary Goldman? What am I? Is there something about me that is before time, and which is unbounded by space? Is there a timeless, soul-traveler "me" that lives forever? Where is this "me"? What is it? Now, none of this is scripted of course, I am just trying to convey generally what happens in contemplation.

Then I might move on to the second part of that verse. '*Beside me there is no God.*' Beside who? Who is this "me"

---

[231] Isaiah 44:6.

that was speaking here to Isaiah? God? Who is God?

Then I might change the verse. Perhaps, I might change it to *"I am the beginning and the end."* I say it out loud, very softly. And contemplate it. Cogitate it. I think about the same questions. Then suddenly, something amazing happens. There is a click. Ignition. Contact!

The first time it happened, that day on my back porch, I did not understand it well. But I knew that something was happening. Something very deep and life-changing.

It isn't easy to describe what happened because what happened is a spiritual happening. Though the body and the mind are impacted by it, still, messianic meditation is an activity of practicing the Presence of God. It is not a physical nor intellectual event. It is something happening in an invisible realm. And here I am trying to explain it in the visible world, using concrete terms. Which is impossible, really. Nevertheless, I am trying to do so, because concrete is all we have to work with.

You see, there was a "click." Contact. What happened was like a contraction. It was a jolt. My body, from head to toe, physically contracted. And then released. I felt something happening within me. Literally. And then came this incredible, overwhelming joy.

I can only describe it as if I was enveloped in an ocean of love. It is the warmest, most serene, blissful and joyful experience imaginable. The love into which I was immersed, was like liquid, but thicker. Instead of being immersed into something like water, it was more like sort of a mush. Like a balm. Or heavy oil. Kind of like soft, mushy butter. Yes, I had known this before. But I did not know how or why.

It was not an out-of-body kind of thing. But I had the sense that I was more than my body. It was as if there was a snap, and from that snap, I was immediately conscious beyond my body. I was conscious in a way that seems as if I was completely congruent with everything that I could see.

I was as much the life of that oak tree in my backyard, and everything that was buzzing and singing in it, as I was the life of my own body. A realization occurred that the thing which I am was far grander than what was normally my immediate, natural self.

As the contraction eased, and the release came, I saw, with eyes closed, the Kavod. Kavod is "Glory." It is the Glory of God, and I saw it with great magnificence and intensity.

Let me just say that being touched by the Holy Spirit was nothing new to me. I was well-familiar with it. But when I started meditating, not only was the communion with God's Spirit far more profound, but also, it was something that I could enter into regularly, intentionally, and pretty much at will. And furthermore, it was personal and private. I get great joy out of public worship events, and no one will ever hear me say that they aren't a necessary part of a healthy and vibrant spiritual life. However, messianic meditation has enabled me to practice the Presence, not just once per week, but on a routine, daily basis. Real-time fellowship with the Messiah has been the key to my personal transformation.

Never had I seen the Kavod with such clarity, and never before did I know how to enter into it on any kind of intentional, regular basis. The Glory I beheld was something like fireworks going off in my mind, as visions of the heavenly kingdom exploded before the eyes of my heart, on the inner screen, but without any thought or action on my part. These visions were not my conception, no, they were being sent by an "other." And I just sat their silently, and beheld the Glory of the Lord.

Then, thoughts began to flow into my awareness. I was not thinking thoughts. They were pop ups on the inner screen. Lots of them. Yes, I'd seen this before, but only a few times, and at isolated incidents. There was never before any understanding on my part as far as how to go and get more. Not on this level or depth, and not, as it would soon develop, on a regular basis.

I didn't see them as words on a screen. The pop-ups came into my mind as thoughts, but I knew they were not my thoughts. Mostly, these pop ups were fragments from scripture verses: "*I am the vine. Abide in me. Peace I leave with you. I am the Lord your God. Be still and know that I am God. I am the I am. I am the Way, the Truth, and the Life. I am the Light."* Stuff like that.

The pop ups just came rolling in. Like waves on the beach. They rolled in. I beheld them. Grasped them. One by one, they came, then retreated, back into the undercurrent of the infinite sea. Then another came, like white water, crashing on the shore, rolling out across the sand, then back inward, swallowed up on the waters. A short pause, and then another came, gloriously peaking, then falling over upon itself, crashing onto the beach, then retreating back out to the sea.

I did not know what was happening. I just knew that it was working. The connection had been made. I was not in a new or better relationship with God. I was in contact with God. And it was transformational.

With each wave, God was speaking to me by the Spirit. I knew this spiritual presence was the voice of God. I did not before know how to enter into this kind of kesher with the Spirit of God privately, on my own, and on a regular basis. But it has become my daily bread.

Now I had learned how. I did not before have any manner of practicing secretly, sacredly and privately the "igud" or "union" with God that was taught to me by the lawn doctor, Carlos Feldman. Now I did. And it changed everything.

I don't like talking about all this. Frankly, I feel that I can't accurately describe what happens during a time of messianic meditation. On the other hand, if I don't talk about it, then I cannot impart unto others, the blessing which was imparted unto me through the lawn doctor, Carlos Feldman.

The Heavens Broke Open:

So, I took Feldman on his word, I did as he said for a day, then two, then three. And on the third day, the heavens broke open. Actually, it was Tropical Storm Alice.

Alice was the first major storm of the season. Formed somewhere down in the Yucatan, it moved right into Tampa

Bay, not terribly windy, but a titanic rainfall event. We were pounded with rain for 48 hours straight.

Due to the overwhelming rainfall, the lakes in our neighborhood were overflowing right into the streets. The roads were still passable if necessary. But one problem when the lakes overflow is that the lakes are teeming with alligators. So, now the lakes, and the gators, are in the street.

Just before what normally would have been sunset time on day two of the storm, I was sitting on the back porch, in my secret place. Since I live on a corner lot, I can see the sidewalk from my back porch. That day I heard a woman's voice shouting rather hysterically. I looked and saw that it was Mother Theresa.

"Pierre !" she shouted to her dog.

Mother Theresa's umbrella was turned inside out, and she was chasing after her Pierre, who apparently had slipped out of his collar, perhaps due to being wet.

Pierre wasn't going to be easily caught. Every time she stopped moving, Pierre would stop. But as soon as she moved ahead to try and get him, Pierre would trot forward, beyond her reach.

No doubt, this little game Pierre was playing was great fun from his point of view. As he trotted along the sidewalk, toward my house, playfully evading his master, Pierre may have been enjoying very much a brief moment of freedom. Yet, being a domestic K-9, he was oblivious to the great threat that lurked ahead. For lying completely still, in the gutter of the street, was a 12-foot alligator. And sunset is feeding time for gators.

Mother Theresa stopped dead in her tracks. I could plainly see her face clearly from where I was sitting. She looked terrified.

"Pierre! Come, Pierre!" she said, pretending to have something in her hand.

He took a step or two toward her, then as soon as he realized she was teasing him, he stepped back again.

Gators are quick on land, but only for short distances. They are lightning fast in the water, but on land, they can dart forward quickly, but only for about five or ten feet. Beyond that range, you are pretty safe, because after that initial burst, they move pretty slow on land.

That is why alligators stalk their prey on land by laying completely still, like a rock, until the victim unknowingly comes within striking distance.

As I watched this scene develop, I would guess Pierre was about fifteen feet from the alligator. And Theresa was about another fifteen feet from the dog. She was out of the gator's reach. But Pierre was not.

I don't know why I did it, but suddenly, without thinking about it, I decided to intervene. I got up from my chair, exited the back porch, and began to briskly walk directly toward the dog. As Theresa saw me coming, she continued calling Pierre. The dog took a few steps toward her. As I quickly walked through the yard, I snatched up a large branch, about five feet long, which had fallen from the live oak during the storm.

Mother Theresa took a step toward Pierre to try and grab him. The dog quickly lurched away, and then back-trotted a few paces away from her. Theresa froze. But the dog continued to move playfully backward along the sidewalk, completely unaware that he was moving right into the reach of a 12-foot alligator.

I knew that was it. Pierre was well within range, and it was do or die for Pierre at this point.

I rushed within about ten feet of the gator, and I hurled the branch right in between the dog and the gator, hoping that it might spook the dog and cause him to run into the arms of his owner. A moment after I let go of the branch, the gator sprung forward, toward the dog, with jaws open. But as it happened, the branch hit the gator right in the snout, just before he was about to clamp down on Pierre.

It wasn't much, but it was just enough to rattle the carnivorous creature, and make him think twice about what he'd be eating for dinner. The gator balked, and missed his opportunity.

Now alerted to the danger, Pierre jumped into the arms

of Mother Theresa, who became quite hysterical and broke down into tears. I quickly grabbed another large branch and threw it right at the alligator, backing away to make sure I wasn't going to be dinner either. That was it. He'd had enough. He crawled off, across the street, and presumably back into the black, mucky lake, where no doubt there were still plenty of good options for him to get a meal.

"Are you ok?" I said to Mother Theresa.

She did not respond. She was hysterical. Gasping for breath, her nose was running, and she could not even speak. Mother Theresa turned around and ran home, with Pierre in her arms.

After the storm cleared out, it continued to rain nearly every day in the late afternoon, all through the next couple of months. The drought was over. And my lawn problems were too. The lawn turned green!

As far as what happened with my lawn, granted, some might say that it's pure coincidence, and no great marvel that the lawn turned green after a good, solid period of rain. Indeed, some might say that I just lucked out. But I don't believe in luck.

Now, was it a miracle? Well, for me, the "miracle" was not the growth in my lawn. But the miracle was in the growth in me. I am referring to the growth of my awareness of the Messiah who lives in me. And who always did. But now I was far more aware.

And the more I became conscious of Messiah in me, the more I understood also the Reality of everything else, knowing, of course, that there is only one God. Therefore, I began to understand the nature of what we call "problems." What I discovered, with Dr. Feldman's help, was that our "problems" are not really "problems." They come to us with the appearance of something other than what they really are. What they really are is nothing. And the Reality is something entirely different than the problem.

The problem is simply something that blinds us from seeing the Reality. Indeed, problems are the illusion, not the Reality. No matter who you are, or what you may be experiencing, the Truth remains what it is. And eternity is in our hearts. Eternity, the ever-present Reality.

I can testify to this. We actually can see the Kingdom of God. It is invisible, but we can learn to see it. We must first be transformed. As the Rabbi said, *"Unless a person is born-again, he cannot see the Kingdom of God."*[232]

If only we can put on the mind of Messiah, things appear quite differently. If only the mind that was in Yeshua could be the mind that is in each of us, then we can see things inside-out. And the problems that this perishing world throws at us are seen for what they are—nothing. Whether we are talking about a brown lawn, or even death itself. It is nothing!

And furthermore, as I have found, when the mind that was in the Rabbi is the operative government of our lives, then it is not just we personally who benefit from it, but we are able to help others as well. As Feldman helped me. And Shlomo, Marley, and the dread Captain Rosenblatt. Oftentimes help comes and goes out in ways that we never imagined. But it's the Spirit of the Lord going about his own business. We who are on the iPath, are the instruments of God. And God only knows how to use us.

I did not come to be transformed by any work of my own. I did not choose it. It chose me. So, it is not me who did it, nor me who is doing it. But the Messiah, who lives in me. It is a work of God's grace, opening my eyes to see things not as men see, but as they are. And that is what I call messianic consciousness. Or as some might say, "Christ consciousness."

Mother Theresa never did thank me for saving Pierre from the alligator. But a few days after the tropical storm cleared, I was sitting upon my back porch, having my quiet time, and as I opened my eyes for a moment, I saw her.

Mother Theresa was walking Pierre. And she saw me, sitting there. As she passed by, for the first time ever, she waved to me. Score!

At that moment, a thought popped into my mind, saying:

---

[232] John 3:3.

"Resist not evil, but overcome evil with good."[233]

Good is not something to be used against evil. True good is the consciousness of God. Whose nature is love. You don't use love against hate. God is one, and there is one Love that transcends the duality of love and hate altogether.

And I am glad to say, that not only was the whole matter of my now green lawn dropped by the Homeowners' Association, but I have not since had any other notices from the Homeowner's Association, or complaints made against me by Mother Theresa.

To be sure, I even tested it out. I left my trash pail out for an entire evening after the pickup. No complaints. Amazing.

By the fourth of July holiday, so green, lush and good-looking was my lawn, that even Larson was impressed. It was on that day, when I happened to come outside to check the mail.

The humidity in Florida in July is off-the-charts. It's hard to imagine that anyone in their right mind would be doing lawn work. But there was Larson, wearing a sombrero-style straw hat, trimming his shrubbery.

I think he was playing the soundtrack from *Mama Mia!*, because "Take A Chance On Me," by Abba, was blasting from Larson's garage. He hollered, over the music, so that I could hear him:

"Your lawn is looking great!"

I gave Larson a thumbs up. He smiled and tipped his sombrero. Then his expression changed. His face turned sour. He grabbed at his chest, and suddenly, as if struck by a bolt of lightning, Larson collapsed.

In an instant, Larson was flat on the ground, nose in the grass, with shrub clippers by his side. I immediately rushed over to Larson and called 911 on my cell. The paramedics were on the way.

I had some very basic CPR training, because it was required to be a head coach of a youth football team. But, frankly, I didn't know much.

---

[233] Rom. 12:21.

I figured it was going to take about seven or eight minutes for the paramedics to arrive in the ambulance. And I knew that if I didn't do something immediately to help Larson's blood flow, he wouldn't make it. Because, from what I could tell, Larson seemed not to be breathing. And I couldn't feel a heartbeat either.

I tried to remember my CPR course training, but it isn't easy when you've never used it. I thought I remembered hearing that for cardiac arrest, it's best to do "hands only" CPR. I really wasn't sure.

But one thing I was sure about is that it is typically better to do something than to do nothing. So, without delay, I flipped Larson over gently and started doing quick chest compressions. About 100 per minute. The music helped me to keep rhythm. That's all I did. Rhythmic chest compressions to the beat of a Swedish pop band. But, apparently, it was enough to keep Larson alive.

The paramedics arrived, Larson was given immediate care at the scene, and then was carted off in the ambulance. The paramedics told me that I probably saved Larson's life. I don't know. I certainly didn't want any credit.

That was the last time I saw Larson. He did send me a "thank you" card.

It seems that the illness he was fighting had progressed to the point where it led to cardiac arrest. He would not return home to live out his days doing lawn work, as I'm sure Larson would have preferred. Instead, he was living in hospice care.

Larson did seem to be quite thankful to still be alive, at least he said so in the greeting card he sent me from Hospice. I would've gladly gone to visit Larson, but he said he wanted no visitors. So, I respected that.

8

The Name

Miracles Do Happen:

It was early September. Rosh Hashana (the Jewish New Year) was just a few weeks off, and my Sabbatical year was coming to a close.

As I signed for a certified letter, and saw a law firm logo on the envelope, right away I thought for sure Mother Theresa was back on the warpath.

Immediately, the thoughts started racing through my mind. I must have a palm tree with dead palm fronds, or too much mold on my driveway. Or maybe the ornament that Laura hung on our front door that says "kindness matters" was somehow violative of a homeowner's association restriction.

But as it turned out, the certified letter was not from the homeowner's association. And although it came from a lawyer, it was not entirely bad news. Which proves that miracles do happen.

For the first time ever, I got a certified letter that had both good news and bad news.

The bad news, sadly, my neighbor, Larson, had just passed away a couple of weeks earlier. I would miss old Larson. My lawn was looking real nice at that point, and Larson sure would have been proud.

The good news, to my astonishment, I had been named as a beneficiary in Larson's will. The letter said that Larson, who had no children or surviving family members, bequeathed a donation of $100,000.00 to me. I called the lawyer to make sure there hadn't been some kind of mistake.

"He left his possessions to a diverse set of beneficiaries," said the lawyer in a teleconference. The lawyer was Murray Spiegelman.

"He divided his estate mainly among charities and philanthropic organizations," said Atty. Spiegelman. "The will was amended a couple of weeks before he passed. Why he wanted to include you in this list, I'll never know. But it's legal. I drew it up exactly as my client instructed me."

I guess you never know what difference you might make in a person's life. But, as I would soon begin to learn, when the infinite grace of God has truly become the operative principle of your life, stuff like this just happens.

When I received those funds later on, I took ten percent off the top, and sent a check for $10,000.00 to the lawn doctor, Carlos Feldman. In the blank in the lower left corner of the check I wrote, "For Resurrected Lawn."

Going Out With a Bang:

A few days later, I was on an airplane, on my way to my favorite hiking spot, the Shenandoah National Park in Virginia. I planned to spend a few days of hiking there. I guess it was sort of a last ditch effort to make the most of my sabbatical. Maybe go out with a bang. Or something like that.

Shenandoah is a Native American word that means "Daughter of the Stars." Shenandoah is the name given to the fertile valley of that region as well as to the river which cuts through the valley. It is truly one of America's treasures, and aptly-named as something which seems to have descended from out of heaven itself.

The airplane backed away from the terminal at Tampa International Airport, and began to taxi down the runway. As the plane took off, I looked out the window, and marveled at the beautiful sight of the beaches, the bay, and the Gulf of Mexico. The Tampa Bay region—with the Gulf of Mexico, the Bay, and all the inlets and lakes—is quite spectacular when viewed from the air.

With great anticipation, I had an abiding expectation

that there would be something of vast significance about to happen to me on this hiking trip to the mountains. I could just taste it. Suddenly a verse of scripture popped into mind:

> *"How beautiful upon the mountains are the feet of him who brings good news."*[234]

I was filled with a warm sense of gratitude. As the plane soon climbed above the clouds, and reached cruising altitude, I pushed the button on the arm of seat, leaned back, and just basked in the peace that I felt at that moment.

But the sense of peace I had quickly changed to fear and trembling, as the voice of the Captain came over the airplane PA system. To my horror, it was, indeed, none other than the dread Captain Rosenblatt.

"Good morning, folks, this is Captain Rosenblatt. We've got some weather up ahead, and we'll do our best to avoid it. But we may hit some rough air, so please keep your seat belts fastened and refrain from moving about the cabin unless absolutely necessary."

He wasn't kidding. The plane bounced around like a rubber ball. People were throwing up into the paper bags. I know that those bags are supplied for that purpose. But I'd never actually seen anyone use one of those bags. I figured they were like the oxygen masks hidden in the compartment overhead. They were only there for extreme precautionary purposes. Yet, I imagine they are quite common on flights flown by Rosenblatt.

Moreover, I never imagined why you are required to wear a seatbelt on an airplane. It seems to me that if, God forbid, a plane should crash, you are going to need a lot more than a seat belt to save your life. I mean, c'mon, when a plane bursts into flames on impact, or dives into the ocean, or is shattered into smitherines—what good is a safety belt going to do for anyone?

Yet, in Rosenblatt's case the purpose of the seat belt was

---

[234] Is. 52:7.

clear. The plane suddenly dropped in space. It felt like that feeling you get when you are on a roller coaster, diving down at high speed. Your stomach is suddenly in your throat. Only this was worse. And if not for the safety belt holding you in place, your head would've smashed into the compartment overhead.

"Woops," said Rosengrubbs over the PA system. "We hit a little air pocket there. Sorry folks."

I figured, yeah, we're back here suffering, while he was probably stuffing a turkey sub into that pie hole of his, instead of focusing on flying the plane.

Whatever it was, there can be no doubt. Captain Rosenblatt is the worst commercial airplane pilot ever. And even though he once did impart unto me great wisdom at the Salt Lake City airport, which I appreciate, that fact does in no way mitigate my firm belief that Rosenblatt has no business being in the cockpit of a passenger jet. And I could not imagine for what good purpose that I, or anyone else, should ever have to endure this experience. Yet here I was, now enduring it for the second time. Indeed, God's ways are mysterious and hidden from man.

I was extremely relieved when we hit the ground at Baltimore-Washington Airport. And I do mean "hit" the ground. Hard. But safely enough. The passengers actually applauded. And not because of the pilot's great skill. They applauded because the plane was on the ground.

I made my way to baggage claim, only to find that my one checked bag was not on the carousel. I waited until everyone else was cleared, and then made my way over to the airline customer service desk.

I soon learned that my bag had somehow been placed on the wrong flight. Lucky bag.

In any case, it had been located and was en route. I was told that I could have it delivered, or I could wait about an hour for it to arrive. My destination in the mountains was at least a two hour drive from the airport. My level of trust for Southern Airlines was grossly depleted at this point. And I do mean grossly.

So, I decided to wait. I contacted the car rental company and told them I'd be late.

One More Cup of Coffee:

One should never underestimate what can happen when killing time. As I often do, when killing time in an airport, I looked for a place to sit and have a cup of coffee. So I found a Starbucks there in the airport, and sat down.

But before ordering any coffee, I opened up my laptop. As often happens, I got engrossed in what I was working on, and forgot all about the coffee.

I was writing a book. And I was nearly finished. But not quite. I was stuck. And I was hoping that, among other things, my hiking trip might provide me with some revelation needed to complete the final draft.

Pretty much all summer long I had been drafting that book. That book as I previously mentioned in chapter 5, was entitled *One God*.

This book that you are reading now—*the iPath*—is the prequel to *One God*. In *One God*, I gave the teaching that was given to me during my Sabbatical period. In this book, *the iPath*, I give the story behind it.

I did not reveal in *One God* where or how the information in that book came to me. Well, now I have.

So, I began reading through the manuscript on my laptop. If only I could finish the final draft, then with some minor editing, it would be ready for publication.

However, there was just one small part lacking at this point—the beginning. Maybe that seems odd. Maybe you would think that the beginning would be written first. I would too. But in this case, it was not so. I had a very rough draft of the first chapter. But that was it.

Now let me explain something: I feel that the opening of a book is the most critical part. Because whether the reader is looking at it online or in person, I think, most people decide after perusing from about page one thru page three, whether they will purchase the book. Or if they already have purchased it, they decide whether they will actually read the book, or shelve it. I know that I tend to do that myself.

That's why I feel the most important part of the book is the opening line. But I did not have the opening line. Nor the first subsection, which is the first few pages of the book. And I couldn't just make it up. This teaching came from real life. So the beginning is not optional. The beginning must be the accurate beginning. But, you see, I didn't know what it was. Therefore, I had to find how it must begin.

But I had hit the wall. I had a nearly complete final draft, but no beginning. And, therefore, only a very rough sketch of the first chapter.

Now, the reason I had hit the wall at that point, the reason I did not know how to begin the book, was because I did not yet understand how to explain the answer to the question I had asked when this journey began—*Who am I?*

If I knew fully how to explain the answer to that question, then I would know how *One God* must begin. Because, in fact, my journey on the iPath came about when I started asking the question—*Who am I?* And by now I had learned so much about that. Almost a year was complete at this point. In my heart, I knew the answer to that question. But I did not quite know how to articulate it. Why not?

Because the nature of the answer is Truth. The whole Truth. Raw, unfiltered, unconditioned and undivided. As I've come to learn in my journey, human beings are not programmed for communicating that. And I include myself in that category. I am human. I will never deny it.

Even when a human comes into contact with God, to such an extent that he or she is reborn and transformed, the human is still human. To be "messianic" means "messiah-like." That is not to say that messianic people are little gods. God forbid. We are not little messiahs or little christs. We are humans. Humans who have come into contact with the Divine, but God forbid any human should make that kind of a claim that they are divine. Such things belong only to the realm of paganism.

God is God. There is nothing human that can ever be

divine. So herein lies the quandry of the human condition. Even when we have, through the Son of God, become God's children, we are still human nonetheless. So, how do humans beings communicate with one another something which can't be communicated humanly? We might as well be speaking Klingon.

I guess, the silver lining in this situation is that everyone has within us the faculty needed to apprehend Reality. If only the conditions are right, we can do it. It just isn't natural. It has to be done consciously, intentionally.

As the scriptures say, "faith comes by hearing,' so, when Truth is spoken, there definitely are always going to be people out there who embrace it.

The Problem:

But the problem is that Truth isn't something you can pick up with your finger, put into a petri dish, and say, "here it is, this is the answer," so that it can be examined, measured, analyzed, studied and discussed.

Over the course of a year, Truth unfolded in me. Yet, do you see my predicament? Even when you know the answer to—*who am I?*—explaining it to others, let alone publishing it to the world, isn't so easy.

Yeshua had the same challenge. Even when the masses followed him, he knew they couldn't understand what he was saying to them. He understood that most of them were coming with the idea of what they might get from him, and what he might do for them. They were not coming because they recognized who he was.[235]

They were hysterical over him. It was like when the Beatles came to America. Only bigger. Even bigger than King Solomon. Yeshua said it himself: "*Something greater than Solomon is here.*"[236]

---

[235] See, John 6;26 – "*Amen, amen I tell you, you seek Me not because you saw signs, but because you ate all the bread and were filled.*"
[236] Mat. 12:42.

He was the son of God. And the people were flocking to him. But why? Was it because he did miracles? Of course. But if he said to them, "Who do you say that I am," they wouldn't have been able to answer. Even the few who might have said, as I would, he is the son of God. So what does that mean? Yeah, I understand it. But how do you explain it?

You might say, well, the son of God IS God. Yeah. I agree completely. But there again, what does this mean? One way or another, inevitably, when you get to the bottom line, God cannot be described nor explained.

Of course, God can be known by humans. But the "knowing" happens, if at all, in an inner sanctuary. And when it happens that God is known, the result is consciousness. Consciousness manifests in a human being, but it cannot be captured in a jar, nor written down.

God in man is consciousness. The fullness of this—fully God and fully man—all in one, that is Messiah Yeshua, the Son of God. But these words fall short. Because human beings must communicate in human terms. Yet, neither God nor consciousness thereof can be put into words. Because humans are still human and God is still God. That's just how it is.

God is a Spirit. The Spirit of God in one person might open the eyes of another. That's how people become followers of the Messiah, and get onto the messianic path. Otherwise, how do you put the Spirit into words? No can do.

The world is full of people who believe that Yeshua is the son of God, but the problem is that they don't know the son of God. They can tell you all day about Yeshua's identity as the son, but they don't know the son.

It's like saying Bob is an elf, and he is the chief of all the elves, but then, what is an elf? In that scenario, if you don't know what an elf is, then you don't who Bob is either. All you know is that Bob is an elf. But that's not good enough. That's the problem.

People flocked to Yeshua, but they weren't getting his message. He was trying to communicate the Truth to them, but they weren't understanding, even when he demonstrated it in the many signs and miracles he did. His message was to reveal God. So that people could know God. If we know who Yeshua is, then we know God. But we don't naturally know this. And we don't know where to look.

What I learned, and what got me on the iPath, was the simple principle, to look within. But there again, what does that mean? How do we explain it?

Yeshua explained this problem He told his inner circle of talmidim that the world cannot receive the Spirit of Truth, because it neither sees him nor knows him; but *you* know him, because he dwells with you and will be in you.[237]

Went to See the Captain:

My sabbatical was nearly over. I had come to the Appalachians of Virginia, hoping to get another transfusion of revelatory, spiritual wisdom, to help me press on in my new vision of life.

If I had known that getting to my destination would in any way depend upon the aviation skill of the dread Captain Rosenblatt, I would surely have opted to stay home. Therefore, if indeed I went to see the Captain, it was not by my own choice. But surely by that of a higher power than my human self.

So there I was, at BWI airport, thankful to be alive. Thinking about life. Asking myself questions like: What is life? And what is the meaning of life? These are the kind of questions you start pondering immediately after you are transported through the air at high speeds by a man who ought to be permanently banned from flying airplanes.

Nothing was coming to me, though. And I was tired. I snapped the laptop closed, and put my head down in my folded arms on top of it. I dozed off. And pretty quickly, I was in a deep sleep.

I distinctly remember dreaming that I was on board a ship, being tossed about at sea by a terrible storm. And in the

---

[237] John 14:17

dream, while everyone was freaking out, and throwing things overboard, I was down below deck, sleeping peacefully through it all.

But someone was trying to wake me up. A voice. It was the Captain of the ship. At this point, I am not sure if I was dreaming, or awake, or partially both. But the voice of the ship's Captain said to me, "How can you sleep? Get up! Call out to your God."[238]

Then, suddenly, I was definitely awake. And I was being spoken to by a voice. A voice with food in its mouth.

"How can you sleep?" said the chewing voice.

It was the Captain alright. The dread Captain Rosenblatt.

"Whatcha doin'?" said Rosenblatt.

"I *was* sleeping," I mumbled, stretching out. "But not anymore, I guess."

"Ha!" he laughed, slapping me on the back, as if I was joking. "Guess not."

Rosenblatt sat himself down at the table with me. He had already placed down two drinks, and quite a wide variety of food items.

"Mind if I join you, Pal?" he said, sliding one of the cups my way. "I got you a cup of coffee."

I really wasn't in the mood. But I could hardly turn away a nice cup of coffee. I accepted, then got up to put in some half and half. As I poured, I noticed a group of female flight attendants sitting at a table across the café. One of them pointed over to Rosenblatt, and it looked like she was talking to the others about him. Probably his flight crew, I assumed. Most likely talking about what a horrible pilot he is.

When I returned to the table, Rosenblatt was busy stuffing in a blueberry scone. I took a few sips of coffee.

"Never thought I'd see you again," I said. "Nice to see you."

"Oh, do we know each other?" he responded.

"Well, yeah," I said.

"I don't think so," responded Rosenblatt.

---

[238] *See*, Jonah 1:1-6.

I was thinking to myself, *is he for real or is he just messing with me?*

After an awkward silence, I popped open my laptop.

"Whatcha working on?" he asked.

"Writing a book, actually," I said. "I just can't seem to finish it."

Rosenblatt wiped his hands together, as if to get the scone crumbs off. But I don't know why. He picked up another scone and started stuffing that one in. Meanwhile the crumbs from his hands were now all over the table.

I said, "So, hey, you're just messing with me, right?"

"What do you mean?" he said.

"I mean, c'mon. Obviously we met once before."

"You know who I am?" said the dread Captain.

"Of course."

"If you knew me, then you would know my Father as well," said Rosenblatt. He swallowed a big chunk.

"But I have seen you before and I do know you," I blurted out.

"Anyone who has seen me, has seen the Father," he said.

"Well, I've seen you," I said. "Salt Lake City airport. Starbucks, just like this."

"If you knew me, then you'd know the Father," said Rosenblatt. "And then maybe you'd know how to finish that book you are writing."

I started packing up my laptop. I was tired. I wasn't in the mood. And Rosenblatt was freaking me out.

"Don't be freaked out," he said.

"Wouldn't you be?" I fired back.

"Okay, listen, pal." He held up his palms, "Take it easy. Maybe I can help."

I put the laptop in its case. But I agreed to sit and stay. I heard Rosenblatt out.

"So, what's the problem?" said Captain Rosenblatt.

"The problem is that I can't figure out how this book begins."

"What's the book about?" he asked. "In a nutshell?"

"It's about the things I've learned since I've been on the

298

iPath."

"Maybe it doesn't have a beginning," he said. "Or an end either."

"Then I would have no book."

"Not necessarily," he said. "The iPath is a journey without beginning and without end," said Rosenblatt.

"How's that?" I said.

"Because *I* am the beginning and the end," he said.

"Okay, I get all that. But that doesn't work for writing a book."

He brushed off his hands again, this time getting the crumbs all over my leg.

"Are you kidding me?" I protested, standing up.

"Sorry," said Rosenblubber. "That was an accident."

As I brushed the crumbs off my pant leg, he offered a napkin, which I refused.

"Forget it," I said.

"Sorry," he repeated, and he went to work on opening up a turkey sandwich.

At that moment, one of the flight attendants, came up to our table.

"Hi," she said shyly to Capt. Rosenblatt. "I'm Tammy. Just flew in from Tampa with your crew."

"Hi, Tammy," said the Captain, as he shoved in a large portion of a Turkey sandwich.

"I was just wondering, if you don't mind, can I please get a photo with you?" she said.

"Sure," he said, choking down the sandwich.

"Thanks," she said.

Tammy the flight attendant handed me her iPhone, which was opened to camera already. She put her face cheek to cheek with the dread Captain, and I snapped a few for her.

"Thanks so much," she said. "I didn't mean to bother you," she said.

"No bother. Happens all the time," said Rosenblatt.

"And if, well, if I could just have your autograph," she said, handing him a Starbucks napkin.

"Sure," he said.

"Hope you don't mind. It's for my daughter," she said sheepishly.

"Your daughter's name?" he asked.

"Uh, Tammy," she said.

"Same as you?" he said, writing on the napkin.

"Uh, yeah. Thanks so much."

Rosenblatt handed Tammy the napkin, which she pressed up to her heart. As she assumed her place back with the other ladies, there was much whispering and giggling going on.

And I sat there, stone-faced, dumbfounded. Did I accidentally walk into a black hole? Was I now living in a parallel universe where overweight Jewish airplane pilots from hell are worshipped as gods?

"What in the world just happened?" I said.

"I used to be pretty famous," said Rosenblatt. "Back in the 70's, I was Dirk Lancer, the lead singer of a group called This."

"What? No way!" I said. "Everyone has heard of them."

"Yep," he said, as he pulled up a photo on his iPhone and showed it to me. "That was me."

"Holy crap!" I said, looking at the long-haired youth, who was quite lean and muscular, and whose face was unrecognizable due to make-up. "That's you?" I said.

"That's me," he said. "At least, it was me anyway. Hard to tell with all the make-up, huh?"

"Unbelievable," I said.

"I was Dirk Lancer. And that was another life. I have no regrets, but I left that scene for good reason," said Rosenblatt. "Joined the military. Got my flight experience. Got married. To a wonderful woman. I am perfectly happy being Captain Morris Rosenblatt. Thanks to the old make-up, nobody recognizes me."

"I see what you mean," I said.

"About ten years ago, the word got out on the internet. You can't hide anything anymore. And then they started pushing me to form a reunion band. Plenty of money to be made on that kind of thing."

"Sure," I said. "So why not do it?" I asked.

"No. I can't go back to that. That's why I put on all this weight. So they'd leave me alone."

"Wow," I said.

"Hey, sorry about those crumbs, pal," he said.

"It's okay. Forget about the crumbs," I said.

"No, no. My bad. But, look, pal. No worries. I'll make it up to you," he said.

"Yeah?"

"I'll tell you how to find the beginning to that book you're working on."

"You're gonna tell me how it starts?"

"No. I said I'm gonna tell you how to find it," said Rosenblatt.

"This I gotta hear."

"You got a bible?" he asked.

I looked through my laptop case. No luck. Then I remembered, I had one on my cell phone. I opened the app. And nodded.

"Pull up John 14:13, and read it out loud."

I did as he suggested.

"*Ask anything in my name and I will do it.*" I said out loud.

"Well, there you go."

"What?"

"Ask in my name, and you will receive. Isn't that what it says?"

"Yeah, but—"

"But what?" said Rosenblatt.

"Look, I mean, I know it says that and everything. But millions of people pray in the name of the Lord. And just because we say "In the name of Yeshua," or "In the name of Jesus," or whatever language, doesn't mean that prayers are automatically answered.

"Well they ought to be," said Rosenblatt.

I thought about this for a moment. He was right. If we prayed in the name of the Lord, then our prayers ought to be answered. That was the plain reading of the verse anyway.

And yet, I knew it didn't work like that. Something was missing. And that missing link, could be the very reason I was sitting in a Starbucks at the BWI airport with Captain Blackbeard.

"Let me ask you this," said Rosenblatt. "Did Yeshua pray?"

"Of course."

"In whose name did he pray?"

"I don't know," I said.

"Well, then, if you knew the answer to that, then do you think maybe you would know what he meant when he said, *'Ask anything in my name.'* I tell you then you'd have yourself a pearl of great value."

"I would?"

"Yeah. And I think you'd know how that book begins and ends. Because even though I don't know what you're writing there, I can tell you one thing. If it has anything to do with the iPath, then the beginning is the end. And the end is the beginning. Because the I of the iPath is the I am, without beginning or end. Remember that, ok?"

I smiled. I felt that was what I needed to know. And he seemed to feel that way too. I finished my coffee, which by now was lukewarm. I shook Rosenblatt's hand and thanked him.

Although I sincerely hoped never to hear his voice over an airplane PA system again, I did indeed feel thankful for the counsel he gave me.

So, off I went to pick up my bag at customer service, and soon, I was on my way to the Shenandoah National Park. I needed to get out there in the mountains, in the woods, isolated on the trails.

The Waterfall:

The waterfall was about 90 feet from bottom to top. I had hiked about three miles in from the trailhead to this remote spot, and was now taking a nice break.

I took out the trail map to get my bearings. It was mostly

downhill so far. Not as grueling as uphill, but definitely tougher than flat ground. This was a nine mile loop trail, so I had about six miles ahead of me.

Per the map, the hike out from here would be three miles flat along the creek bed, and then three miles uphill back to the trailhead. It was going to be a long, tough day ahead, so I figured I'd better make the most of the quiet, restful mid-morning break.

I was sitting on a granite rock, next to the stream. A beautiful spot. I had just finished a wonderful time of messianic meditation. I was soaking in the awesome Presence of the Ruakh HaKodesh, that was flowing from within me, much like the waterfall before my eyes.

I must've been in it for thirty minutes. Or was it an hour? I don't know sometimes. When I am in fellowship with the Spirit of the Lord, time seems to not even exist. It sometimes goes just a few minutes, sometimes over an hour. If I don't clock it, I really wouldn't know how long it went.

It was a Monday in mid-September. Not being a holiday season, no one was anywhere in sight. I sat there alone. Just me and the eternal, abiding Presence. As I was admiring the beauty, and listening to the peaceful roar of the waterfall, a slight mist from the fall seemed to drift my way. It was still summer and hot. The cool mist felt nice upon my face.

With my teeth, I tore open the wrapper of a Clif bar. Crunchy peanut butter flavor. My favorite. As I chewed on this delicious morsel, I took the print bible out of my pack. The Tree of Life, messianic Jewish version, of course.

I opened the book, somewhere in the middle, I didn't even see where. I continued enjoying the Clif bar. Suddenly, there was a strong gust of wind. The pages of the book turned. And then the wind stopped.

I looked at the book, and it was open to John 17. My eyes somehow fixated on one verse. And there it was. Glowing like a burning coal. Not really glowing, but just something about it immediately grabbed my attention.

Just a simple little statement. Just one sentence. But it poured off of the page like it was written in my soul. It had always been written there. But I read that verse a thousand times before and nothing happened. I had never got from it what I was supposed to get from it, and which I did in fact get that day in the Virginia mountains.

In that verse, John 17:6, Yeshua says to the Father:

*"I have made **your name** known to the men of this world that you gave me."*

Those two words "your name" stood out to me as if they were written in bold.

I thought to myself, *what name?*

When Yeshua walked through the land of Israel, preaching, teaching, healing the sick, raising the dead, performing miracles of all kinds, there were thousands of people who heard and saw. They may not have understood that he was the promised Messiah. They may not have realized that he was the son of God. Nor what that meant. Yet, they darn sure knew his name—Yeshua. There was no mystery or secret about that. Everybody knew his name.

So, I wondered, what is this "name," about which Yeshua spoke, as recorded in that bible verse, John 17:6, that seems to only have been revealed to Yeshua's closest followers? That's the name in which he himself must've prayed. That's the name I wanted to know about!

An Age-old Tradition:

We Jews have a long-standing, age-old tradition which says that the name of the Lord in the Torah and the Old Testament is not to be spoken. It is held to be an ancient secret that has been lost to antiquity. What is this all about? No one really knows for sure. It's a strange tradition.

A brief explanation is as follows: In the Torah there is a four-letter name, often called the "tetragrammaton." The Latin letters are YHVH. It appears over 5000 times in the Old Testament. Nobody knows for sure what it means. Nor how to pronounce it. Or if maybe it is an acronym. Or whatever.

It was a closely guarded secret at first, and eventually became something that was lost. The tradition in Judaism says that the secret of the name was known only to the elders and spiritual leaders of Israel, who passed it down orally. Aside from the written scriptures of both the old and new Testaments, the Jewish people have a rich oral tradition in which many teachings have been handed down orally throughout the generations.

The name of God, according to Jewish tradition, is said to be part of the oral tradition. Something known to the Patriarchs, to Moses, Joshua, the elders of Israel, the Prophets, High Priests, and so forth. But not to the people at large.

Now, this is all just tradition, of course. If you were to ask me whether the written bible is true, I would say absolutely yes. As for whether or not the oral tradition of Judaism is true, I would say, some of it is, some of it isn't.

It's a very complex thing. In terms of its reliability and authority, Rabbinical Judaism often puts the oral tradition practically on the same level as written scripture. Or even higher. I do not see it that way. On the other hand, it is a tradition rich in wisdom, and some of it is of great value.

Regarding the secret name of the Lord, Judaism has a widely accepted tradition which says that in ancient times, when the Temple was standing in Jerusalem, the High Priest of Israel used to say the secret name once per year. No one could hear him, because he did it when he entered the inner sanctum of the Temple, the holy of holies, on Yom Kippur, which is the day of Atonement.

Nobody is really sure if this story of the High Priest is true. Nor when this practice of saying the name in the Temple may have actually started or stopped. After the Temple was destroyed by the Romans in the year 70 C.E., obviously we don't have this rite anymore.

Nevertheless, since the time the Temple was destroyed, right up until today, there have been Rabbis who claim they know the name. But generally, they won't tell anyone. So, nobody really knows if there is just some posturing going on there, or is there something to it?

To the amusement of the Jewish community, the Christian world has invented the names "Yahweh" and "Jehovah" which are mispronunciations of the four-letter name of the Lord in the Torah.

Linguistically, those attempts make no sense. The four letters in Hebrew cannot be pronounced as a word. Nor more than YHVH can be pronounced as Yahweh or Jehovah or anything like that.

All of this mystery about the secret name of God is very strange. The bible says so much in black and white. Why does it not give us the name of the Lord, instead of referring to it over and over, and instead of giving us four letters that make no sense when read them together? Why leave such an important matter as a mystery? That is a question for God.

But I personally believe it is because the world wouldn't understand it, even if it was written in black and white. Even if it could be put into a petri dish, and handed over for examination, inspection, dissection, and discussion, the world would still not understand it. That is why the scriptures quote the *fact* that Yeshua revealed the name to his inner circle of disciples:

> *"I have made **your name** known to the men of this world that you gave me."*[239]

And yet, the same is completely devoid of any information as to what name was it that he revealed unto them. I mean, c'mon John. If you are going to tell us that the Rabbi revealed some name to you, why not tell us what it is!

I reiterate, the reason that the answer is not given in print concerning the name is because the world would not understand it. Because putting it in print wouldn't mean a thing. Just like it wouldn't have meant a thing if Yeshua told the disciples over a campfire one night. They would've said,

---

[239] John 17:6.

"Huh?"

And as it happened, he didn't just tell them straight up one night the meaning of the name. No, he as the Son of God was with them for over three years teaching them. In one way or another, he had been teaching them the name all along. But they were no different than anyone else. They could not see it. And even after they saw it, they still couldn't explain it to anyone else.

No, Yeshua didn't just tell them one day—"okay guys, here it is. Let me tell you now about this name thing." It wouldn't have worked. They wouldn't have understood. Yeshua planted the seed. By his teaching. He was with them for so long, but most of the time they didn't know who he was. They knew his name, of course, from day one. His name was Yeshua, no mystery about that. Seven billion people in the world today know that, and 1/3 of them believe he's the Messiah. No mystery there.

The "mystery" about the name is that the name points to who Yeshua is. Not what his first name or last name is. And not a title either. Not Lord of Lords or King of Kings, even though he is all of that.

If Yeshua was to ask, *Who do you say that I am?* then Bingo! If you can answer that, then you have the name. But even his closest disciples couldn't answer it. And even Peter who did answer, well, he forgot shortly afterward. Knowing the name of the Lord, is to know who he is. And you can't put that in a petri dish for examination under a microscope.

For the talmidim of Yeshua, it was the Spirit that opened their eyes to understand. The same Spirit by which he came, and the same Spirit which raised him from the grave. And the same that is in us today—if we have become conscious. And if so, then we are reborn. And we are children of God. And the children know the Father, because they know who the Father is.

The name is a mystery. And it only ceases to be a mystery when the Spirit of Messiah in you makes it known, even as the same Spirit made it known to the talmidim of Yeshua.

In Judaism the name of the Lord has become either "Adonai" which means "Lord," or "HaShem," which means "the name." Jews actually call God "the name," because our traditions teaches that we don't say the name of God out loud.

Yet, the New Testament seems to say that in spite of all this secrecy and mystery and tradition initiated by the priests of Israel and the Rabbis after them, the "name" was revealed to the inner circle of Yeshua's followers.

As I read on in my bible, I quickly saw that Yeshua continued speaking to the Father in this manner:

*"Father, keep them **in your name** that you have given me, so that they may be **one just as we are one.**"*[240]

This immediately sent the wheels in my mind into motion, raising many questions. I pondered them for a few minutes. Obviously, the scripture is saying that this name of God has something to do with "oneness" through the Messiah.

The Word:

Then, something clicked in my thoughts, and I suddenly thought of another verse, in a completely different book of the New Testament, but also written by John. So, I quickly turned there, to the book of Revelation:

*"His eyes are like a flame of fire, and many royal crowns are on His head. He has **a name** written that no one knows except Himself. He is clothed in a robe dipped in blood, and **the name** by which He is called is the word of God."*[241]

Again, I had read that passage of scripture countless

---

[240] John 17:11,12.
[241] Rev. 19:12,13.

times before. As millions of people before me have done. And, yet, like them, I never saw anything in it.

I didn't understand it. But I had to wonder. I had to consider and ask the questions. There were many questions forming in my mind. What is this "name that no one knows except Himself"? Could this be a name which, by grace, Yeshua has revealed to his inner circle? And if so, unto whom did they reveal it?

I was overwhelmed with enthusiasm as I thought about the part that says, "...and **the name** by which He is called is the word of God." The mystery of the "word of God" or "logos," as they say in Greek, must be connected to the "name."

The name, as it were, must be something that reveals who God is. Something that tells us the secret of his nature. A hidden truth that the bulk of the world, even the religious world, is missing.

I quickly turned the pages to another book by John, the gospel of John:

"In the beginning was the Word. The Word was with God, and the Word was God. He was with God in the beginning."[242]

So, I contemplated this. And I wondered. For I know that humanity is a fallen race of beings, who have become alienated from the Truth, and thereby, separated from God. But the Logos remains our link. Something which we once knew. All of us. And yet, as time went by, we forgot it. We lost our way.

But then, by God's grace, there have always been those who, through consciousness, have kept the link. So that the human race would not perish from the face of the earth. Messiah is the word made flesh, who dwelt among us, that mankind might grasp onto that link, the word, which is our lifeline.

---

[242] John 1:1,2

309

Because God so loved the world, the Son has been revealed to the world so that it would not perish, but have everlasting Life.

But the world has not grasped this revelation. Worst of all, the world thinks that it has grasped it, but it hasn't. Because it doesn't know what it is, nor how to deal with it.

There is something about the Son that is so revelatory, if we knew this, then we'd know the Son of God. But without it, it is the blind leading the blind. The Apostles must've known it. The holy men and women of the old Testament era knew it. Even in the darkest and most twisted generations, there has always been a remnant. So too, there is a remnant today.

The Logos. What is it? The word of God? As much as we know that Spirit cannot be conceptualized nor conveyed through human terminologies, is there a single word, which reveals more in one word than we could ever know conceptually about the nature of God? And that if we were to dwell upon that word early and often, it would be sort of a Rosetta stone, that opens our understanding to the scriptures, and helps us to be more and more filled with the Spirit of the living God?

All of these questions were coming to mind. And as I have said, I think that one should never underestimate the power of questions. So I kept going. Because I had more.

Could it be, I thought, that there is some simple truth about the nature of God that is revealed in the simplicity of one word, a simple word that if dwelt upon, could reveal a wealth of Truth about God's nature? And could it be that from that revelation, the cornerstone of all creation has been laid, and so too, the cornerstone is laid for a person's individual life to be a person who walks in the abundant, overflowing grace of the Lord?

And if so, isn't it only natural that Yeshua would have kept this hidden from the world, because the world could never understand it? Because they would make it cliché, write love songs about it, put it in a petri dish and study it, marginalize it to the point where it would become ridiculous to even mention it, because everybody already knows it and it hasn't seemed to work, it hasn't brought peace on earth, even though it has been said and done a million times before? It's only because they haven't understood it. But they don't understand that either. So, no one would grasp it. And it would be dismissed as a cliché.

If there is a name, hidden from the world, isn't it only natural that the Master would have guarded it in secret, just like all the Rabbis and elders of the Jews before him always guarded the things they believed to be sacred?

But, also, wouldn't he have shared this Truth at least with his inner circle, in order to reveal unto them something about God, something that the world generally would not accept, even if they knew this name? And moreover, if there even is such a name, then wouldn't it likely be found in the writings of the scriptures?

Another verse in John 1, came to mind, and so I continued to read:

"The word became flesh and dwelt among us."[243]

What was it that became flesh? The word. Yes, but what is that? What word? What is the word? Could the word be this "name" to which the scriptures seem to allude? You could say the word of God is God, but that only begs the question! What word? What is it?

You could say the same about Yeshua. You could say Yeshua is Lord. But what Yeshua? Who is Yeshua? Or Jesus? Or Iesus? Language doesn't matter. What matters is who is he?! Obviously, people disagree on that.

Someone might say, the bible tells us. If you'd just read the bible, then you'd have the answer. Well, men have read of Jesus in the bible for centuries, yet they still didn't get who Jesus is, nor is there global agreement among bible readers about who he is. Without a spiritual revelation there is no understanding.

So I had many questions such as this. I like to ask

---

[243] John 1:14.

questions. And contemplate. For when I contemplate, the Spirit of God comes, oftentimes with answers.

And, in this manner, I mulled over these questions, sitting upon the rock at the foot of the waterfall, by the mountain stream in Shenandoah National Park.

And as massive amounts of water flowed down over a 90-foot cliff, the sound, and the power of that moving water lulled me into a tremendous sense of peace and harmony in that place.

Visitors:

I definitely picked a good day to be alone in the woods. There were very few other visitors to the Shenandoah National Park that day. I still hadn't seen hardly a soul all day. Just a few in passing along the trail.

But then, I heard the sound of people walking. It sounded like a whole group of hikers. Bummer. This spot by the waterfall was a beautiful place, and I really wanted to be alone. Hopefully, they would press on past me, and find their own secret place in these mountains. For I had staked my claim here. This place was mine.

But they did not see it that way. The hikers approached, I could hear them. I turned around, and there they were. All four of them.

To my astonishment, it was Marley, Capt. Rosenblatt, Shlomo, and Dr. Feldman. They now stood in front me, in sort of a semi-circle, as I stayed seated on the rock.

Rosenblatt was totally gasping for breath. His hands were on his hips, Marley took a bottle of water out of his backpack, and offered it to Rosenblatt. The dread Captain downed about half the bottle.

Dr. Feldman said, "I hope we are not interrupting anything?"

"Well, yeah, sort of," I said.

They all laughed.

"Did you find what you were looking for?" said Rosenblatt, still panting for breath. He dumped the rest of the water over his head.

"You mean the name?" I asked.

Rosenblatt nodded.

"No. Not really," I said.

Marley said, "The name is not really a name."

"True," said Rosenblatt. He reached out to Marley, snapping his fingers. Marley handed him what looked like a peanut butter and jelly sandwich, wrapped in cellophane.

"The name of God?" asked Shlomo.

"Yes," I said.

"It's not really a name," Shlomo said. "Not like Bob or Suzy, you see. It's more like a principle."

"A principle?" I asked.

"Yeah," said Marley. "It's a principle of the nature of God."

"But at the same time," said Feldman, "if you are on the iPath, then you know it already."

"Even if you don't know that you know it," said Marley.

"Well," I said, "Whatever it is, I'm lost."

"Not as lost as you think you are," said Capt. Rosenblatt, as he desperately tried to unravel the cellophane from the sandwich. Unsuccessful in this, he ripped it with his teeth, and tore it off.

"So I'm not lost?" I asked.

"We're here to help you," said Shlomo.

"Cool!" I said.

"Pay attention. Because after this, you won't see us again," said Marley.

"But first," said Feldman, "you have to understand, there are no shibboleths."

"Huh?" I said.

"No passwords or open sesames," said Feldman.

"Right," said Marley. "That's not what the name is. Remember that."

"Okay. Will do." I said.

"Because if we gave it to someone who wasn't ready, it wouldn't mean a thing to them," said Rosenblatt, stuffing the PBJ into his hole. "Unless you're on the iPath, it wouldn't do you any good."

"Because the name is not really a name. It's just a principle of God's nature," added Shlomo.

"Even though it is a name," added Marley.

"That makes about zero sense," I said.

"They're trying to tell you not to get weird about it. You don't necessarily have to know it," said Rosenblatt while chewing. He swallowed a big chunk. "It's just to help you."

"And it will help you," said Shlomo.

"You already know the principle," said Feldman. "But you don't know it as well as you will know it when you know the name. Does that make sense?"

"No. But I'm all ears," I said. "So, help me out here. Where do I find the name of God?"

"Anywhere and everywhere," said Rosenblatt, laughing. He stuffed the remainder of the PBJ sandwich into his hole, and wiped his fingers on a rock.

"Do you understand?" asked Marley.

"No," I said. "Does it matter?"

They all four looked at each other. Rosenblatt shrugged. Feldman pointed at me with his thumb. Shlomo seemed to consent.

So Marley walked close to me, and sat down beside me on the rock.

"What you are about to hear," said Rosenblatt, "you must keep locked away secretly and sacredly."

"Reveal it only to your closest talmidim (students)," said Dr. Feldman. "Men and women, who you trust are on the spiritual path. The same path that you are on."

"The iPath, that is. No one else will understand it anyway," said Shlomo.

"That is the tradition," said Marley, putting a hand on my shoulder. "So, are you ready?"

I nodded. As the other three watched, each of them seemed to have a slight grin, such as a father might have when his son is about to receive an award.

Marley flipped back his dreadlocks with a flick of the head, and leaned toward me. He went right up to my ear and whispered the name in my ear.

They were right. The name is very simple. It was something that was there all along. It is throughout the scriptures, but I never before saw it.

And now my mind was illumined to see this not only in scripture, but in myself, in others, and in all manner of creation. But that's all I will say about the name at this point, at least as far as this book. It is all I can say.

After this, Marley stood up and walked into the stream, until he was about knee deep. Then the other three joined him there. They were all about 25-30 feet or so from where I was sitting.

Rosenblatt rubbed his hands together in the water, presumably to get the peanut butter off his fingers.

Marley spoke up first. It was necessary now to speak quite loudly, in order to be heard over the roar of the waterfall.

Marley said: "In a moment you will not see us anymore. Even as we are about to go out, in this same manner, we shall return, together, with the anointed One, who is Lord of Lords, King of Kings."

Shlomo continued: "Yeshua will appear, and the whole earth will tremble. The Son of God will take the throne of David in Jerusalem."

Feldman added: "No one knows the date nor the hour. Not even him. But write down what you have witnessed, along with all that you have learned, and publish it in your book."

I said loudly: "If they ask me why I have written these things, whom shall I say told me to do so."

"Tell them that *I am* told you to do this," said Rosenblatt.

"Can you be a little more specific?" I asked.

"Yes," said Marley. "I am that I am."

"Ok. But surely they will not believe me."

"You are right. They will not believe you" said Rosenblatt.

"Thanks for the encouragement," I said. "What then shall I say unto them?"

Shlomo added: "But my sheep hear my voice. And there will be those who hear my voice in you, and they will believe."

And Marley said: "And all who believe in me, out of their innermost being shall flow forth a river of living water."

"But why me?" I asked. "Can't you give this asignment to someone else?"

"Have no fear," said Shlomo. "By this, they will know that you speak the truth. In that I will be with you."

"What do you mean you will be with me?" I hollered.

"I have been with you from the beginning," answered Marley.

"Only now you know it," said Rosenblatt.

"Yeah, but no one else will know it. They'll never believe it." I argued.

"Some will," said Marley. "There will always be a remnant."

Dr. Feldman continued: "Go forth. Teach the children well. Teach them what you have learned. Raise up new talmidim."

Marley went on: "From every nation tribe and tongue. Both Jew and Gentile. Rich and poor. Young and old."

"I don't know if I can do this," I protested.

"You cannot do it," said Capt. Rosenblatt.

"I appreciate the vote of confidence," I said.

"But *I* can!" said Capt. Rosenblatt. "And *I* will."

"So, what do you need me for?" I shouted.

"I don't need you. You need me. And I am with you always, even to the end of the age."

At that moment, each of them helped one another to unzip from the back the clothing that they were wearing. Underneath the clothing, each was now dressed in a white garment. The finest, purest white I have ever seen. This garment resonated with a brilliance that I cannot describe.

On the front of the garment, each had something like an emblem across the chest of it.

Marley had the face of a man. Rosenblatt an ox. Shlomo a lion. And Dr. Feldman an eagle.

Now the four of them huddled together, shoulder to shoulder, facing me. Capt. Rosenblatt took something out of his pocket and held it in his hand. He nodded to the others, and then he spoke into the thing that was in his hand.

And with that, suddenly, a bright light flashed down from the sky. Rosenblatt, Marley, Shlomo and Feldman were all encased in this bright beam of light. The light shone bright only for a few seconds, and then when it disappeared, the four men disappeared into the beam of light. With that, they were gone from my sight.

But I looked up and saw this great, disc-shaped, spinning ship overhead. And then like a flash of lightning, it suddenly departed through the sky, and out of my view.

"Wait! Come back!" I hollered. "Don't go!"

And suddenly I was awake. The whole incident by the waterfall, it was all a dream. Or at least, I had been in a deep sleep.

I woke myself up as I was shouting "Don't go!" Now I knew I was dreaming. I felt a tremendous peace. All I heard now was the sweet song of a bird, and the rushing waterfall that must've lulled me to sleep.

My head was propped up on a rock, where I had taken my rain poncho out of my backpack, and placed it as a cushion on the rock.

"Ma nora hamakom hazeh,"[244] I said softly.

I don't know how much time had passed, but I had some hiking ahead of me, and I figured I'd better press on. So I packed up, put on my backpack, and pushed ahead, into the wooded trail along the stream.

I could still hear the sound of water. I love that sound of a stream. It's like the sound of life. As I continued along the trail, I reflected on what had just happened at the waterfall. Quite frankly, I don't know what happened.

Were the four men really there with me? Or was that just a dream? I guess it was a dream. I mean, yeah, it was. But then, what is a dream? Isn't everything a dream—except for

---

[244] Gen. 28:17 – *"How awesome is this place!"*

Reality? So, was any of this real?

I remembered Jacob. When Jacob dreamed a dream, and saw a stairway to heaven, and the angels going up and down the stairway, and the voice of the Lord spoke to him, and said "Anokhi Imakh" (*I am with you*) was that all a dream?[245] Or was it Reality?

. And what about Jacob's son Joseph and his dreams? Sheaves of barley, bowing to him. The moon and the sun and the stars bowing down to him. Dream or Reality? I thought about this as I meandered along the trail by the stream.

How about when an angel appeared to Yeshua's parents when he was a newborn, and warned them to flee to Egypt, saving the child's life—was that just a dream?[246]

Or what about Solomon, when he became King, and the Lord came to him in a dream, and said, "*Ask for whatever you want me to give you.*"[247] Surely that was a dream, but was it not also real?

Two Things:

Whatever the incident by the waterfall was—a fiction or actual Reality—I came away from the Shenandoah with some important information. Two things, really:

First, the name. Of course, I can't actually write the name in this book. Marley told me the name in a dream. Was it a dream or was it Reality? I don't know. I just know that the name is real. And I can't put it into concrete. Not only because I was instructed in the dream not to publish it, but also because I realize that if I did, it wouldn't make sense to most people anyway. The most I could do is teach it orally, and then only to a chosen few who I knew could grasp it.

Secondly, the beginning to my book. I got the answer. I drafted it in my villa that night after the incident by the waterfall. Then I finished the whole first chapter before I left

[245] Gen. 28:10-15.
[246] Mat. 2:13.
[247] 1 Kings 3:5.

to return home.

As it turned out, the beginning of the book, *One God* opens like this:

> *"Who is God? If someone were to ask you that question, you would not be able to answer. Oh, you might think you can answer. Most people do think they can."*[248]

So it seemed, that my journey ended there. Or should I say it began there. Because actually, it never ended. But I'm not sure where it began either. Or if it even has a beginning. Let alone, an end. Because the iPath is a journey without beginning or end.

I was now on the iPath. Not a path to God. But the path *of* God. And it all started when I asked the question—*Who am I?*

The answer to that question, which, as I said, is difficult to articulate, came fully to me in the Shenandoah. The answer is this—*Who is God?*

I am sorry to answer a question with another question. But it's the only way to explain it. Because if I poured it into concrete, it wouldn't be an answer at all. Not to that question anyway.

As far as the name, well, the name is the answer to both of those questions. But again, if I put it into a petri dish to be examined, inspected, dissected, and rejected, it wouldn't make any sense—unless you happen to be on the iPath. And in that case, you already know the answer anyway.

End of the Year:

It was Rosh HaShana. The end of one year. The beginning of a new year. My sabbatical was over. It was a packed house. And I was back in the saddle.

As I stood at the bima (pulpit), for the first time in a

---

[248] Stepakoff, Michael, *One God*. 2015, p.1.

year, the congregation was singing a beautiful song led by the Cantor. I had tremendous renewed confidence in what I was doing. What a sense of excitement, hope, and exuberant joy for whatever might lie ahead. Many things flashed before me.

A year earlier, I had left the pulpit for sabbatical, soon to discover that I had no real answers to the very questions about which I had been preaching and teaching for years.

Now I had answers. I wasn't sure how I would explain them. Or even if people would receive whatever I might have to impart. But I knew for certain, that an inner spring, a fountain of life, was flowing from within me. And therein, there were answers to all manner of problems. Not the "written in concrete" kind of answers. But the inarticulable, ineffable, free-flowing "river of living water" kind of answers.

Those answers, and that river, was always there before. But it was not flowing freely in me. And now it was. I had woken up. I was conscious. The Light of Messiah had dawned in me.

And I was thankful to Yeshua. Because whatever was going to happen from here on in with my life, it would glorify him. That's why he paid my debts by suffering in his own flesh. He took away my sins by paying the penalty for me on the tree of sacrifice. Exactly as Isaiah the prophet said that he would.[249]

And as I was being transformed into the rightness of God through Yeshua's work,[250] I knew that somewhere in the heavens, Yeshua HaMashiakh, in the manner of a true Kohen HaGadol (high Priest) was intervening for me.[251] He was the one who orchestrated my transformation. He was the one who sent the messengers into my life to impart wisdom, and he was the one who brought me to the iPath. Because it's his path. And being on the iPath, I am walking in messianic consciousness, seeing the created world through his eyes.

There have been quite a few times during my messianic

---

[249] See, Isaiah 53.
[250] 2 Cor. 5:21.
[251] See Heb. 7:25.

meditation periods, that Yeshua has come to me. I see him. Not every time. But oftentimes. Even when I don't see him, I know he is the one behind the revelation of the Spirit.

Because Yeshua reveals the Spirit, and the Spirit reveals Yeshua. Yeshua immerses his followers in the Spirit, in the same way that his cousin, Yochanan the immerser said he would: *"I immersed you in water, but he will immerse you in the Ruakh ha-Kodesh.*[252]

All of this was happening to me through the infinite intelligence of the one God. It is a work of grace, and my only role is to be an instrument in the hand of God. I walk along the iPath, always in this awareness, that God is doing his work in me. The more I do, the more I grow.

And when Yeshua does come into my consciousness, during meditation, all I can say is that it is glorious! When he comes, he simply meets with me. It might last for ten seconds or for a minute. Not long. He has a word with me. He shows me things. Speaks to me.

Yeshua is enveloped in a Light that is so glorious, it is impossible to describe. But when it happens, there is such a deep sense of Joy. Sometimes I laugh. Sometimes uncontrollably. I am glad I am in a private place where no one can hear me. The laughter is something God put in my soul. It is healing. It is wonderful. It has changed the way I preach, and the way I write. Sometimes I can even be very funny. Which is not my normal personality. This is the gift of God.

I don't know what else to say about it. Messianic consciousness is infinite Joy beyond anything imaginable. I truly know what it means to say "the Joy of the Lord is our strength."[253]

I know Yeshua. Personally. He is not an historical figure that I read about. He is real. And he lives in my consciousness—or as some would say, in my heart. But he doesn't just live there. We fellowship together. For real.

---

[252] Mark 1:8.
[253] Neh. 8:10.

Frankly, I don't know how this all works. But in regard to the personal transformation that happened to me during my sabbatical period, I can testify to this: Yeshua, the Lord of Lords, is the one who ordained this and he is the one who is carrying out in me the purpose for which I was formed in the womb and brought into this perishing world to begin with.

I still do not know all the details of what will happen or how this life to which I am called will be fulfilled. But what a joy it is to know that your life is being governed from above, and you are being watched over. This has been my experience since I got on the iPath.

So, on Rosh HaShana, I took my place behind the pulpit. They were signing Avinu Malkeinu. The Cantor was leading. And the people were singing along. It was the chorus. Such a deep, soulful, moving melody.

I looked out, to a packed house, and there, in the front row, center aisle, was Evan, the totally-tattooed-Jew. He was singing Avinu Malkeinu. And he had a woman with him. Which appeared to me that they were together. It was Latasha.

I don't know how she knew the song. Maybe she just picked it up as it was going, and was reading the transliterated Hebrew. Or maybe she'd heard it before. I do not know. But Latasha knew it. And she sang it. And man that girl could sing.

The song stopped. I spoke my first word of the new year to the congregation: Shalom.

About the Author

Michael Stepakoff is the Rabbi of Temple New Jerusalem, a messianic synagogue in Dunedin, Florida. He is a key leader in the international movement known as Messianic Judaism.

Rabbi Mike is a frequent speaker at national, regional and local messianic Jewish conferences and events. He is active in social media, and reaches a broad audience internationally through regular livestream video teachings.

Rabbi Mike speaks most Friday nights at Temple New Jerusalem. For schedule see: www.templenewjerusalem.org.

Rabbi Mike is married with four children. He enjoys hiking, jogging, playing pick-up basketball, coaching youth sports, snow skiing, the beach, and entering into oneness with God and the universe while sitting on his back porch listening to the song of crickets and birds.

66541441R00182

Made in the USA
Lexington, KY
16 August 2017